El Lobo

READINGS ON THE MEXICAN GRAY WOLF

Edited by Tom Lynch

THE UNIVERSITY OF UTAH PRESS
Salt Lake City

Cover photo by Frans Lanting/Minden Pictures.

 The Defiance House Man colophon is a registered trademark of the
University of Utah Press. It is based upon a four-foot-tall, Ancient
Puebloan pictograph (late PIII) near Glen Canyon, Utah.

LIBRARY OF CONGRESS CATALOGING-IN-PUBLICATION DATA

El lobo : readings on the Mexican gray wolf / edited by Tom Lynch.
    p. cm.
  ISBN-13: 978-0-87480-835-3 (pbk. : alk. paper)
  ISBN-10: 0-87480-835-9 (pbk. : alk. paper)
  1. Mexican wolf. 2. Mexican wolf—Reintroduction. I. Lynch, Tom, 1955-
QL737.C22L62 2005
599.773'097—dc22

                                                              2005019172

CONTENTS

||||||||||||||||||||||||||||||||||||||||

Tom Lynch | Introduction: Rewilding the West | 1

To the Brink

Grenville Goodwin | Wolf and Mountain Lion Hunt Together | 13

Amadeo M. Rea | *shee'e* | 14

James C. Burbank | Great Beast God of the East | 16

Steve Pavlik | Will Big Trotter Reclaim His Place? | 31

David E. Brown | The Long and Dismal Howl | 53

A. Starker Leopold | Wolf. *Canis lupus* | 65

Ben Tinker | Timber Wolf (*Canis lupus*) | 71

Estela Portillo Trambley | Wolf Boy | 74

G. W. "Dub" Evans | Wolf Cunning | 77

Aldo Leopold | Thinking Like a Mountain | 84

And Back

Roy T. McBride | The Mexican Wolf (*Canis lupus baileyi*) | 89

Norma Ames | Mexican Wolf Recovery Plan (excerpts) | 107

Dale D. Goble | Reintroducing the Missing Parts | 130

David E. Brown | A Tale of Two Wolves | 138

Sharman Apt Russell | The Physics of Beauty | 143

Rick Bass | The Feds | 156

Joan Moody | El Lobo's Homecoming | 164

JANE SUSAN MACCARTER | Road Trip with Mexican Wolves | 169

J. ZANE WALLEY | Caught Twixt Beasts and Bureaucrats | 176

ALEXANDER PARSONS | Strip Mall Lobos | 183

J. ZANE WALLEY | The Wasting of Catron County | 197

JOHNNY D. BOGGS | Living with Wolves | 203

DASHKA SLATER | Signs of the Wild | 207

LAURA SCHNEBERGER | Caught between the Pack and
the Hard Case | 215

PETER FRIEDERICI | Welcoming Home an Old Friend | 220

MICHAEL J. ROBINSON | Mexican Wolf Fate Teeters between
Science and Politics | 224

TOM DOLLAR | The Mexican Wolf | 228

JON TRAPP | Mexican Wolf Guardian Reports, 2002 | 236

Coda

DAVID HIDALGO and LOUIE PÉREZ (LOS LOBOS) | Will the
Wolf Survive? | 247

Acknowledgments | 249

Contributors | 253

About the Editor | 258

INTRODUCTION:
RE-WILDING THE WEST

Tom Lynch

When you stand at the Blue Vista overlook in the Apache-Sitgreaves National Forest and peer out over pine-forested mountains receding to the remote horizon, or when you pull off at the Clinton P. Anderson wilderness overlook on the road to the Gila Cliff Dwellings and gaze over high rugged plateaus that seem to encompass all the world, you think surely, surely here, if anywhere, there would be room for wolves. Surely here, if anywhere, the Wild West, the truly wild West, still lives.

But as we know, looks, even from scenic viewpoints, can be deceiving.

Mexican gray wolves, referred to locally as lobos, co-evolved in complex interaction with this landscape and its peoples. For tens of thousands of years lobos trotted through these groves of Ponderosa pines, sipped water from these creeks on hot evenings, chased terrified deer across these meadows to a bloody struggle and kill, snuggled in dens among these rocks nursing a passel of pups, and echoed their harmonic howls off these canyon rocks. Lobos wandered the edges of Mimbres settlements, entering the Mimbres imagination as their images became transformed onto pottery. Later, they watched from the cliff edges as Apaches followed the river bottoms to summer encampments in the cool mountains. Geronimo, born in what is now the Gila Wilderness, no doubt heard tales in which the wolf figured as a powerful presence. But by the 1940s, after less than one hundred years of American occupation of the Southwest, the wolves were all but gone. Up until the 1970s a few stragglers wandered in from Mexico. But these were hunted relentlessly until the very last one was dead.

After tens if not hundreds of thousands of years roaming the mountains of the desert Southwest, the Mexican gray wolf was, in the blink of an eye, driven to the brink of extinction. By the early 1980s, when the U.S. Fish and Wildlife Service, responding to the requirements of the Endangered Species Act, established a plan to recover the lobo, there were probably none living in the wilds anywhere in the United States. A precious few held out in Mexico while only a handful lingered in captivity. At one point the total number of Mexican gray wolves known to be alive in the world was a scant twenty-three, all in captivity. Currently, as I write this, nearly two hundred Mexican gray wolves live in captivity, and more than fifty are living in the wild. Further releases are planned until a goal of one hundred is reached.

How this subspecies of wolf came so close to annihilation, only to be saved—or so it seems—at the last possible moment, is a dramatic tale told from a variety of perspectives in the pages that follow.

The view from the Blue Vista overlook is indeed spectacular. The view from the Clinton P. Anderson wilderness overlook is certainly grand. This is very wild country. But what you don't see from these heights, what isn't obvious in these distant views, is that down beneath those trees, down among the rocks of those canyons, a lot of cattle are grazing and a lot of peoples' livelihoods depend upon the welfare of those cattle.

There exists, as we know from our religions and folklore, an ancient enmity between wolves and the herders of pastoral stock, for there's no denying that wolves will, from time to time, dine on domestic animals. And so it was at the behest of ranchers that the U.S. government, in the early part of the twentieth century, set about the systematic extermination of the wolves in this area. Killing wolves made the land safe for cows and safe for civilization. What we now think of as icons of the Wild West, the cowboy and his cow, were in fact participants in a de-wilding process, they were outriders of civilization penetrating these remote canyons and transforming them into feedlots for distant cities. Ironically, the same federal government agencies that worked so hard to destroy the wolves are now undoing some of that work, and many of the ranchers in the area are understandably perplexed at this change of policy.

In European cultures, the wolf was often the embodiment of evil, the functionary of Satan, the threatening wilderness at the edge of a nascent and fragile civilization, the symbol of our own inner wildness threatening to break free; to kill a wolf was to strike a blow for God and for civilization and for sanity. In this context, then, restoring the wolf can seem evil, barbaric, insane.

⁓

In assessing the wisdom of the reintroduction of wolves, we find ourselves engaged in a sort of cost-benefit analysis. The benefits include satisfying the ethical and legal imperatives to save an important subspecies of wolf from extinction. They include helping to restore a disrupted balance of nature. They include the economic possibilities of wolf tourism. They include, for many of us, the enormous but unquantifiable benefit of even the possibility of seeing or hearing a wild wolf in the Southwest. In short, to many people, myself included, the benefits of wolf reintroduction seem to vastly outweigh the costs. But I also realize that this is easy to say because I'm not the one paying the main costs. It's not my calf being disemboweled by the lobos. I'm not lying awake at night worrying about what carnage I might find in my pasture in the morning, or how that carnage might affect my ability to pay my bills. And I think it's only fair to appreciate and acknowledge the depth of anger, fear, and hostility some people feel for the wolf. While not all ranchers oppose the wolf reintroduction program—in fact some, like Jim Winder of Nutt, New Mexico, and Jan and Will Holder of Safford, Arizona, are active supporters of it—most do. These ranchers and their rural neighbors have some legitimate concerns and grievances that ought to be addressed. Though the exact numbers are in dispute, there's no denying that wolves have been and will continue to kill cattle. The compensation program run by Defenders of Wildlife, which pays ranchers a fair market value for confirmed cattle predation, is a sincere effort to ameliorate these losses, but we must recognize its limitations. There are cultural, practical, political, and emotional reasons why many ranchers find the compensation program inadequate. To these ranchers and other opponents, the costs of wolf restoration seem high and all too tangible in blood, worry, and dollars, while the benefits seem negligible and amorphous.

Furthermore, the successful return of the lobo will inevitably force ranchers to change some of their traditional husbandry practices. I don't doubt that if they felt wolf restoration were a valuable thing, most ranchers would be happy to make these accommodations. But if they think, as many of them do, that the restoration of the wolf is an absurd undertaking foisted on them by ignorant if not downright malicious city-slickers, then they will resent and resist any changes in their traditional ways of doing things. These opponents of wolf reintroduction clearly have some legitimate concerns and I think wolf supporters should be sympathetic to them. Local people in the wolf recovery area should be given significant and meaningful input into the program's implementation and management process and the costs to them in time, trouble, anxiety, and money should be reduced to the extent practicable.

But some of the more extreme concerns expressed by reintroduction opponents are unfounded, especially the risk of human predation. The likelihood that people will be seriously injured or killed by a restored Mexican wolf is almost zero. Rural people certainly accept many other more threatening risks to their safety and to the safety of their children. Statistics will show that people are far more likely to be seriously injured or killed by horses, by firearms, by all-terrain vehicles, by loose dogs, and by other commonly accepted aspects of rural life, than they are by wolves.

On the other hand, proponents of wolf reintroduction often claim that there has never been a documented case in North America of a healthy wild wolf killing a human being. But determining the veracity of this claim is not as easy as one might imagine and much hinges on what one accepts as reasonable documentation. Recent studies (Linnell, 2002; McNay, 2002) suggest that the claim is probably true, at least for North America. However, wolves certainly have killed people elsewhere in the world, most notably in India and Europe. And there are enough not-quite-adequately documented incidents of wolf predation on humans even in North America (Mader, 2004) that I would be wary of accepting the claim as absolutely true. But I don't think this matters, because I think this is a misguided line of argument. I think we need to accept the possibility, however remote, that Mexican gray wolves might seriously injure or kill someone. If we don't accept this possibility, then how can we justify the restoration elsewhere of animals that indeed do kill and maim human beings, like grizzly bears? It is extremely unlikely that Mexican gray wolves will seriously harm anyone, but it is not impossible, and the reintroduction program should not be predicated on that impossibility. Still, the risk is incredibly remote and it hardly seems the sort of thing that the rugged descendants of the pioneers ought to be fretting about.

Stepping back a bit, we can recognize that this struggle is not just about the wolf. It's about competing visions of life in the American West. While it can be characterized as a conflict between the Old West and the New West, I think it's more complex than that. We are engaged in a difficult transition from a frontier to a bioregional vision of the West. No one epitomizes that transition more than Aldo Leopold, who records in his essay included here—one of the most influential essays in the history of environmentalism—his own transformation from wolf killer to wolf lover, from an agent of the frontier process to a pioneer in environmental ethics and bioregional thinking. In the frontier vision of the West, whatever stands in the way of the march of progress, be it the native peoples or the native animals, must give way. The frontier moves across the land, transforming the "wild" into the "civilized." And though some of the frontier's participants—and the life they lead—may seem terribly wild, they are in fact engaged in a process of de-wilding the landscape. A frontier is a moveable process, not an actual terrain. The frontier seems to belong to a place, but in fact it's just passing through. A frontier moves across a landscape, and when it rides off into the sunset, the land remains, usually much diminished. Animals that are driven to extinction by the frontiering process are extinct forever. For a variety of reasons, however, this transitory frontier West has come to seem to many people to be the true, the authentic West. Frontier ideology continues to dominate the perceptions of many people and to control the politics in many Western states. There's no doubt that frontier history is colorful and exciting and can make for great stories, but it can also be a curse, trapping us in outmoded ways of thinking. Surely there is some way to honor the struggles and heroism of our pioneer ancestors without also being condemned to repeat their errors.

The bioregional vision, on the other hand, is deeply emplaced. Unlike the frontier, it doesn't move along to greener pastures. It has to make due with the overgrazed ones. Therefore, bioregionalism can be considered re-inhabitory. It's about restoring, to the degree possible, a damaged landscape. It's about learning to inhabit a place for the long haul, in a sustainable way, without diminishing the natural heritage. It's about adjusting our culture to respect the limits of the nature that surrounds and sustains us. Many ranchers have been on the land for several generations; this fact confers both bioregional status and a certain moral authority, as well as political clout. Many of these multigeneration ranchers would like to pass their land and lifestyle on to their children and grandchildren, and they are therefore some of the people with the greatest stake in making the transition from frontier to bioregional thinking. The restoration of the wolf, I think, serves as a litmus test for people's ability to make this transition. It's hard to claim to care about the health of the land and yet oppose the restoration of the wolf, one of the quintessential embodiments and determinants of that health. But the frontier is a powerful myth, hard to resist; its icons, its customs and culture, are alluring, and thus far bioregionalism finds it hard to compete with the romance of the frontier. The wolf (and its restoration) is one of the few elements of bioregionalism that can compete in the public imagination with the cowboy as a romantic icon of the West.

Ultimately, restoring the wolf is part of the larger bioregional process of undoing some of the ecological damage we've done. Though many of us might be glad to hear wolves howl again in these hills, though many of us might be thrilled to glimpse a wolf trotting past our campsite, these experiences are not the main purpose of the reintroduction program. Restoring the wolf is not, fundamentally, about thrills for us; it's about healing the land.

⁓

While the restoration of wolves to Yellowstone National Park has received an enormous amount of public and scientific attention, with scores of books and several TV documentaries, the restoration of the lobo to the Southwest has received much less notice. Yet in many ways it is of more compelling interest. To take just one example, the wolves released in Yellowstone were all wild wolves, captured while living in the forests of Canada and moved to Yellowstone. They had all been socialized to the complexities of wolf behavior; they had all learned how to behave as wolves. But in the Southwest there were no wild lobos to draw upon. All the Mexican gray wolves being released are captive-raised and are many generations removed from the wild. They've never seen their parents cooperate to hunt and kill prey. They've never been integrated into the sophisticated social network of a wild, free-roaming pack. For several generations now, they've never had to fend for themselves.

Wolf restoration opponents fear, not without some justification, that the wolves being released in the Southwest will not predictably behave like wild wolves elsewhere. These wolves raised in captivity may not be able to survive on their own. Hungry, confused wolves may increasingly turn to preying on domestic livestock or on pet dogs. They may turn to raiding campgrounds. They may linger around rural homes. They may stalk humans. While the restoration program has taken great steps to minimize these problems, they can't be entirely eliminated, for we simply don't know how much of wolf behavior is learned and how much is innate. If it's mostly learned, this restoration effort is probably destined for failure. So far, however, the wolves seem to be adjusting. They are cooperating in the hunting of large animals such as elk—no easy task. They are forming pair bonds and packs, finding den sites, and rearing pups. The evidence so far seems to indicate that nature, more than nurture, makes a wolf a wolf. But this is a complex matter and the evidence is incomplete and far from certain.

⎯⎯⎯∽⎯⎯⎯

I compiled this anthology, initially, for myself. When I moved to southern New Mexico I realized that I was living near the proposed Mexican gray wolf recovery zones, and I wanted to know more about this wolf and the recovery project. I found that such information was hard to come by. At the time only one book, David Brown's *The Wolf in the Southwest,* was readily available. Though it provided useful historical information, it was dated and had concluded gloomily that there was no hope for the survival of the Mexican gray wolf. As I searched for, photocopied, and filed away a series of articles, book chapters, and other writings, I realized that other people might be interested in these materials as well. I also noticed that the public debate over the wolf reintroduction program was often shrill and, I thought, ill-informed. It seemed to me that a collection such as this one might help to create a better-informed discussion. Such is my idealistic hope.

This anthology is arranged in two broad sections that explore various aspects of the lobo in roughly chronological order. The first section, "To the Brink," contains pieces that describe the role of the lobo in Native American cultures and in Mexican folklore; the wolf's biology, range, and behavior; and the campaign to exterminate wolves in the Southwest, including consideration of ranchers' hostility to wolves.

The collection pivots on several key documents that represent a transformation in public attitudes and government policy toward the wolf: Aldo Leopold's famous "Thinking Like a Mountain" essay, Roy T. McBride's 1980 report on the status of the Mexican wolf, and excerpts from the U.S. Fish and Wildlife Service's 1982 recovery plan. Following this transition, the concluding section of the anthology, "And Back," traces the steps that led to the current recovery program. This section looks at the politics and personalities involved in that process and includes dissenting voices who believe the recovery program is misguided and harmful to ranchers and other rural populations. Some of these voices speak in harmony. But many also speak in contradiction to each other. I have tried to include as wide a variety of perspectives as possible, given the limitations on a project such as this. I do not agree with all the voices included here—no one could—but I do believe they should all be heard and taken to heart. I have not sought to reconcile conflicting opinions or disagreements on facts. To do so would be to falsify reality. These sometimes harmonious and sometimes discordant voices are all part of an ongoing dialogue; they are all part of the multi-vocal bioregional narrative of what it means to be a human being inhabiting, and seeking to re-inhabit, this area we call the Southwest at the beginning of the twenty-first century.

Readers will notice that some of these pieces directly engage with each other, sometimes overtly and sometimes just by implication. Most notably, many of the essays in favor of wolf reintroduction quote from the Aldo Leopold essay, affirming its importance in American environmental thinking. In this brief tale, told in a few short paragraphs, Leopold distills the change in thinking about environmental matters in the United States, the change made manifest in the transition from wolf killing to wolf restoration that this collection seeks to document. Leopold's tale has achieved mythic status in the environmental community, serving as a foundational story for a new environmental ethos. Also of note, Dub Evans's essay, "Wolf Cunning," eloquently describes his hatred for wolves and his gratitude to the government for removing them from his Slash Ranch. At the end of this anthology, however, Jon Trapp describes his work with cowboys at the same Slash Ranch to help restore wolves in that area.

⌒〜◦

In Cormac McCarthy's novel *The Crossing*, Don Arnulfo, the oracular old wolf trapper, tells young Billy Parham that "the wolf is like the copo de nieve." And he explains:

> "You catch the snowflake but when you look in your hand you dont have it no more. Maybe you see this dechado. But before you can see it it is gone. If you want to see it you have to see it on its own ground. If you catch it you lose it."

If you're reading this, you're probably interested in wolves. But the wolf is not in this book. The wolf is not in any zoo or captive breeding pen. If you want to see a wolf worth seeing, you have to see it on its own ground. Hike into the Blue Range of Arizona or the Gila Wilderness of New Mexico. If you get lucky, you'll see the wolf. If you get lucky, you'll hear the wolf. Or maybe you won't. But still, you'll know it's out there, you'll know that you *could* have seen it. And that's lucky, too.

⌒◞

As this book goes to press, the success of the Mexican gray wolf re-introduction program is far from certain. Eleven packs and a number of lone stragglers, totalling 51 to 56 wolves, inhabit the high forests of Arizona and New Mexico. Whether they will remain, how they will fare, and whether they will substantially increase their numbers, are matters we must wait to discover. For readers interested in keeping track of the progress of the program, the websites noted below provide regular updates.

⌒◞

U.S. Fish and Wildlife Service's Mexican gray wolf "Field Notes"
http://mexicanwolf.fws.gov

Defenders of Wildlife "Wolf Guardian Field Reports"
http://www.defenders.org/wildlife/wolf/wolfupdate/fieldreports.html

Center for Biological Diversity's "Track the Packs"
http://www.biologicaldiversity.org/swcbd/species/mexwolf/wolf_track.html

Gila Wilderness dot.com's "Wolves Reintroduction Homepage"
http://www.gilawilderness.com/local/wolfhompag.htm

Bibliography

Linnell, John D. C., et al. 2002. *The Fear of Wolves: A Review of Wolf Attacks on Humans*. Trondheim, Norway: NINA. <http://www.nina.no/archive/nina/Publikasjoner/oppdragsmelding/NINA-OM731.pdf>

Mader, T. R. 2004. *Wolf Attacks on Humans*. Abundant Wildlife Society. <http://www.aws.vcn.com/wolf_attacks_on_humans.html>

McNay, M. E. 2002. *A Case History of Wolf-Human Encounters in Alaska and Canada*. Alaska Department of Fish and Game. Wildlife Technical Bulletin 13. <http://wildlife.alaska.gov/pubs/techpubs/research_pdfs/ techb13_full.pdf>

To the Brink

WOLF AND MOUNTAIN LION HUNT TOGETHER

|||||||||||||||||||||||||||||||||||||||||||||||||||||||||||||||||||||||

GRENVILLE GOODWIN
from *Myths and Tales of the White Mountain Apache*
(1939)

Long, long ago, Mountain Lion and Wolf were killing all kinds of animals in a contest to see who was the best hunter. So they said one time, "We will go out at dawn and see who is the first to get something before sunrise." They bet on the outcome. Mountain Lion said to Wolf, "I don't think that you will bring in anything, but I will bring in a deer." Wolf answered, "I am the one who will get the deer and you will get nothing." They started off to hunt. Just about sunrise, Mountain Lion brought into camp *'id·lgije'* and a little while afterwards, Wolf brought *ni·ya·ge'ilgij.** Both these deer were big. Thus Mountain Lion was the first to bring in something, but Wolf said, "You crawl along on your belly and hide yourself. That is why you have sores on your belly and on your knees. That is the way you hunt." Mountain Lion answered, "You chase the deer all over and get them hot. Then you kill them and eat the meat when it is hot. It is no good that way." The reason that these two hate each other so much is due to this argument and contest of long ago.

---

*These two terms are descriptive of the horns of the deer. The first implies the largest of the bucks.

SHEE'E

||||||||||||||||||||

AMADEO M. REA

from *Folk Mammalogy of the Northern Pimans*
(1998)

shee'e, [pl.] sheshe'e
Canidae
Canis lupus
Gray Wolf, Mexican Wolf; Lobo

The Gray Wolf of Pimería Alta, the smallest of the North American subspecies, has a head and body length of three to four feet, in addition to a long, full tail. It aboriginally ranged from about the Mogollon Rim southward through the Sierra Madre Occidental, hence one of its names, Mexican Wolf. In the Southwest it weighs from 60 to about 90 pounds. Resembling a heavy, overgrown Coyote, the wolf has more rounded and relatively shorter ears. The hind footprint of dogs and Coyotes is roughly square, while that of the wolf is distinctly longer than it is wide.

Brown (1983a) maps the original range far to the east of Gileño country, but Hoffmeister (1986) maps the distribution westward to include all of Gila Pima country, the entire Santa Cruz drainage, and at least the eastern part of the Papago reservation in the vicinity of the Baboquivari Mountains. There is no specimen documentation for any of this desert country. However Pima oral history contends the wolf was once part of the local fauna.

Sylvester Matthias said, "*Shee'e* is the wolf. It sounds almost like a blood hound. You can tell it from *ban* [Coyote] by higher and hunched back, but different tail." According to Joseph Giff, "*Shee'e* sounds like a Coyote, but has different tune or ring. Coyote has sharp howl, wolf sort of a drowning howl. We used to hear them, my brother and I. There may be a few of them in the Muhadag [South Mountains]."

The Piman Creation Epic includes this account of the two great hunters immediately following the episode of Coyote eating Cottontail's heart on South Mountain:

Mavit, Puma, and RsU-U-u [Shee'e], Wolf, joined their fortunes and went hunting together. One day Wolf said, "I wonder where is our brother, Coyote; suppose I call him." So he took the kidney of a deer and roasted it and the wind carried the appetizing odor toward the south. When Coyote smelled it he said, "Surely, these are my brothers, who wish me to return." So he ran to the place where Puma and Wolf were living. When he reached them he was in great distress, for when he ate food it fell from him as wheat falls from a broken sack. Finally, Puma and wolf stitched his skin until it retained the food he ate. (Russell 1908:217)

The wolf in the Southwest and in much of its range across the border in the Sierra Madre was deliberately exterminated by federal trappers of the U.S. Biological Survey because it conflicted with the cattle raising industry, itself a questionable enterprise in arid and semiarid regions (Bahre 1991; Brown 1983b).

～

Comparative Linguistics: The name for the wolf is pan-Piman. In addition to *shee'e* among Akimel and Tohono O'odham, we find *shee'i* (desert Pima Bajo), *shee* and *shee'i* (pl. *shéshee*) (Mountain Pima), *séi* (Northern Tepehuan), and *seeg* (Tepecano). Colonial Névome records *suhi* (pl. *susuhi*), where *e* was not distinguished from *u* in the orthography.

(Author's note: The "e" symbol in Pima is not an "e" at all but a spread-lipped "u," sort of like the second vowel in "roses.")

Bibliography

Bahre, Conrad Joseph. 1991. *A Legacy of Change: Historic Human Impact on Vegetation of the Arizona Borderlands.* Univ. of Arizona Press, Tucson.

Brown, David E. 1983a. *The Wolf in the Southwest: The Making of an Endangered Species.* Univ. of Arizona Press, Tucson.

Brown, David E. 1983b. On the Status of the Jaguar in the Southwest. *Southwestern Naturalist* 28:459–60.

Hoffmeister, Donald F. 1986. *Mammals of Arizona.* Univ. of Arizona Press, Tucson.

Russell, Frank. 1908. *The Pima Indians. Ann. Report Bureau American Ethnology* 26:3–389. Re-issue, with introduction, citation sources, and bibliography by Bernard L. Fontana, Univ. of Arizona Press, Tucson, 1975.

GREAT BEAST GOD
OF THE EAST

||||||||||||||||||||||||||||||||||||||||||||||||||

JAMES C. BURBANK

from *Vanishing Lobo: The Mexican Wolf in the Southwest*
(1990)

*So he went out and came to a large court. He was in an upper story
with somebody. Below them were different kinds of animal—
mountain lion, bear, wolf, fox, wildcat, dragonflies, also bees,
the big and the little ones. He was frightened. They said, "We
are your friends." They jumped up on him and scratched him.
They had power.*

— ELSIE CLEWS PARSONS, TEWA EMERGENCE MYTH

*E*arly in March, I phoned anthropologist Alfonso Ortiz to discuss my wolf book. I told him I was interested in discovering
what the wolf meant to Pueblo tribes. Originally from the
Tewa village of San Juan, Ortiz is one of those amazing people who
has in a single lifetime spanned two cultures, maintaining a foothold
in both the Indian and white worlds.

He referred me to some basic readings and graciously agreed to
meet with me in two weeks after I had time to study the works he
suggested. I immediately obtained the two or three books he recommended and began to scour them for material relating to the wolf.

My research was disappointing. There were few references to the
wolf and those that I managed to uncover were obscure and difficult
to decipher. My search seemed to be going in a confusing circle. I felt
less and less sure of my direction. I wondered if I even had the right
to be considering such an enormous and demanding undertaking.

On a cold blustery day, I headed across the University of New
Mexico campus to meet Ortiz at his second story office overlooking
an open courtyard of the anthropology building. His door was open
as I approached and I could hear he was on the phone. Cautiously, I
knocked.

WHITE MAN'S THINKING

"Come in, come in," he said. "So, you're the wolf man." His boom-ing, melodious laugh filled the room cluttered with books stacked in random piles in and around his desk. I thought, if I am the wolf man, Ortiz is the bear man. Large, but full of energy, he seemed constantly on the verge of exploding with the excitement of discovery. He wore his hair long in a traditional Tewa *chungo* wrapped at the nape in a figure eight with a piece of yarn. He motioned for me to sit.

"Well, what have you learned?" he asked, pushing his glasses back on his nose.

I told him I had discovered that the wolf was the Beast God of the East.

"Maybe in Zuni," he replied. "I've thought about your problem driving back and forth from Santa Fe. There's nothing on the wolf that I know of, and if there is, you'll have to talk to men who are in their eighties now...men who were hunters. There's a lot on the coy-ote, but nothing on the wolf...Nope, nothing."

He explained that the coyote was an intermediary. I mumbled something about heaven and earth and asked if the wolf being Beast God of the East meant the same thing to Pueblos as to Plains Tribes. Ortiz scowled.

"That's white man's thinking," he said. I felt foolish and embar-rassed.

"No, I think you misunderstand," I said. "I meant if the Beast Gods are the same to the Plains Tribes and Pueblos."

"*I* misunderstand!" he said.

I asked Ortiz why he thought the wolf had been exterminated by ranchers and the government. He compared the fate of the wolf to genocide and continued persecution of Indian tribes. He commented that wildness in any form had to be eliminated by the white culture. He paused, his brow furrowed in thought.

"If there is something on the wolf," he said, "you can find it by going west to Zuni or Acoma. Don't go north or south. You'll waste your time."

"I have some contacts at Taos," I said. "Maybe I should try going up there."

"Maybe," he said. "But I think you'll find it's a waste of time. Head west if you want to learn about the wolf. I wish I had more for you, but you'll have to talk to the old men. I've thought about your problem a lot and this is all I can tell you. I'm sorry. I wish I could be more helpful. Go west and maybe you can learn something." We shook hands and my encounter with Alfonso Ortiz was at an end.

I was deeply disturbed and baffled by our meeting. I stayed awake most of the night turning over in my mind our meeting. On the one hand, Ortiz had expressed genuine concern for the project. On the other, he seemed impatient, secretive, and defensive. Then there was the issue of our misunderstanding and his comment about my white man's thinking. I felt ashamed and vulnerable, my efforts to make a favorable impression obviously unsuccessful.

CLARITY EMERGES

Not only was I confused by my encounter with Ortiz but I found my research continually perplexing. I knew prey animals were associated with the cardinal directions and that each direction, in turn, was associated with a color. The color for north was yellow, for west it was blue, for south it was red, for east it was white, and for zenith and nadir it was black and variegated. Plants, trees, animals and birds likewise had this directional association—mountain lion with north, bear with west, badger with south, eagle with sky, moles with underground...and wolf with the east.

Plains tribes had similar associations between animals and directions, but the wolf was associated with the color red. Interchange between Plains tribes and Pueblos was common, so it seemed reasonable to assume the Pueblos could have adapted this way of thinking. I pondered what these associations meant. Could animals, directions and colors be elements in a secret system of symbols which was totally closed to outsiders?

Two weeks after my meeting with Ortiz I read in one of the most extensive studies of Pueblo traditions published in 1939 by anthropologist Elsie Clews Parsons that a certain doctor by the name of Kroeber had been given the name Onothlikia, or Oriole, by the Zunis because he had originally come from the north and had worn khaki clothing. According to *Pueblo Indian Religion,* the two-volume study recommended by Ortiz, the oriole is the bird of the north and yellow is the color associated with the north.

In Pueblo legend, Wolf Boy, suitor of Yellow Corn Girl lived in the east as is to be expected because this direction is associated with the wolf. Suddenly, Alfonso Ortiz's advice came back to me. He had suggested I go west in my searches for wolf knowledge. How appropriate his suggestion seemed.

If I arrived from the east and told residents of Zuni or Acoma I was interested in the wolf, chances for a good reception were enhanced. I would be arriving from the east, the wolf's direction.

I decided to open my investigations to a whole other mode of thinking that seemed to be emerging for me. Ortiz had given me my first instruction and demonstration in Pueblo thought modes, not through explanation and question-answer format, but through demonstration, participation, and example.

He was right. My mind was so bound up with my white man's presumptions and my reporter's questions that I was failing to take seriously the subject of my inquiry and I was failing to understand, honor, and respect the traditions I was studying.

Ortiz's instructions had been a vivid example of one phase or part leading to the whole and involving all other parts. A more vivid example of this principle came from Ortiz's penetrating exposition of Pueblo life and thought, entitled *The Tewa World: Space, Time, and Becoming in a Pueblo Society*. The wolf plays an important role in the Tewa's most important myth, the emergence story.

As revealed in the previous chapter, questioning and discovering the origin and causes of particular phenomena or events is not seen as a way of learning in Indian thinking. The sacred infuses everything and is akin to a kind of sentient-being spirit. In Judeo-Christian beliefs, God is an outside agency, a kind of grand mover who shapes the universe. The creation story is for European cultures, therefore, very important because it explains *how* and *why* the world was created.

Interest in origins or explanations is not the central focus for Tewa mythology. The Pueblo world is multidimensional, extending in at least six directions. The gods are not "above," and down is as important as up. Humans are in the middle and the village is in the center of the Pueblo universe.

The most important story for the Tewa is the myth of emergence, just as it is for many Native American tribes. In emergence stories, people, animals, divine beings, and others originally lived in a world beneath the present world. Often this ancestral underground universe is described as a place of darkness and social chaos. In the Tewa story the underground universe is located beneath a lake.

The collective unconscious with its dream images and subterranean archetypes may be compared to pre-emergence existence in which animals, gods, and humans can communicate. The pre-emergence world is the realm where the dead go and the magic place where shamans descend in their soul travels. The universe before this one is the womb-world. By intercession of a hero or powerful animal the people climb through a hole or up a tree into the present world.

The analogy to the birth experience or parturition has been noted by anthropologists. Emergence stories may record mythological memories of an ancient past when ancestral prehumans had yet to take the first tentative steps on the long journey of human discovery. These myths record the evolution of human awareness and dawning consciousness. In this sense emergence myths trace the birth and growth of social awareness. In some Pueblo traditions humans emerge from four womb-worlds into the present world. In each world social chaos, imbalance, and disorder erupt and the people repeat their initiation in another universe until they emerge in our present world.

The emergence of humankind is not a creation in the Tewa myth. Humans are seen as already existing. There is little if any interest in telling how or where humans or the world came from or ascribing such origins to a moral, purposeful God who rules the world from on high. Myths serve as a way of instructing people about habits of mind, tradition, and ways of doing things that are in accord with the sacred which infuses everything, not just in explaining how or why things evolved the way they have.

Of particular importance in the Tewa emergence myth is the role played by the wolf and other predators in the entrance of the People from the previous world into the current world. The wolf teaches predator lessons and survivor skills, and bestows hunting tools.

When I first read this story of Tewa emergence, I felt only my usual confusion. The legend seemed to yield to me no meanings whatsoever, like a dream half-remembered the next morning after a fitful sleep. I decided I would let the story speak to me without forcing meaning from it. I resolved to read the legend over and over, to memorize it, and to repeat it to myself, allowing whatever meanings to surface in my conscious awareness by emerging from deep within my own mind. My process was intended to imitate the very story itself. Like the ancient hero who undergoes rites of initiation to journey from the realm of darkness to the world of sunlight, I struggled toward insight by abandoning my reason and relying on intuition.

I drew pictures of the myth with colored pencil and I imagined the story over and over until the legend saturated my experience. What emerged from my studies gave me a deeper knowledge than my initial confused readings of this myth, in which the wolf as predator plays a most important role, a crucial part in the development of an awareness that infuses all of Tewa life.

According to Elsie Clews Parsons, who conducted her detailed studies of Pueblo life in the early to mid-1900s, a white woman asked a man from Taos Pueblo what Indian religion was.

"Life," he answered, meaning that religion was a means to life, that it covered life as a whole and that everything of meaning was alive and vibrantly part of religion. It is in this sense that the myth of emergence must be understood. The Pueblos form analogies for everything they see and life is permeated with sympathetic magic which informs all experience.

A DAWNING CONSCIOUSNESS

Far to the north of the present Tewa world located in the Rio Grande Valley of New Mexico there was a large lake called *ohange pokwinge*, or Sandy Place Lake. The "lake of the dead" is an actual place located in the Sand Dunes National Monument northeast of present day Alamosa. It is a forbidding site, a place of death.

In 1892, an old rancher who lived nearby in the Sierra Blanca said the lake was about a hundred yards in diameter, the water black, the shore surrounded by a perpetual ring of dead cattle that had mistakenly drunk the waters.

In the primordial time before this world people, animals, and supernaturals lived beneath this lake in a place called *Sipofene*. This world was dark, and time and death were unknown. Two of the supernaturals, Blue Corn Woman (the Summer mother of the people) and White Corn Woman (the Winter mother), asked one of the men to go forth and discover a way through which everyone might be able to leave the lake.

Three times the man pondered this request, and, on each occasion he refused. Finally, after a fourth demand, he agreed, going first to the north. He found only mist and haze, saying the world was unripe (*ochu*) or green. On successive tries he went to the west, then to the south and east. The two mothers instructed him to go to the above. He came to an open place and here he saw gathered all the *tsiwi*, or predators.

The wolves, mountain lions, coyotes, foxes, vultures, and crows were waiting for him. He was afraid. On seeing him, the predators rushed him, knocked him down, and fiercely scratched him. Then they told him to get up, that they were his friends. His wounds disappeared and they bestowed on him a bow, arrows, and quiver. They dressed him in buckskin and painted his face black and they tied feathers of carrion-eating birds in his hair.

"You have been accepted," the wolves and other predators told him. "These things we have given you are what you shall use from now on. You are ready to go."

The Tewa emergence story recounts a shamanic initiation journey of an anonymous hero who represents the entire people as he travels from the darkness of unconscious underworld existence where only a pale moonlike dimness resides. Here the people grope about lost in social chaos.

According to Santa Ana tradition, beneath our world there were four womb-worlds, each of a different color, from which humans and animals originally emerged. The Tewa version seems a condensation of four worlds into one. In no way is the underworld personified, but the womb analogy seems a most apt description. Emergence from the dark womb-like underworld can be seen as a kind of journey of human consciousness as it travels from dim semiawareness toward self-knowledge and social conscience in the upper world, where the sun resides and blesses all life.

The corn mothers, associated with winter and summer and agricultural cycles, give birth to the people, but ability to survive comes from this journey of initiation. The teachers who bestow survival knowledge on the hero are Wolf and other archetypal predators who test him by scratching him. Knowledge comes with pain. Perhaps by scratching him, the predators make the hero aware of his own frailty, his own mortality, and his dependence on the prey he must hunt and kill for his own survival.

The knowledge that Wolf and other predators give to the Tewa hero is not knowledge of good and evil as in the Biblical story of Adam and Eve, but knowledge of life and death and the interdependence of animal and human life cycles. It is an ecological knowledge.

The Tewa call the world 'opa which includes all that is. Their universe is considered as a living being and is worshipped as Universe Man.

The Tewa, when asked why they practice certain rites or why they do certain things, say that such practices came up with them in the emergences. They also say that in the beginning they were one people and that they later divided into Summer and Winter people. This explains how the Tewa divide themselves into moieties or primary subdivisions of the people into two seasonally identified parts. At the same time they recognize the essential wholeness of the people.

Thus, they are simultaneously both divided and "at one." Their traditions and this mode of thinking, they say, stems from the time of emergence.

As a part stands for the whole, so hunting practices are reflected in the emergence myth. The hero's initiation by predators allows him to be given magical tools of the hunt. He has proved himself worthy. The relationship Pueblos developed with prey species is based on identification with wolves and predators.

Animals in their mortality resemble humans, but they are more closely associated with gods because they are considered to be ultimately mysterious. They have powers not possessed by men. Predators and the wolf play a special role in Pueblo life because of their spirit power. Due to their power, they bestow hunting knowledge on men. The talismans of this special knowledge—bow and arrow, quiver, dress made of animal skins, black face paint, and feathers of carrion birds—are given to the mythical hero ancestor at the dawn of this world as a sign that he has been provided with the power to hunt. All Tewa hunters from this time forward get their power to hunt from the mythical ancestral hero who led the people from the world of darkness into the world of light and who was given hunting magic and ritual by Wolf and the other great predators at the beginning of this world.

The successful hunter who led tribal communal efforts to kill deer depended on a spirit helper such as the wolf that was possessed of special hunting magic. Predator power, as pictured in the emergence myth, was evoked in tribal hunting practices when the hunt chief relied on the wolf or other prey animals to give him power and knowledge.

Ritual dances to stimulate vision power for the hunt leader were enacted during communal hunting rites. Sexual continence, proper eating and personal conduct were carefully observed to ensure successful hunting. Through his vision power a hunt chief might locate a herd of antelope or charm them to tameness after beaters had scared them from the chaparral into a corral where they might be shot.

Deer magic was conjured at camp before the hunt so prey would give themselves to the hunters. Rituals, offerings, dances, and display of sacred objects ensured the arrival of Wolf and other hunt gods known as supernaturals. Individual ritual behavior was believed to please prey. For the Zuni and Keres, supernaturals invoked through proper rites, eating, and behavioral observations were the beast gods of the four directions, including the Wolf of the east. Prey gods were considered guardians of the prey. In other Pueblos a deity called Mother of Game Animals was evoked. Rites, dances, and prayers culminated in the appearance of Wolf and other prey animals.

SOFT WORDS AND SPIRIT ANIMALS

Quarry, when hunted successfully, were believed to return to an animal spirit world where they reported on the treatment they had received. Others of their kind were encouraged in this way to undergo giving their lives to hunters who honored them through ritual and ceremony. Dances and rites involving Wolf of the east, the Game Mother, and other supernaturals were also held to promote the general good will of prey species.

During these rites dancers imitated animals and supernaturals. In singing ceremonial songs involving the Wolf god of the east, other supernaturals and prey animals, so-called "soft words" were used to avoid offending prey by using their direct names. The wolf, coyote, and crow were often given secret allusive names. To what extent the spirit wolf was an independent being or a helper or intercessor is hard to tell.

The nature of spirit wolf identity was confused by the tendency to preserve social integrity through keeping exact traditions secret or deliberately lying to outsiders. The spirit wolf and other prey animals are sometimes known as "pets" or spirit companions. Anthropologist Elsie Clews Parsons thought spirit animals participated in a collective identity. Perhaps such confusion arises because of the desire not to offend prey by referring directly to the supernaturals or prey.

Among the western Pueblos, killing deer without damaging buckskin held special value. It may be that the value and power obtained by such hunting practices came from imitating the wolf. The wolf was observed to run after his prey, while the mountain lion killed by springing on his quarry. Indian hunters ran down the deer until it fell down exhausted and they smothered it. This practice may account for many of the running games so popular among Indians of the Southwest.

These traditions evoke mindfulness of the total dependence people have on resources provided through earth's bounty. Understanding that the earth freely gives a harvest of corn is an obvious reason for seeing earth as a powerful living being. Game animals give themselves to hunters and require propitiation for their sacrifice. Compassion for animals who are hunted, suffer and die is embodied through elaborate ritual conduct and ceremony so participants are always reminded of a fragile balance preserved between species.

WOLF OF LEGEND, WOLF OF MYTH

The association between use of prayer sticks and the wolf is strong among Pueblos. Prayers sticks were used almost universally by Pueblos except in Tewan and Tiwan villages. They were buried under trees and shrubs, or in other propitious locations, sunk under water, carried to mountain tops, placed on altars or in kiva or house walls, or they were simply stuck in the ground or "planted."

In one Pueblo story, a boy cuts prayer sticks in honor of Yellow Wolf. He brings them to Wolf's house and presents them to Father and Mother Wolf and their sons and daughters.

"It won't do to have him [Wolf] living near us. We shall have to send him away," says the boy who presents prayer sticks to the Wolf family. Then he commands Father Wolf to go north, Mother Wolf to go west, the Wolf Boys to head south and their sisters to head east. This is said to explain why wolves were found in all the hills in every direction. In this brief story ambiguity about wolves and wolf nature leads the boy to desire to keep Wolf at a distance. Despite reverence for Wolf's power, wolf nature embodies the dangerous and unpredictable that produces antipathy in the human spirit.

Wolf was not viewed as the most powerful Beast God as he was portrayed in Wolf Ritual stories of the Northwest. Anthropologist Ruth Benedict related a Zuni tale about the Beast Gods who were angry with people because they didn't know how to make prayer sticks or offer prayers.

Wolf, Bear, Mountain Lion, and other Beast Gods were living in Ice Cave thirty miles east of Zuni. They held a council there and they were very angry because, if the people did not know the use of prayer sticks, their ceremonial omission would upset vital balances that preserved harmony essential to the well-being of the entire universe. They sent Wolf down to the village each night to kill the women and girls. Wolf's attack represents this imbalance through powerful sexual symbolism. It might be tempting to explore Freudian interpretations of this story, but perhaps more meaningful in the imagery of Wolf's attack is the sense of a world turned upside down because of a seemingly unimportant oversight or lack of knowledge. How dire the consequences of this imbalance are is manifested in the terror of Wolf's attack, which overturns all social order and wreaks havoc and destruction through the murder of women and defenseless girls.

The men were afraid to go out. Local priests bathed a virgin girl and boy and made from the slough of their cuticle a fetish of Ahaiyute, War Patron. Thus empowered, the fetish was sent to protect the village from Wolf's ravages. When the image of Ahaiyute confronted Wolf, he retreated to Ice Cave.

"There is someone down there who has more power than we have," Wolf told the other beasts. "I do not think I can go there any more." Badger rebuked Wolf for his cowardice, choosing to go himself, but he was chased back to Ice Cave by Ahaiyute who fearlessly challenged the Beast Gods. White Bear, when he saw Ahaiyute coming, told the animals to scatter.

This, according to the legend, is the reason why predators were to be found everywhere and why they no longer attacked people. Both these stories also seem to be dealing with the dread that predators have always evoked in humans. Cowardice when presented with danger, or outright panic when confronted with wolves in the wilds, was to be avoided if calm heads were to prevail and survival was to be secured.

As a hunter, the mountain lion was considered to be more powerful. This may be because of the prominent role mountain lions play in the Southwest ecosystem. Wolf's reduced stature in Pueblo beliefs may also be because as myths and legends circulate, characters may change in importance, while content remains relatively stable.

A writer about Pueblo mythology, Hamilton Tyler recounts that Wolf and Mountain Lion were considered to be companions and that they visited each other constantly and talked about hunting. Wolf was thought to make his kills rather directly and easily. Mountain Lion could not run as swiftly, and did not kill as many as Wolf. He sang a song and sprang on his prey, while Wolf pursued his quarry and never gave up the chase.

In one story, Mountain Lion and Wolf held a contest to see who was a greater hunter. Wolf chased some deer without fatigue, but Mountain Lion hid himself and waited until the deer that Wolf was chasing passed his hiding place. Then he sprang out and quickly dispatched the deer. This happened several times and Wolf was left to gnaw the bones and other leavings of Lion's kills. Tyler suggests Wolf's lesser position in Pueblo mythology was due to wolves that could often be observed cleaning up lion kills.

Wolves are capable of killing mountain lions and will try to eliminate them as competitors, just as they will more effectively eliminate coyotes. Given Tyler's theory, the Pueblos would not have known or observed how wolves play a pre-eminent role in the predator cycle. Provided the emphasis in Pueblo thinking on close sense observation of all natural phenomena, obvious predator interaction like the relationship between wolves and lions probably could not have escaped their notice.

Just as the story of Ha-Sass in the previous chapter credited Wolf with superior guile, considered a mark of wisdom, in this story Mountain Lion outsmarts Wolf and shows the same trait. Guile as a component of survival wisdom seems to be the lesson to be learned from this tale. Other attributes such as strength, endurance, and concentration perhaps were less important than such cleverness. In a version of the White Bison myth, Zuni legend credits Wolf for being a steadfast guardian of the young hero who gives Wolf an eagle feather that he covets. As a reward, Wolf guards the boy all night, wakes him, and taking his leave, trots off into the east from where he has come.

Tyler compares the wolf with coyote and fox, an association that probably would not enter the minds of Pueblos, or at least might not interest them. Pueblo nomenclature recognizes differences, not relationships. Pueblos are not given to the habit of classifying animals by species, order, and family except in the most obvious of cases. Usually an animal is considered a distinct creature not related to any others.

POWER WOLF AND MEDICINE SOCIETIES

Much of what can be surmised about Southwest Pueblo wolf beliefs relies on information gathered through the early part of this century. With the increase of non-Indian populations, the larger game animals such as the deer, elk, mountain sheep, and antelope either were greatly diminished or disappeared from the wilderness entirely. The wolf as an important predator was also being rapidly depleted.

As the population of prey species diminished, so did the importance of hunt societies and traditions. By the late 1930s, the hunt society had become virtually extinct in Keresan and Tewan towns. What is known of Wolf must be told from the faintest outlines sketched in the anthropological accounts of Elsie Clews Parsons, Ruth Benedict, and other observers.

These hunting traditions, which were once central to lifestyles developed by Pueblo and other Southwest Indians, show how predator magic typified by the wolf was vitally important to their beliefs. The Tewa emergence myth taught how predators gave the people their hunt magic. The wolf and other predators were honored for their knowledge, but the prey animals themselves were also honored. Everyone, through myth and rite, was led to constantly be reminded of the dependence people had on the game animals who gave themselves in death that the people might live. Wolf and other prey animals were also associated with war, especially in the west and at Jemez.

Wolf, as a power animal, also played an important role in Pueblo medicine, as did the other prey beasts. Disease was cured through an agent, or an animal such as Wolf, having power for good or ill over disease. Shamans having vision power belonged to societies devoted to curing. Priests and temporary healers also served to cure patients. Disease in Pueblo cultures of the Southwest, however, was defined differently than in Western medicine tradition.

Maladies were brought about through intrusion of objects into the sufferer's body, loss of soul, spirit possession, breaking taboos, or sorcery. These causes were assigned to all disease. Shaman medicine societies each had their power animals with control over disease and their own distinctive songs and rites.

The spirit wolf and other prey animals, as patrons of medicine societies, had quite independent identities. The bear was considered the most powerful sponsor, but wolf and the other prey animals also had healing powers. All beast gods had their home in a mythical place called *Shipap* (Zuni *Shipapolima*) in the East despite the association each beast god had with a primary direction and color.

During Zuni medicine society initiations, predators were imitated, and, reminiscent of Tewa emergence, clawed and bit the initiate like wolves. Eastern Pueblo medicine societies involved re-birth rituals. Animal images were used by the Tewa in such rites.

Breach of hunting rituals or disrespect for remains of prey was thought to cause disease. At least two animal societies in Zuni were thought to have the power to create disease. This idea appears not to have been as well developed in other pueblos.

Pueblo ideas about disease were closely tied to traditions about witchcraft, which often involved the wolf. Doctors possessing animal powers could transform themselves into animals. Witches, having the same power, could do likewise. Doctors could over-power witches or sorcerers through the same means. Essentially witches, like doctors, were thought to know all, but they used power for personal gain.

Elsie Clews Parsons defines *nagualism* as the transformation into wolves or other animals and receiving power from animals. Parsons's definition is more narrowly focused than that found in other cultural traditions of the Southwest and Mexico, in which the individual human becomes identified with a particular spirit or animal counterpart. Nagualism is practiced either by individuals or collectively through societies. Even witches sometimes belonged to societies but most often operated alone.

OF WITCHES AND WOLVES

Nagualism and the practice of witchcraft among the Pueblos was shot through with Spanish influence. A witch was considered to possess all the traits people thought to be antisocial. Anyone who was cantankerous, assertive, or quarrelsome could be subjected to accusations of witchcraft. Insomniacs who wandered at night were also under suspicion. In accusations of sorcery lie the dark side of Pueblo tendencies to sacrifice individualism for the social welfare of the entire group.

Witch baiting and trials were conducted by Pueblo alcaldes and war captains. Where proximity to Hispanic villages was common in New Mexico, witch lore was more fully developed. European ideas associating witches and wolves influenced Pueblo beliefs, making it difficult to distinguish Hispanic ideas from Pueblo concepts. Accusations of witchcraft and nagualism were used by both Spaniards and Pueblos for social control. Popé, instigator of the Pueblo Rebellion of 1680, was accused of witchcraft. After his release, following pressure from Tewa warriors he began his rebellion against the Spanish.

The growth of witchcraft and absorption of Spanish concepts began the negative association between wolves and witches. Werewolves and witches were minions of Satan in the European mind. Pueblo terms not originally associated with witchcraft became so. For instance, the Hopi runner called Wolf Boy became known as Witch Boy in the east pueblos.

Intertown antagonism or suspicion between Pueblos often took the form of imputing witchcraft. In the early part of this century, Taos Pueblo secretly referred to Tewa as Wolf Dung and the Tewa in turn called them Taos Rats.

As late as 1906, Laguna war captains executed a woman named Tsotsi as a witch after a wolf skin with tie strings and paws made into moccasins was found nailed to her wall. She had been known as particularly quarrelsome and as a gossip and braggart. She and her husband, like many another accused of witchcraft, always seemed to have plenty though they were known to be poor. In the 1920s during Parsons's extensive study of Pueblo culture she developed contact with a Pueblo individualist accused and subsequently persecuted as a witch.

Transformation into wolves was thought to be effected by either wearing a wolf pelt or by passing through a hoop or ring and in this way the witch was said to turn over and assume wolf form. A witch who practiced nagualism could be identified because the wolf's snout could be seen pressing against the witch's forehead.

While belief in witches certainly existed before the arrival of the Spanish, their appearance marked the infusion of European ideas about the wolf which spilled over into Pueblo beliefs about nagualism and the negative association between witches and wolves. Witches were a manifestation of social imbalance and personal misuse of power. They were not seen as extensions of evil. The association of witches and satanic forces is a European idea, an idea that has marked the relationship with the wolf ever since that belief was brought to this continent.

In Pueblo culture the wolf was a spirit animal who bestowed his power on hunters or those who sought his aid in curing diseases. The Great God of the East, the wolf stood at the door of the world when time began and taught humankind hunting secrets and served as guardian of deer, antelope, and other prey upon whom life depended. Close to nature, indeed, embedded in the natural world, the Pueblos saw Wolf as a great teacher, sometimes frightening, but always to be honored and respected.

WILL BIG TROTTER RECLAIM HIS PLACE? THE ROLE OF THE WOLF IN NAVAJO TRADITION

Steve Pavlik

(2000)

*T*he wolf was long an important factor in Navajo life. With the destruction of the wild wolf in the American Southwest, a vital link to the past—and perhaps the future—has been lost to the Navajo people. In recent years, however, an effort has been made to restore wolves to their native habitat. If the wolf recovery program is successful, what effect will it have on the Navajo people? Will the return of the wolf help restore the balance and harmony that once existed?

THE WOLF IN THE SOUTHWEST AND NAVAJO COUNTRY

Sometime shortly after his arrival into the Southwest in 1917, US Forest Service biologist Aldo Leopold participated in the killing of a wolf somewhere in the White Mountains, which stretch across the borderlands of south-central Arizona and New Mexico. Leopold and a number of companions were eating lunch on a high rimrock position overlooking a river when they spotted a female wolf and her six grown pups playing in an open area below. Immediately, the men pulled out their rifles and "with more excitement than accuracy," began blasting away at the family. When the rifles were empty and the shooting stopped, only the female wolf was down and one pup was seen dragging its leg into a rockslide. Leopold, who would go on to become perhaps the most famous conservationist in American history, described the death of this wolf—and his own personal transformation—in one of the most quoted passages in the literature of wildlife conservation:

> We reached the old wolf in time to watch a fierce green fire dying in her eyes. I realized then, and have known ever since, that there

was something new to me in those eyes—something known only to her and to the mountain. I was young then, and full of trigger-itch; I thought that because fewer wolves meant more deer, that no wolves would mean hunters' paradise. But after seeing the green fire die, I sensed that neither the wolf nor the mountain agreed with such a view.[1]

The gray wolf, *Canis lupis*, had long been part of the Southwest American landscape—and an integral part of Navajo mythology and culture.[2] The Leopold incident described above took place during the heyday of the war of extermination against the wolf. With the arrival of cattle ranchers and sheepherders in the 1880s, and the subsequent destruction of the native herbivore species on which the wolves preyed, wolves became a serious threat to the livestock industry. Consequently, a program of wolf extermination was soon initiated by the Predatory Animal and Rodent Control (PARC) branch of the US Biological Survey, predecessor to the US Fish and Wildlife Service. Using firearms, traps, poisons, and denning—digging wolf pups out of their dens and clubbing them to death—the professional "wolfers" of PARC were relentless in their efforts to eradicate the wolf. By 1925 the wolf ceased to be a major predator in the Southwest with all resident animals eliminated except for a few holdouts on isolated pockets of land such as the San Carlos, White Mountain, and Jicarilla Apache reservations, and on the Navajo Reservation. By the 1940s the wolf was all but extinct in the Southwest with the last wolves killed in Arizona and New Mexico in the early 1970s. Although documentation is scarce, it is believed that wolves were once relatively abundant on the Defiance Plateau and in the Lukachukai and Chuska mountains of the Navajo Reservation.[3] In all probability the last wolf on the Navajo Reservation was killed before 1950.

In 1973 the United States Congress passed the Endangered Species Act (ESA). This law directed the secretary of the interior to develop and implement a recovery plan for species and subspecies of wildlife that were in danger of human-caused extinction. The act also mandated the reintroduction of endangered species when feasible. In 1976 the Mexican wolf, *Canis lupus baileyi*, or the lobo as it was once commonly called, was listed as an endangered species under the ESA. Two years later the entire gray wolf species in North America south of Canada was listed. The listing of the entire species served to initiate efforts to reintroduce wolves to the West.

In 1996 wolves captured in Canada were released in Yellowstone National Park in Wyoming, and in Montana and central Idaho.

Encouraged by the success of this program, plans were made to re-introduce Mexican wolves to the Southwest. In the spring of 1998, three family groups of eleven captive-bred Mexican wolves were released in the White Mountains of Arizona—the site of Aldo Leopold's encounter with a dying wolf almost eighty years earlier. Other family groups would be reintroduced over the next three to five years until the recovery goal of one hundred wolves was sustained through reproduction within the wild population.

Although the return of the wolves has been highly controversial, public opinion surveys have shown overwhelming support for reintroduction programs. Environmental groups view wolf reintroduction as the cornerstone of their efforts to promote biodiversity and restore balance to the natural world. However, livestock ranchers, hunting organizations, and a number of other special interest groups see no place in the modern world for wolves and have posed stiff opposition to reintroduction.[4] Regardless of one's position, wolves have certainly re-entered the minds, hearts, and lives of the American public.

One indication of the resurgence of interest in wolves is the proliferation of books and articles written about the animal. A visit to any decent-size bookstore usually reveals an impressive selection of wolf-related publications, most published since 1980. One author has termed the past decade the "Decade of the Wolf."[5] Most of these books include some reference, and often at least one or more chapters, regarding wolves and American Indians.

Writers, especially environmental writers, tend to emphasize the special and positive relationship between wolves and this country's Native American inhabitants. In general, the literature reflects on the fact that most American Indian tribes hold the wolf in high regard. For many tribes, the Cheyenne, Sioux, Pawnee, and Nez Perce, to name a few, the wolf is an important figure in their origin stories and is usually portrayed as a powerful being possessing admirable qualities such as courage, strength, wisdom, family devotion, and the ability to work cooperatively with others. Many tribes have wolf clans and some tribes have warrior and hunting societies that associated themselves with the wolf and draw power from this animal. An extensive list could be compiled of Native American warriors, hunters, spiritual leaders, and diplomats who adopted or were given wolf-related names of honor.

One tribe stands in sharp contrast to others regarding views and attitudes toward the wolf: the Navajo. In writing about the relationship of the Navajo to the wolf, some writers, most notably Barry H. Lopez and Robert H. Busch, unfortunately focus on the question of witchcraft.[6] In doing so I believe these writers are perpetuating a false impression of the relationship that actually existed between the tribe and the wolf. In reality, the wolf, *Ma'iitsoh*, or Big Trotter as he is known to the Navajo, was an important and positive figure in tribal tradition.

One purpose of this article is to provide a deeper analysis of this relationship. The second goal is to provide a close examination of the wolf-witchcraft association and how it came into being. By doing so, I hope to correct what I believe to be a misinterpretation of this issue. Finally, I will offer a few observations and comments regarding the future relationship between the Navajo and the wolf.

Three books have been published in recent years specifically on the Mexican wolf: David E. Brown's, *The Wolf in the Southwest: The Making of an Endangered Species* is the standard work on this subspecies and provides basic background in regard to natural history and especially man's efforts to eradicate the animal.[7] Brown, however, does not address the topic of the wolf's relationship to Native people in the Southwest. James C. Burbank's *Vanishing Lobo: The Mexican Wolf in the Southwest* does focus more on the nature of the wolf-human relationship and includes excellent chapters on the role played by the wolf in Pueblo and Navajo cultures.[8] Most recently, Rick Bass has written *The New Wolves: The Return of the Mexican Wolf to the American Southwest*.[9] As the subtitle suggests, this book documents the early efforts to reintroduce the Mexican wolf back into its historic range in the Blue Range of the White Mountains. Again, no mention is made about the role of the wolf in Southwest Native American cultures and lifeways.

THE DIVINE WOLF

The people who we now know as the Navajo are a result of the coming together of two traditions: the Athabascan or Apachean hunters who migrated into the Southwest around 1500, and the largely agricultural-based Pueblos with whom the hunters made extensive contact after 1680. What we now recognize as "traditional" Navajo is a syncretism of these two traditions with most religious and ceremonial beliefs, including their emergence stories, actually deriving from the Pueblo side of their heritage. However, the role of Wolf in the Navajo stories originates mostly from the Athabascan hunter tradition. This aspect of the relationship between the wolf and the Navajo has been studied by W. W. Hill and Karl W. Luckert and will be discussed in the next section of this article.[10]

In the Navajo emergence story, the earth was first inhabited by Holy People, beings of supernatural power, and some Animal People, who preceded and then coexisted with humans. Anthropologist Gladys A. Reichard summarized that:

> The Holy People might well be considered those who, in mythological times, were able to help man in cases where he could not help himself. In those days snakes, birds and other animals could speak and behave like men and to human powers they added supernatural powers. Nowadays they no longer speak but their powers remain for good or evil to man depending on how he receives them and upon the side which they allied themselves in ancient times.[11]

Wolf, the deity, and wolf, the animal, fall into such categorization. In the beginning he existed as an anthropomorphic figure, a being possessed of considerable supernatural power. Today we see him only in his animal form retaining only a remnant of the power he once held. However, these powers are still considerable. Consequently, wolves are thought (along with bears and coyotes) to be among the so-called dangerous animals in terms of the sickness they can bring to people who have offended them in some way. More will be said about wolf sickness later in this article.

In Father Berard Haile's version of the Upward Moving and Emergence Way myth, as told to him by Gishin Biyé, the Red Underworld is the home of Wolf who lives in a white house in the east. In one of his first appearances in the narrative, Wolf attacks the house of First Man, whose guardians, Wildcat and Puma, catch the arrows he shoots at them. First Man then uses those arrows to kill sixteen Wolf People. In return for First Man restoring life to their slain kin, the Wolf People create four songs for each member restored, a total of sixty-four songs, which they give to First Man. Haile notes that this story explains the presence of wolf songs in Navajo ceremonials.[12]

In another emergence story, again recorded by Haile from Gishin Biyé, a separation of sexes occurred when Wolf, chief of the east, finds his wife to be irresponsible and disrespectful. Because of this he leads the other male beings to the opposite side of a great river to live away from the female beings. In time, however, the two sexes find they need each other. It is Wolf who calls a meeting of the chiefs and proposes a reconciliation. This series of events suggests that Wolf is held in the highest esteem and was considered the leader of the other chiefs who are quick to accept his proposals.[13]

Wolf is also the first to raise the alarm over the omens, which ultimately foretell a great flood brought on by Coyote stealing Water Monster's baby. As the floodwater rises, Wolf, along with Mountain Lion and Bear, help dig a hole through the roof of the Underworld so they can escape into the Upperworld.[14] Upon entering the new world, Wolf continues his role as chief.[15]

The other side of Wolf's character is his impatience and short temper. In another emergence story, Wolf becomes angry over the introduction of foods he sees as inferior, including certain plants and salt. In his anger he offends Salt Woman. This story explains why people today take offense at different things.[16]

Another origin story, as recorded by Washington Matthews, deserves mention because it draws a comparison between Wolf and his cousin Coyote. In this story, Coyote visits Wolf who buries two arrows with wooden heads in the hot ashes beside his fire, then pulls them out to reveal two fine pieces of meat, which he serves his guest. Later, Wolf visits Coyote, who tries to impress him by attempting the same magical act. However, when Coyote pulls the arrows out of the ashes, he has only burnt wood to show for his efforts.[17] Clearly Wolf and Coyote do not share the same character and abilities.

Wolf's most prominent role in Navajo mythology can be found in the stories associated with the Beadway ceremony and the related Eagle Way ritual. In the version of the Beadway story as told by Miguelito to Reichard, the hero, Scavenger or Holy Boy, wanders off and is buried under a pile of rocks. The Eagles, who have befriended Scavenger, call upon the hunters, Wolf, Mountain Lion, Lynx, and Bobcat, to rescue him. Although the hunters fail in their attempt, Badger eventually recovers his bones. A ceremony is then held to bring him back to life using four feathers from different birds: Bald Eagle, Blue Hawk, Yellow Hawk, and Magpie. These feathers are transformed, respectively, into Wolf, Mountain Lion, Beaver, and Otter. When the transformation is complete, Scavenger is restored to life. It is for this reason that the skins of these four animals are used in the Beadway ceremony.[18]

Wolf appears several other times in the Beadway story. At one point, in Haile's version, Wolf is chosen as the meal sprinkler and, traveling supernaturally on sunrays, is sent to spread the word of an impending Beadway ceremony.[19] In Reichard's version, Wolf is portrayed as traveling to perform a Beadway himself. In both versions Wolf encounters his friend and fellow hunter, Mountain Lion, who is on a similar mission. Since neither wants to miss the other's sing, they agree that Mountain Lion should postpone his ceremony for one night. To bind this agreement, the two great hunters exchange quivers. A sandpainting used in Beadway depicts this event, showing Wolf wearing a quiver made of mountain lion skin.

Another sandpainting from Beadway shows the Wolf People joining the Mountain Lion People in a Fire Dance performance. Yet another Beadway sandpainting shows both the Wolf People and the Mountain Lion People dancing while wearing packs of corn on their backs—corn secured by the Hunters through use of their magical powers to plant, cultivate, and harvest the crop, all within minutes, before performing their dance.[20]

Wolf also plays an important role in another life-restoring origin story associated with the Flintway ceremony. In this story, White Thunder destroys the hero, Holy Young Man. Wolf is one of the deities summoned to help restore him. Wolf, because he did not devour the hero's flesh at the time of his death, is asked to regulate the Flintway method of administering liquid medicine. An accompanying Wolf song is also sung. One such song imitates the growl of Wolf and mentions him four times in which he represents both himself and other animals whose fur and body parts are used in the Flintway ceremony. Dark Wolf represents the bear, White Wolf represents the wolf itself, Yellow Wolf represents the mountain lion, and Glittering Wolf represents all three collectively, the wildcat, or possibly the otter.[21] The wolf, along with the mountain lion, is one of the key animals whose death blood, tallow, marrow, and menstrual flux are utilized in Flintway.

In looking at the role played by Wolf in the emergence story, and subsequent stories leading up to various ceremonies, it is clear he is a figure of considerable power and prestige. He is highly respected by the other Holy People for his wisdom and powers and is looked to for advice and often given important assignments upon which the welfare of the people depends. Consequently, Wolf must certainly be ranked as one of the important Animal People. Most critically, Wolf appears throughout Navajo mythology as a divine personage who, on the whole, is a positive and beneficial figure to the Navajo people.

WOLF AND THE NAVAJO HUNTER TRADITION

Of his many attributes and abilities, Wolf was formally recognized for his skills as a hunter. It is not surprising, then, that in the stories of the Navajo hunter tradition, Wolf plays a major role. Indeed, the Navajo use the word *naatl'eetsoh*—which literally refers to wolves—for all hunters and predators, including man.[22]

As noted earlier, the origin of these hunter stories traces back to the Athabascan period of Navajo prehistory. Luckert, whose work I draw from extensively, credits this period with providing the foundation for Navajo hunting stories, especially regarding the role of animal elders and hunter tutelary. Later contact with the Pueblos, with the consequent incorporation of an emergence mythology, elaborated and enriched the Navajo hunter tradition. This contention is supported by the fact that the Navajo did not arrive at many of the geographical places mentioned in their hunter stories until the late 1700s.[23]

In the Deer Hunting Way, as told by Claus Chee Sonny to Luckert, the deer gods themselves provided the divine hunters, Wolf, Mountain Lion, Tiger (Jaguar), Bobcat, and Cat, with the necessary knowledge to pass down through the generations.[24] Presumably, the deer gods taught man how to hunt them, but man also acquired his specific knowledge of hunting from the divine predators.

In a second version of the Navajo hunter tradition, as recorded by Luckert from Billie Blackhorse, a definite hierarchy of gods exist who preside over animals: Black God, who ranks highest, Talking God, and Calling God. Since these gods presumably preside over the hunt, they are theoretically the leaders of the *naatl'eetsoh*. Consequently, Luckert feels that all *naatl'eetsoh* should be called gods. However, it should be noted that the animal gods predate Black God, Talking God, and Calling God. Since Wolf bestowed his mythical name on all hunters, of both animal and human form, he was in the truest sense the highest ranking of the hunter deities.[25]

The Navajo traditionally distinguished between two types of hunting: ritual and nonritual. The wolf itself, whose body parts are sometimes needed for certain ceremonies, was killed nonritually. Only deer, antelope, bear, and eagles were hunted ritually.[26] Perhaps a dozen specific hunting rituals or "ways" existed. These animals were apparently singled out for ritualistic hunting due to their importance in Navajo tradition and lifeway and certainly because of the degree of power they possessed. For example, deer were very powerful and could cause deer sickness called *ajiłee*.[27] For these ritual hunts, the hunter was obligated to follow certain procedures that regulated all aspects of the hunt, from preparation and planning through breaking camp when the hunt was over. Only by strictly observing ritualistic procedures could the hunter honor the game he hunted, ensure his success, immunize himself against *ajiłee*, and cleanse himself of the guilt associated with taking a life. Most of these procedures were used to hunt deer—the most important of the game animals.[28]

The Wolfway was one of the most popular of the hunting rituals and was primarily used to hunt deer and sometimes elk in the fall, especially from the first of November until the full moon of December. Usually four to ten men made up the hunting party. This party was under the direction of a medicine man or singer who initially called for the hunt and would instruct and lead the hunters throughout the activity.[29]

The Wolfway hunt began with the participants retiring to a sweathouse. In doing so, they not only purified themselves, but also, through prayer and the recitation of songs, entered the mythic world of preemergence and animal gods, which gave birth to the hunter tradition. Hill states:

> The most outstanding feature of the ritual hunt was the complete reversal of the psychology of the participants. Through the hunt, they found release from ordinary restrictions. In everyday life around the hogan, the hunters were normal individuals of the group. They shunned speaking of death, blood, or killing. Their hunting songs could not be sung because of their danger to women, children, and sheep. However, as soon as the party left on a hunting trip, the individual behavior underwent a complete change. The hunters did everything possible to emulate the animal in whose way they were hunting: eating from branches, sleeping like animals and using animal cries to call other members of the party. Topics that dealt with blood and death, which, under ordinary circumstances were avoided, were spoken of with the utmost freedom. The hunters were charged to keep their minds on killing and things pertaining to death.[30]

In summary, the hunters emerged from the sweathouse transformed into the predator whose power they sought. Those who hunted in the Wolfway did not simply imitate the wolf, they assumed the wolf identity. During the hunt they referred to each other as *naatl'eetsoh*. They thought, behaved, and even communicated like wolves. In the story behind the Wolfway ritual, Wolf gave permission for hunters to use his voice. If a hunter howled like a wolf four times to the north, he could fend off bad weather. Also, hunters used the howl of the wolf to signal each other. Indeed, it was the only form of communication permissible while on the hunt. As one hunter familiar with hunter tradition stated:

> The Wolf's voice may be used in hunting to signal one another if more than one person is hunting together. The wolf gave them

that and today those people who know about this make use of it in their hunting. You never talk to another hunter in your own voice. You always imitate the voice of the wolf. If you recognize the importance of this in hunting, you will observe it. If you do not, then you may see deer all around you but you will never hit one.[31]

When a hunter killed a deer, he used the call of the wolf to attract the attention of his fellow hunting partners. Reportedly this tradition traced its original to an earlier story in which the wolf, after running down a deer, gave a call to signal others of his success. "This was to invite everyone to come and eat of his meat, crows, coyotes, etc."[32] It is interesting to note that among Chiricahua Apaches, who had their own "wolfway" of hunting, howling was also used to communicate after a kill was made.[33] In addition, both Navajo and Chiricahua warriors used the howl of the wolf to communicate with each other in times of war.[34]

In most ways, other than those aspects already discussed, the Wolfway did not differ significantly from the other hunting ways. However, one additional element that deserves mention are the songs associated with this hunting ritual. It is thought that at an earlier time, the Athabascan Wolfway had a long litany of songs attached to it. Unfortunately they no longer exist. Nevertheless, the following wolf identification is found in a Stalking Way song and might originally have been a Wolfway song:

> He goes out hunting
>
> Big Wolf am I
>
> With black-bow, he goes out hunting
>
> With tail-feathered arrow he goes out hunting
>
> The big male game through its shoulder that I may shoot
>
> It death obeys me.[35]

The Wolfway hunt ended as it began, with a purifying sweat. Luckert notes that hunting involves the "…dirty business of killing." It was for this reason that the initial sweat was held to turn man into a predator. The closing sweat allowed the hunter to cleanse himself of the death, to shed his wolfish identity, and to transform himself back into a man. With the hunt over and the transformation completed, Blessingway songs were sung to bring closure to it all.[36]

THE WOLF AND THE SKINWALKER TRADITION

In 1987 I was an administrator at a high school on the Navajo Reservation. One day our secretary walked into my office to show me the following note from a parent excusing her son for missing school:

> To Who It May Concern:
> Please excuse my son, Wilson [pseudonym], from being absent on Thursday and Friday, the 6th and 7th. He was very ill and we took him to a medicine man. The medicine man told us that a Skinwalker had witchcrafted him, so we took him to another medicine man so he would be OK.
>
> Mary Yazzie [pseudonym]

This note provides testimony to the Navajo's strong belief in witchcraft and its most popular manifestation—the skinwalker—a human witch who dons the skin of an animal and goes out at night to wreak havoc, destruction, and even death on its human victims. Clyde Kluckhohn, who has written the definitive study on Navajo witchcraft, notes that skinwalkers take the shape of many animals: the bear, mountain lion, fox, owl, or crow, but most commonly a coyote or a wolf.[37] The Navajo word for the skinwalker is *yenaldlooshi*, a term that translates to "it walks on all four feet." Kluckhohn states that he found this word, as well as the Navajo word for wolf, which will be discussed shortly, to be the common colloquial term for *witch*.[38] However, Will Tsosie, a Navajo orthodox traditionalist and noted traditional scholar, states that the word *yenaldlooshi* would be used for any form of were-animal, and would not necessarily mean a wolf. If a person said they saw a *yenaldlooshi*, a typical Navajo response, according to Tsosie, might be "What kind did you see?"[39] Navajos generally believe that witches are initiated by others of their kind, commonly relatives, in secretive rites usually held in a cave. After putting on the skin of one of the aforementioned creatures, these were-animals then set out to do their evil deeds. They are said to frequent cemeteries where they dig up the dead, sometimes for the purpose of performing sexual acts with corpses. In addition to necrophilia, skinwalkers also engage in incest and cannibalism. Most commonly, the skinwalker climbs on top of a Navajo hogan at night and drops powder made from the ground bones of dead children down the smoke hole. This powder causes its victims misfortune, illness, and death.

The Navajo skinwalker phenomenon is well known to the general public. In large part this is due to popular fiction writers, especially

Tony Hillerman, who wrote a best-selling murder mystery entitled *Skinwalker* in 1986.[40] Unfortunately, some environmental writers have chosen to single out the relationship of wolves to skinwalkers and witchcraft as their primary focus regarding the role of the wolf in Navajo culture. Two such examples deserve special mention.

In his classic work *Of Wolves and Men*, Barry Holstun Lopez dedicated three chapters to documenting the close, special, and often sacred, relationship that existed between Native Americans and the wolf. The Nunamiut, Naskapi, Pawnee, Cheyenne, Hidatsa, Bella Coola, Sioux, Arapaho, Cherokee, Nez Perce, Arikara, Crow, Ahtna, Kwakiutl, Blackfoot, Nootka, Quillayute, and Makah are all tribes Lopez discusses or mentions for their positive attitude toward the wolf. Only the Navajos are singled out as a contrast. Lopez writes: "Other tribes, notably the Navajo, feared wolves as human witches in wolves' clothing. The Navajo word for wolf, *Mai-coh* is a synonym for witch."[41]

Another writer, Robert H. Busch, in his otherwise excellent *The Wolf Almanac*, states: "Almost unique in North American Indian wolf mythology is the Navajo werewolf myth. The Navajo word for wolf, *mai-coh*, means witch."[42] Both books are outstanding publications and, along with L. David Mech's *The Wolf: The Ecology and Behavior of an Endangered Species*,[43] probably stand as the three most popular books written about wolves. It is unfortunate that the information they give on Navajos and wolves is so scant. Moreover, the distinction they give for *mai-coh*, or more correctly *ma'iitsoh*, is inaccurate and misleading.

The Navajo name for coyote is *ma'ii*, and the wolf is called *ma'iitsoh*, or simply "large coyote." The origin of this word is probably *ma'i*, an Apachean term for "animal." For example, in the Chiricahua Apache language the word for coyote is *mbai* and the wolf is called *mbai'tso*. That this Athabascan or Apachean term extends to all animals can be seen in the Chiricahua word for lizard, *mba'ishoi*.[44] None of these words in themselves have anything to do with witches.

In one version of the Navajo creation stories, Aileen O'Bryan states that First Man and First Woman named the Wolf *ma'iitsoh*.[45] According to this version, Wolf had stolen something and, although a chief, would from that time be called *ma'iitsoh*, the "big wanderer," because he now had to "travel far and wide over the face of the earth." O'Bryan offers no explanation as to the exact origin of the term but, again, no inference is made about werewolves or witchcraft.

The verbal concept of the wolf as Big Trotter comes from the mythical name for Wolf as used in ceremonies: *naatl'eetsoh*. For this reason *naatl'eetsoh* is usually considered the ceremonial or sacred name for the wolf. This term brings together the words *nadleeh*, which means "to become or revert to," and *tl'eeh* which translates to "trots." *Naatl'eetsoh* thus translates to "big one who becomes a trotter," "big one who trots," or simply "big trotter."[46] Again there is no inference of werewolves or witchcraft in this term.

Interestingly, Gladys A. Reichard, in her classic 1950 study, *Navajo Religion: A Study in Symbolism*, does make such a connection. In describing the ceremonial usage of words, she writes:

> The special terms of one chant may differ from those of another; all are not necessarily understood by every singer. In one chant the names of characters may be lay terms; in another, they may be completely or partly changed. For instance, the ordinary name for 'wolf' is 'large coyote,' but ceremonially he may be called 'large-one-who-trots-like-a-person,' *doubtless a reference to the werewolf.*[47]

It is difficult to determine how Reichard came to her conclusion that "large one who trots," refers to a werewolf. To anyone who has ever seen the long-legged, mile-eating gait of a wolf the term *trot* comes quickly to mind. I am confident the Navajo, who were keen observers of the natural world and tended to relate what they witnessed in a highly descriptive manner, were simply describing and naming the wolf as they saw him. In the Navajo language he was *ma'iitsoh*, big coyote. In Navajo ceremonies he was *naatl'eetsoh*, the big trotting animal-god.

How then did the wolf become associated with witchcraft? What is the origin of the Navajo werewolf tradition? Unfortunately no scholar or writer has yet addressed these questions.

The belief in witches and witchcraft is almost universal, and was certainly common among most Indian tribes. In Navajo culture, witchcraft goes back to the earliest times. The most commonly accepted belief is that Navajo witchcraft traces back to the emergence stories and, specifically, to First Man and First Woman.[48] Another view is that witchcraft originated with Coyote.[49] The association between Coyote and witchcraft might also explain what I believe to be the much later association of the wolf with witchcraft. Wolf and Coyote were traditionally viewed as two very different deities, especially in regard to their character and the way they used their powers. This diametric view of Wolf and Coyote carried over to their animal counterparts. However, this distinction became blurred in later times when Navajo life turned toward livestock and farming and away from hunting and its traditions. As a consequence of this move the wolf came under attack, both physically and in thought. In time, almost all traditional knowledge of the animal was lost. At that point, the wolf, now extinct in Navajo country, was remembered and viewed simply as "big coyote."

The Athabascans who entered the Southwest undoubtedly brought with them their own set of witchcraft beliefs. Moreover, as hunters who ritually transformed themselves into predators, they probably recognized that a fine line existed between humanity and the rest of the natural animal world. It is exactly for this reason—namely that this fine line needed to be maintained at all costs—that I believe the Navajo concept of were-animals, and specifically werewolves, does not trace its origin to the Athabascan hunter tradition. Evidence for this view can be seen in that other southern Athabascans, various Apache tribes, possess strong beliefs in witchcraft but have no were-wolf tradition. For example, the Western Apaches, who are closest to the Navajo in terms of shared traits, including similarities in witch-craft beliefs, have no werewolf tradition.[50]

Luckert believes what he calls the "defamation" of the divine predators, such as Wolf, began when the Athabascan hunting culture came into contact and consequent conflict with the agriculture-based Pueblos. Luckert notes "all hunter gods eventually suffer defama-tion if their human proteges cease to be hunters and if they learn to answer to different types of gods."[51] After the Athabascan-Pueblo merger, and the subsequent transformation into the people we now know as Navajo, a new worldview emerged. An accompanying reli-gious and ceremonial system, one that was more a product of an agri-cultural rather than a hunting way of life, emerged. I do not believe, however, that this alone explains the defamation of certain Navajo animal gods, especially the wolf. Nor does it explain the association of the wolf with witchcraft. The Pueblos, like most tribes, tended to view animals rather favorably. Wolf, in particular, played an impor-tant and positive role in many Pueblo stories. He was the Beast God of the East, playing the role of warrior, guardian, and healer. Most Pueblos also had hunting societies whose members drew their powers through association with the wolf.[52] Since hunting societies remained strong well into the 1900s, it can be assumed that the Pueblos with whom the Navajos made contact three and four centuries earlier, had little direct influence in defaming the divine predators of the Athabascans. Indeed, the knowledge of Pueblo hunters may have enriched, at least initially, the stories and rituals associated with the Navajo hunter tradition.

Pueblo mythology contains many witch-related stories. Animal transformations, which may or may not be associated with witch-craft, usually involve Coyote and are central themes in Pueblo stories. It is interesting to note that among some Pueblos witchcraft is believed to have begun with Coyote, which is similar to a version of Navajo witchcraft origin mentioned earlier in this article. For example, in one Tewa tale Coyote married Yellow Corn Girl and taught her how to transform herself into a wolf by jumping through a hoop. Before this mythical event took place, the Tewa say that there were no witches.[53] Other Pueblo stories credit witches with transforming into animals and prowling cemeteries to rob graves of their possessions and corpses.[54]

In summary, it seems highly probable that the Navajo skinwalker tradition came at least in part, from a Pueblo origin. But what about wolf defamation? The most likely initial source for this seems to be Christianity passed through the Pueblos to the Navajo.

Parsons states that while the precontact Pueblos undoubtedly possessed their own "black magic," such traditional Native beliefs and practices, including wearing animal skins and taking on powers associated with these animals, were certainly "enriched by Spanish witchcraft theory."[55] Spanish witchcraft beliefs, founded on the Christian tradition, included animal transformation. Moreover, Christianity, in contrast to most Native American religions, has long associated particular animals (snakes, bats, owls, lions, and wolves) with evil. Schaafsma reports finding Spanish crosses carved on boulders in the West Mesa area near Albuquerque, New Mexico, in association with Tewa rock art images of mountain lions and snakes.[56] This, along with written documentation, reveals Spanish attempts to exorcise, or at least neutralize, what they perceived to be demonic symbols. Without doubt the Spanish transferred their fear (and defamation) of certain animals to the Pueblos. This attitude might have then been passed from the Pueblos to the Navajo.

Will Tsosie, a Navajo traditionalist, sees a later, more direct connection. Since the Navajo wore animal skins as hunting disguises and for personal adornment well into the present century with no apparent negative associations, he believes it is more likely that wolf defamation and the skinwalker tradition is a twentieth-century response to Christian missionary activity among his own people.[57]

Elsewhere I have written about the history, development, and impact of Christianity on the Navajo people.[58] For the purposes of this paper it is enough to say that missionary work among the Navajo began in 1868, increased in intensity after 1912, but did not really take hold until the 1940s. Early missionary efforts were made by various Protestant churches and were characterized largely by their attempts to discredit, condemn, and suppress traditional culture and religion. By the 1930s, the Native American Church (NAC), a pan-Indian religious movement based on the use of peyote and incorporating elements of Christianity, began to attract large numbers of Navajo followers. Alarmed by what they perceived to be a threat to their traditional lifestyle, the Navajo Tribal Council banned the use of peyote from 1940 to 1967. Despite such obstacles, the NAC increased in popularity to become the dominant religion on the Navajo Reservation with perhaps as many as 70 percent of tribal members involved to some degree in peyotism. Today most Navajo engage in multiple affiliation; that is, they belong to a primary religion, and also practice a second and often a third religion. Most often the NAC serves as the primary religious affiliation, with members also attending Christian church services, or perhaps, traditional ceremonies. In addition, NAC peyote meetings may incorporate elements of traditional Navajo beliefs. For the most part there are few orthodox traditionalists—individuals who strictly adhere to the original teachings and ceremonial practices associated with the Holy People—left today on the Navajo Reservation. The new traditionalism now prevalent is far removed from the knowledge and values once passed down through the generations from the emergence stories and the Navajo hunter tradition. Along the way, much has been lost to time, including, I believe, the sacred knowledge, understanding, and respect for animals like the wolf.

THE FUTURE OF WOLVES IN NAVAJO COUNTRY

A 1908 survey conducted in the Chuska Mountains of the Navajo Reservation noted that "wolf tracks were found common in the trails over the tops of mountains where most of the cattle and great numbers of Navajo sheep ranged during the summer. Evidently they were thriving there unmolested by the Indians and with an abundance of food."[59] However, this situation soon changed as efforts were made to exterminate predators on tribal lands. It is difficult to document this event because most written records have been lost to time. The pattern, however, seems to generally have followed what was then taking place throughout the American West. Market hunting, carried out to satisfy the needs of border towns along the Santa Fe Railroad, reduced the deer population to less than one hundred on the entire reservation. With the deer gone, predators increased. Predators were a threat to Navajo livelihood. It was a threat that had to be eliminated. PARC hunters, with the support of the Navajo tribe, initiated a serious predator control program on the reservation. This soon resulted in the extermination of wolves and grizzly bears. Black bears, mountain lions, and coyotes were also hunted relentlessly.

The purposeful destruction of predators was not without its price. The coyote was hunted because of his predatory raids against sheep and because of his association with witchcraft. Luckert noted so many coyotes were killed in the Black Mesa area in the 1940s that an epidemic of "coyote sickness" broke out in the area, a problem serious enough to create an increased demand for medicine men to perform the Coyoteway healing ceremony. Luckert's Navajo consultant explained the situation in the following manner:

> When a Coyote person is shot and left to die, his last spasms and twitchings, as they suddenly cease in the animal person, leap onto the killer. This happens most easily if somehow in the process of killing the hunter has eye contact with his victim—Coyote continues to recognize and haunt the offender. But this can also happen through physical contact with the dead animal's body or even with the decayed remains of a Coyote person. And, in this regard, no shepherd who strolls through the sagebrush pastures can be sure of his personal immunity. Killing a Coyote person means offending him. The symptoms of the animal's suffering which are thrown onto the offender continue as a sort of nervous malfunction, a shaking of the head, hands or of the entire body.[60]

Coyote sickness, and related wolf sickness (the two are actually the same) can be remedied through the same Coyoteway ceremony. These illnesses are not caused by the animal but by the transgressions of man. It is a sickness caused when man shows disrespect toward one of the animal people. In a sense, it is an example of defamation coming full-cycle back to the offender.

In Navajo thought, at least the way it has been taught to me, no animal is inherently good or bad. Like man, other beings with whom we share this earth, including the wolf, generally go about their lives in a manner ordained by the Creator and other Holy People. Over the course of time, however, and for whatever reasons, Navajo attitudes toward the natural world, and particularly toward some animals, have changed. Once, the howl of a wolf or the call of an owl was interpreted as a warning sent from a more powerful but benevolent being. It was a warning to be heeded. With the loss of knowledge and change in attitude, these same howls and calls came to be interpreted as omens of evil and sounds to be feared.

The howl of wolves can still be heard echoing in the red rock canyons of Navajo country. The source of this sound, however, is not the beautiful Chuska or Lukachukai Mountains, but the confines of the Navajo Nation Zoological Park in Window Rock. For the past ten years the tribal zoo has been the home to Mexican wolves, the most endangered of the gray wolf species. These animals—there are two females at the zoo today—are the descendants of two of the last wild Mexican wolves known to have existed in the Southwest: a male live-trapped near Tumacacori, Arizona, in 1959, and a female captured in Sonora, Mexico, two years later. Together this breeding pair served as the nucleus of what is known as the Ghost Ranch Lineage. Initially, some question existed regarding the genetic purity of this bloodline.[61] However, subsequent DNA testing verified the status of this bloodline and today the Ghost Ranch descendants are one of only three DNA-certified genetically pure lines of Mexican wolves in existence. In all, there are only about 180 Mexican wolves on earth. With the exception of the animals that have been reintroduced in the White Mountains, there are no other Mexican wolves left in the wild, either in Mexico or the United States.

The Navajo Nation Zoo is one of thirty zoological parks in the world that has Mexican wolves. More importantly, it is one of only a handful of zoos approved as a breeding facility for the purpose of the reintroduction of Mexican wolves into their native habitat. Over the years the Navajo Nation Zoo, like other zoos around the world, has been criticized for keeping wild animals locked in pens. Some tribal members have expressed their concerns that zoos are not consistent with Navajo cultural values. On 26 December 1998, two Navajo deities, or Holy People, reportedly visited a family in the remote community of Rocky Ridge. Included in their message to the Navajo people was a denouncement of the imprisonment of sacred animals in the zoo. Some tribal leaders called for an immediate release of all zoo animals back into the wild. Zoo supporters countered that to do so would mean certain death for the animals. In the end, Navajo Nation President Kelsey Begaye, in part due to the large number of letters sent to him by Navajo children, elected to keep the facility open.[62]

It is not one of my goals in this paper to debate the merits or cultural appropriateness of zoos. However, it is quite clear that the future of the Mexican wolf lies in the hands of captive breeding populations like those held at the Navajo Nation facility. For this reason I will close this paper with personal hope that the Navajo people support the efforts now underway to restore the Mexican wolf to its historic Southwest habitat. As demonstrated in this paper, Wolf has long been an integral and positive part of Navajo life. The Navajo people are poorer without him. While the day will never come when wolves again roam freely through the Navajo mountains, it is important that their physical and spiritual presence remain for the Navajo people to draw upon.

Will Tsosie best summarized the importance of the wolf to the Navajo, and indeed to us all, when he stated:

> Wolves are the most misunderstood creature in the Navajo world. People fear what they do not know. It is sad to think that we have the capability to destroy an entire species of fellow beings—the "ones who trot people." We, as humans, are perhaps not that far behind. Maybe this is a prelude of what is to come. Maybe we are orchestrating our own demise.[63]

The foundation of Navajo culture has been the maintenance of harmony with all life. But their harmony with the wolf has been destroyed. Support of the Mexican wolf program provides the Navajo people with an opportunity to correct the defamations of the past and, in doing so, restore the harmony that once existed. Only when this is done will Big Trotter reclaim his rightful place in the minds and hearts of the Navajo people.

Notes

This paper was originally presented at the Eleventh Navajo Studies Conference held 23 October 1998, at Window Rock, Arizona. I wish to extend a note of appreciation to a number of people who helped give me the information and insight to make this paper possible: author Dave Brown; Kathleen McCoy and Rick Winslow of the Navajo Nation Department of Game and Fish who were kind enough to discuss with me their ideas on the historic occurrence of the Mexican wolf in Navajo Country; Bobbie Holaday of Preserve Arizona Wolves; Peter Siminski of the Arizona Sonora Desert Museum; and Lolene Hathaway of the Navajo Nation Zoological Park, who provided information on the history and status of the Mexican wolves that are being kept at that tribal facility. Finally, I wish to thank my friend and colleague Will Tsosie, who again helped me find my way through the complexities of Navajo traditional thought and lifeways. As always, I alone assume responsibility for the content and analysis offered in this paper.

1. Aldo Leopold, *A Sand County Almanac* (New York: Oxford University Press, 1949), 130.

2. Originally, there were twenty-four recognized subspecies of the gray wolf, *Canis lupus*, inhabiting North America. The subspecies that once inhabited what is today the Navajo Reservation, *C.l. youngi* is now extinct. Considering the historic range of the early Navajo people, tribal members undoubtedly encountered at least two other subspecies, *C.l. mogollonensis*—also extinct—and *C.l. baileyi*, the Mexican wolf.

3. David E. Brown, *The Wolf in the Southwest: The Making of an Endangered Species* (Tucson: University of Arizona Press, 1983), 24. See also Vernon Bailey, *Mammals of New Mexico* (Washington, DC: US Department of Agriculture, Bureau of Biological Survey, 1931), 310.

4. Three Apache tribes, the White Mountain, San Carlos, and Mescalero, also officially opposed introduction of the Mexican Wolf. While it is not within the scope of this paper to discuss in depth the reintroduction program, it should be noted that the first year of the project experienced major problems and setbacks. Of the eleven wolves initially released, only two remain free. At least five were shot and killed, some deliberately by individuals out to sabotage the reintroduction effort. Several wolves exhibited undesirable traits, mostly the tendency to roam too far afield or too close to human habitation, and were consequently recaptured. However the program continues with additional animals being released and several litters of young being born in the wild. As of this writing, there are almost thirty Mexican wolves living wild in the White Mountains recovery area. For additional information on the Mexican Wolf Reintroduction Program and Apache attitudes toward wolves and the reintroduction program, see Steve Pavlik, "San Carlos and White Mountain Apache Attitudes Toward the Reintroduction of the Wolf to Its Historic Range in the American Southwest," *Wicazo sa Review* 14 (1999): 129–145.

5. John A. Murray, ed., *Out Among the Wolves: Contemporary Writings on the Wolf* (Anchorage: Alaska Northwest Books, 1993), 11.

6. Barry H. Lopez, *Of Wolves and Men* (New York: Charles Scribner's Sons, 1978); and Robert H. Busch, *The Wolf Almanac* (New York: The Lyons Press, 1995).

7. Brown, *The Wolf in the Southwest*.

8. James C. Burbank, *Vanishing Lobo: The Mexican Wolf and the Southwest* (Boulder: Johnson Publishing Company, 1990).

9. Rick Bass, *The New Wolves: The Return of the Mexican Wolf to the American Southwest* (New York: The Lyons Press, 1998).

10. W. W. Hill, *The Agricultural and Hunting Methods of the Navaho Indians* (New Haven, Conn.: Yale University Publications in Anthropology no. 18, 1938); Karl W. Luckert, *The Navajo Hunter Tradition* (Tucson: University of Arizona Press, 1975).

11. Gladys A. Reichard, *Navajo Medicine Man Sandpaintings* (1939; reprint New York: Dover Publications, 1977), 16.

12. Father Berard Haile, *The Upward Moving and Emergence Way* (Lincoln: University of Nebraska Press, 1981), 11–12.

13. Ibid., 39–43; 93–94. It should be noted that in other versions of this story, it is First Man, not wolf, who is wronged by his wife and leads the male beings in separating from the female.

14. Ibid., 111, 116–17. See also Franciscan Fathers, *An Ethnologic Dictionary of the Navajo Language* (St. Michael's, Ariz.: St. Michael's Press, 1910), 351.

15. Haile, *The Upward Moving and Emergence Way,* 128.

16. Ibid., 144.

17. Washington Matthews, *Navajo Legends* (1897; reprint, Salt Lake City: University of Utah Press, 1944), 87–88.

18. Reichard, *Navajo Medicine Man Sandpaintings,* 32.

19. Haile, *The Upward Moving and Emergence Way,* 90.

20. Reichard, *Navajo Medicine Man Sandpaintings,* 34–35, Plate VII.

21. Father Berard Haile, *Origin Legend of the Navaho Flintway* (Chicago: University of Chicago Press, 1943), 53–54.

22. Luckert, *The Navajo Hunter Tradition,* 169.

23. Ibid., 11–13.

24. Ibid., 18.

25. Ibid., 172–75.

26. Hill, *Agricultural and Hunting Methods,* 97.

27. Karl W. Luckert, *A Navajo Bringing Home Ceremony: The Claus Chee Sonny Version of the Deerway Ajiłee* (Flagstaff: Museum of Northern Arizona Press, 1978), 30.

28. See Francis H. Elmore, "The Deer and His Importance to the Navajo," *El Palacio* 60 (1953): 371–84.

29. Hill, *Agricultural and Hunting Methods,* 97, 101.

30. Ibid., 98.

31. Luckert, *The Navajo Hunter Tradition,* 51.

32. Hill, *Agricultural and Hunting Methods,* 109.

33. Morris E. Opler, *An Apache Life-Way: The Economic, Social, and Religious Institutions of the Chiricahua Indians* (Chicago: University of Chicago Press, 1941), 320.

34. W. W. Hill, *Navajo Warfare* (New Haven, Conn.: Yale University Publications in Anthropology no. 5, 1936), 36; Opler, *An Apache Life-Way,* 347.

35. Hill, *Agricultural and Hunting Methods,* 136.

36. Luckert, *The Navajo Hunter Tradition,* 142–46.

37. Clyde Kluckhohn, *Navajo Witchcraft* (Boston: Beacon Press, 1944), 25–28.

38. Ibid., 26.

39. Will Tsosie, interview by Steve Pavlik, Tsaile, Arizona, 26 September 1999.

40. Tony Hillerman, *Skinwalkers* (New York: Harper and Row Publishers, 1986).

41. Lopez, *Of Wolves and Men,* 123.

42. Busch, *The Wolf Almanac,* 99. The language used by Lopez and Busch is strikingly similar in content and wording. It is interesting, however, that in Lopez's

book *mai-coh* is a synonym for wolf, whereas in Busch's publication *mai-coh* is said to mean wolf, especially since it appears from his bibliography that Busch's source for his Navajo werewolf comment must be Lopez. In turn, Lopez cites two sources for his Navajo werewolf information: William Morgan, *Human Wolves Among the Navajo* (New Haven, Conn.: Yale Publications in Anthropology no. 11, 1936)—the single most important but largely anecdotal work on the topic—and a special edition of *El Palacio* (1974) dealing with Southwest witchcraft and includes an uncredited article on Navajo witchcraft. However, neither of these sources use the term *mai-coh* for wolf. This word seems to be first used by Kluckhohn (1944) in *Navaho Witchcraft* (see note 37). I can only assume that Lopez also used this work but did not include it in his bibliography.

43. L. David Mech, *The Wolf: The Ecology and Behavior of an Endangered Species* (Minneapolis: University of Minnesota Press, 1970).

44. Luckert, *The Navajo Hunter Tradition,* 7.

45. Aileen O'Bryan, *The Dine: Origin Myths of the Navaho Indians* (Washington, DC: Bureau of American Ethnology Bulletin 63, 1956), 33–34.

46. Fathers, *Ethnologic Dictionary of the Navajo Language,* 140–41, 175.

47. Gladys A. Reichard, *Navajo Religion: A Study in Symbolism* (1950; reprint, New York: Pantheon Press, 1950), 268. Author's emphasis.

48. Kluckhohn, *Navajo Witchcraft,* 25.

49. O'Bryan, *Origin Myths of the Navaho Indians,* 3.

50. Keith Basso, *Western Apache Witchcraft* (Tucson: University of Arizona Anthropological Paper 1, 1969), 34.

51. Karl W. Luckert, *Coyoteway: A Navajo Healing Ceremonial* (Tucson: University of Arizona Press, 1979), 10.

52. Hamilton Tyler, *Pueblo Animals and Myths* (Norman: University of Oklahoma Press, 1975), 154–75; Elsie Clews Parsons, *Pueblo Indian Religion,* Vol. I (1939; reprint, Lincoln: University of Nebraska, 1939), 187.

53. Elsie Clews Parsons, "Witchcraft Among the Pueblos: Indian or Spanish," *Man* 27 (1927): 1226–27.

54. Parsons, *Pueblo Religion,* Vol. I, 106, 136.

55. Parsons, *Witchcraft Among the Pueblos,* 128.

56. Polly Schaafsma, *Rock Art in New Mexico* (Santa Fe: Museum of New Mexico Press, 1992), 149.

57. Will Tsosie, interview.

58. Steve Pavlik, "Navajo Christianity: Historical Origins and Modern Trends," *Wicazo sa Review* 12 (1996): 43–58; Steve Pavlik, "The Role of Christianity and Church in Contemporary Navajo Society," in *A Good Cherokee, A Good Anthropologist: Papers in Honor of Robert K. Thomas,* ed. Steve Pavlik (Los Angeles: UCLA American Indian Studies Center, 1997), 189–200.

59. Bailey, *Mammals of New Mexico,* 310.

60. Luckert, *Coyoteway: A Navajo Healing Ceremonial,* 8–9.

61. Peter Steinhart, *The Company of Wolves* (New York: Alfred A. Knopf, 1995), 202–6, 209–10.

62. Bill Donovan, "Navajos May Close Zoo," *Arizona Republic,* 8 January 1999, 21; Bill Donovan, "Navajos Weigh Options to Keep Tribal Zoo Open," *Arizona Republic,* 1 February 1999, 1; Catherine C. Robbins, "Tradition Clashes With Some Needs to Endanger Zoo," *Gallup Independent,* 30 March 1999, 2.

63. Will Tsosie, interview by Steve Pavlik, Tsaile, Arizona, 30 July 1999.

THE LONG AND DISMAL HOWL:
EARLY ACCOUNTS

||||||||||||||||||||||||||||||||||||||||||||||||||||||||||||

DAVID E. BROWN
from *The Wolf in the Southwest: The Making
of an Endangered Species*
(1983)

olves have been present in the Southwest since at least the late Pleistocene. Their remains are well represented in the fossil record in Arizona (Lindsay and Tessman 1974) and New Mexico (Findley and others 1975), and wolf bones have also been identified from a number of the region's pre-Columbian archaeological sites (Martin and Plog 1973). The Big Game Hunters that appeared at the close of the Pleistocene some twelve thousand years ago (Martin 1963) must have vied with wolves for game. Men and wolves have been at odds ever since. It was not until the arrival of the Spaniards and their livestock, however, that conflict really began.

HISTORIC OCCURRENCE

By the end of the seventeenth century, cattle, sheep, and goats were being introduced to the Southwest in increasing numbers. Livestock, given to sedentary Indians to raise, had to be continually protected from both Apaches and wolves. Describing conditions in northern Sonora in 1763, Jesuit priest Juan Nentvig (1763) wrote, "The wolves do damage among cattle, and the coyotes and foxes, among sheep and poultry."

Apaches and wolves quickly became addicted to this steady food source. Although a number of cattle ranches were established on large land grants, they were generally unprofitable because of these two forces. Apache raids sometimes resulted in the abandonment of many fine haciendas, with the cattle turned loose to the benefit of both predators.

The large, poorly guarded livestock herds of the Spanish and Mexican periods may actually have led to an increase in wolves. Certainly American explorers found wolves plentiful enough near what was to become the Arizona-Sonora border (Tyler 1964). In 1847 the Mormon Battalion found numerous wild bulls, remnants of some hundred thousand head of Andalusian cattle left behind when Rancho San Bernardino was abandoned in the 1830s; most of the more susceptible cows and calves had succumbed to predators, leaving only the large, formidable bulls (Tyler 1964 and Davis 1973). These and other cattle left behind on Mexican land grants generally disappeared by the 1860s (Wagoner 1952). Conditions were not entirely one-sided, however. Members of John R. Bartlett's 1849–1851 boundary survey noted that Mexican ranchers defended their stock against wolves and coyotes by lacing fresh livestock kills with strychnine (Baird 1859).

On entering the Southwest, American frontiersmen found wolves common if not particularly numerous. Emory (1848) reported wolves on several occasions on the upper Gila River in New Mexico. In 1851 Bartlett (1854) described "wolves" as abundant on the plains and valleys of southern New Mexico, southeast Arizona, and northern Mexico. Although Bartlett, leader of the first U.S. Boundary Commission expedition, did not always differentiate between coyotes and wolves, he did list "the large wolf or lobo" as one of the large mammals of the mountains and riparian groves of the rivers and creeks of the Southwest.

Early American boundary and railroad route surveys were usually accompanied by naturalists, who kept accounts of wolves both from the thinly settled Mexican areas and in the wilderness. These accounts, though brief, provide valuable insights into the abundance and distribution of wolves when the Southwest was in a nearly natural state.

The first naturalist to travel extensively in the Southwest was S. W. Woodhouse, a physician with the Sitgreaves expedition of 1851. Captain Lorenzo Sitgreaves and his party traveled west from Santa Fe, down the Zuni and Little Colorado rivers, across north-central Arizona and southern California to the Pacific coast. Dr. Woodhouse, in his biological report of the expedition, found wolves "very common throughout the Indian territory [Oklahoma], Texas, and New Mexico" [Arizona was then still part of New Mexico Territory] (Sitgreaves 1853).[1] Woodhouse found wolves particularly common on the thin, open grasslands west of San Francisco Mountain in Arizona.

A more descriptive account was given in 1853 by C. B. R. Kennerly, naturalist and physician with a railroad route survey along the thirty-fifth parallel. Traveling much the same country that Woodhouse had traversed two year earlier, Kennerly discussed the natural history of the region of the Zuni and Little Colorado rivers in east-central Arizona:

> At night the prairie jackal or coyote rarely failed to approach our camp, and serenade us with his loud and varied notes. The long and dismal howl of the larger species [wolf] was occasionally heard in the distance; but the latter is much less numerous than the former, and was not often seen. It, too, prefers the wooded regions, and depends mainly upon the deer for subsistence, which it hunts, and rarely fails, after a long pursuit, in overtaking and conquering (Kennerly 1856).

This account is of more than casual interest considering later opinions on the exclusivity of coyotes and wolves, since it has the two species existing together under pristine conditions.

During the winter of 1853 and 1854, Kennerly and H. B. Möllhausen (1858) noted that the men of the Whipple party, while camped on the Little Colorado River near Chevelon Creek, entertained themselves by trapping wolves and hunting. One night their remuda of mules was stampeded by a pack of wolves howling close to camp. Later on the same trip, west of Mt. Sitgreaves, Möllhausen (1858) noted:

> Here and there we saw solitary specimens of the black-tailed deer and antelope, and more frequently wolves and coyotes announced their presence by howling and chattering as they prowled around us in the scanty cedar woods. A wolf was also seen on the Partridge Creek and others heard in the foothills of the Juniper Mountains.

Kennerly was again involved in southwestern exploration in 1854 and 1855, as the naturalist accompanying the Emory expedition surveying the new United States–Mexico boundary created by the Gadsden Purchase. Kennerly made notes concerning wolves:

> Near Santa Cruz, in Sonora we found this animal more common than we had observed it elsewhere on our route. It, as well as the coyote, were often destructive to the flocks around the village (Baird 1859:15).

Kennerly also observed a large number of coyotes west of the Rio Grande, howling nearly every night near camp. Thus, his notes indicate that coyotes apparently coexisted with wolves in early rural Sonora.

The first naturalist to reside for a significant period in the South-west in presettlement times was Elliot Coues. A surgeon in the Army, he was stationed at Fort Whipple in central Arizona, near present-day Prescott, in 1864 and 1865. While in Arizona, Coues traveled a good deal, collecting specimens and gathering natural history information from soldiers, hunters and trappers. His *Quadrupeds of Arizona*, published in 1867, is the first attempt at a comprehensive treatment of the mammals of the region. Concerning wolves Coues wrote:

> They are common enough about Fort Whipple, though shy and wary, and seldom making their appearance by day; and notwith-standing their size and imposing appearance, the part they played was insignificant compared with that of their smaller relatives, the coyotes.... This latter animal...is by far the most abundant carnivorous animal in Arizona, as it is also, in almost every part of the West (Coues 1867).

On one occasion Dr. Coues noted a mixed chorus of coyote and wolf howls:

> A short sharp bark is sounded, followed by several more, in quick succession, the time growing faster and the pitch higher, till they run together into a long drawn lugubrious howl in the highest possible key. The same strain is taken up again and again by different members of the pack, while from a greater distance the deep melancholy baying of the more wary Lobo breaks in, to add to the discord, till the very leaves of the trees seem quivering to the inharmonious sounds (Wheeler 1875).

Coues (1867) also reported that a number of wolves taken in winter were grizzled white and that many had been poisoned for their fur, which made fine robes.

That the wolf was never especially numerous in the Southwest is suggested by the paucity of place names. There is no Wolf Moun-tain or Wolf River, no Sierra Lobo or Rio Lobo. Wolf Creek Pass in Colorado and the two Wolf creeks in the Bradshaw Mountains near Prescott, Arizona come to mind. The largest of these creeks is per-haps so named because one Daniel Ellis Conner (1956) saw a large pack of wolves there in 1863.

With the return of the Army to the Southwest after the Civil War, the Apache menace was gradually reduced and then eliminated. Transcontinental railways began to penetrate the country, providing a link to eastern and California markets. By the late 1880s, the region was relatively settled, and cattle were abundant and widespread.

Wolves were conspicuous if not abundant, and their conflict with ranchers was acute. W. W. Price, a zoological collector in southeast Arizona, observed in 1894 that the lobo "is the terror of the cattle and sheep men.... It is found over the entire region, though more especially in the mountainous parts. We saw it on several occasions during our stay in the country" (Allen 1895). To rid the Southwest of this "terror," a campaign requiring more than sixty years and millions of dollars was mounted—an effort almost as great as that devoted to neutralizing the Apaches.

FORMER DISTRIBUTION

Except for the so-called buffalo wolves or loafers (*Canis lupus nubilis*) reported to inhabit the grasslands of Texas and eastern New Mexico, wolves in the Southwest generally have been associated with montane forests and woodlands (Bailey 1931, McBride 1980). Almost all collections have come from pine-clad mountains, oak woodlands, pinyon-juniper forests, and intervening or adjacent grasslands above 4,500 feet. Surprisingly, virtually no wolves have been recorded in California despite an abundance of what appear to be suitable habitats (McCullough 1971). Wolves were also largely absent from the Mohave, Sonoran, and Chihuahuan deserts; wolf records from Arizona and Mexico are almost entirely above the elevations of desertscrub and even semidesert grassland.

Evidence that wolves did not frequent the originally open semi-desert grasslands is provided by Scudday (1977) who quotes Judge O. W. Williams of Fort Stockton, Texas. Williams was educated at Harvard, came to Texas as a surveyor in 1877, and noted all that he observed. In 1884 he opened a law office in Fort Stockton and later became judge of Pecos County. In 1908 the *Fort Stockton Pioneer* published a series of Judge Williams's observations on the county's animal life. An excerpt from that series offers interesting insight into the early status and distribution of wolves in that part of the Trans-Pecos:

> These animals are not now and have never been numerous in our country. Twenty-five years ago there was said to be one pack of lobos in Pecos County. They ranged on the Pecos River about 30 miles above Sheffield. Then, as now, they depended upon herds of cattle for sustenance. The cattle of "S" and Mule Shoe brands were the principal prey of this pack. Cattle had been introduced into Pecos County only for a short time before, and I am unable to say whether or not the lobo made its appearance here before

we brought cattle. Early settlers believed that it came here after the cattle appeared. I am disposed to think, for several reasons, that this was probably the case.

As its English name "timber wolf" indicates, the wolf prefers to inhabit wooded country and forests. Our area is a land of plains. We have no forests, trees are exceedingly rare, and coverts of small brush are infrequent. The country was even more sparse 25 years ago. There must have been good and sufficient cause to bring the wolf into the type of environment that animals avoid. It wouldn't be too puzzling if an abundance of food were present. Within historic time the buffalo doesn't appear to have ever been abundant in this section. The deer and antelope were not copious, and were also animals capable of escaping wolf's pursuit.

Apparently in early times, nature did not allow for the wolf in the economy of this country. But when cattle moved in, large herds ranged over an immense area of the unfenced country. With such huge herds and vast pastures, cattlemen could give their herds only minimal protection. The cattle were necessarily turned loose to fend for themselves.

This condition was favorable to the appearance and increase of the lobo population. Though the forest and glade were absent, the mesas and the rocky caverns around the mesa furnished shelter for the lobo....

Such conditions allowed the lobo to extend its range. First we began to hear of its ravages at the Tunas Spring, 22 miles east of Fort Stockton. Then we heard of it about the old Neighbors ranch, 40 miles south of Fort Stockton. Later, it became troublesome in the foothills of the Glass Mountains both on the north side and the south side. Very early, the wolf marked himself a well-defined area of territory in which it is always found. Ravages outside this territory are rare and transitory.

The northern and western end of the country have remained free from lobos. These portions are fairly level, destitute of caves and good hiding places, and are without mesas or rocky hills. But the southern and southeastern parts of the country are land with high, but small table lands separated by valleys of various widths. Here, the lobo has found a congenial home and safe retreat. If a straight line were drawn on the Pecos River to the Glass Mountains, this line would mark approximately the northern and northwestern limits of damage done by wolves.

Because of their natural hunting method of running deer to ground, southwestern wolves probably avoided rough, precipitous, and brushy terrain. Most reports indicate that they frequented high mountain ridges, rounded hills, mesas, bajadas, and wooded stringers extending into grassland valleys. These accessible landscapes contributed to the wolf's demise since they allowed wolf hunters and their pack animals to cover wide areas.

Since wolves regularly traveled between mountain ranges, occasional stragglers occurred outside this regular range. With the ubiquitous prey base offered by livestock introductions, individual wolves may have operated far from their normal haunts. Old Aguila was such a wolf, ranging the Sonoran Desert and semidesert grasslands north and west of Wickenburg for eight years before being poisoned in 1924. Wolves were also reported on the Papago Indian Reservation in southwest Arizona (Young and Goldman 1944, Gish 1978). Roy McBride (1978) reported taking what he considered a transient pair of wolves in the Chihuahuan Desert north of La Ascensión, Chihuahua. Such individuals were unusual, however, and the wolf's range in the Southwest has generally been overstated.

ARIZONA

In southern Arizona the wolf regularly ranged as far west as the Madrean evergreen woodland in the Baboquivari Mountains. George Ballesteros, who worked on the Redondo Ranch, stated that the last resident wolves in the Baboquivaris were trapped in 1943. He recalled that at least one of these was a female and, like other wolves he remembered, she did not cower like a coyote but met the trapper's club vicious and defiant to the end.

The Santa Rita, Tumacacori, Atascosa-Parjarito, and Patagonia mountains were all well known as wolf country, as were the Canelo Hills. At least equal numbers inhabited the steeper and rougher, but larger Chiricahua, Huachuca, and Pinaleño mountains. A number of wolves were also recorded from the Catalina Mountains—some of them as recently as the 1950s (Lange 1960). All these mountain ranges were, and are, good Coues white-tailed deer country.

Northward, wolves ranged through the oak- and juniper-studded mesas and broken chaparral-covered hills of Greenlee, Graham, Gila, and Yavapai counties through the Apache Indian reservations and the Mogollon Rim. Here the Mexican wolf integrated with the so-called Arizona wolf of the Mogollon highlands. These wolves extended west from the New Mexico boundary through the forested Escudilla and

White mountains, along the Mogollon Rim and Coconino Plateau, to the San Francisco Peaks, Kendrick Mountain, and Bill Williams Mountain. From here small numbers of wolves reached northward to the South Rim of the Grand Canyon and westward to the pinyon-juniper woodlands as far south as Peach Springs (Young and Goldman 1944).

Still further north and to the east one might have encountered wolves, presumably the intermountain variety *youngi*, on the ponderosa-covered Defiance Plateau and in the Lukachukai and Chuska mountains of the Navajo Reservation. This race of wolves extended north into the Manti-LaSal and Blue mountains of Utah and beyond. A few wolves also occupied the North Kaibab Plateau until the mid-1920s before being brought to justice by the U.S. Biological Survey (Rasmussen 1941, Russo 1964). Since they fed primarily on the then dense population of Rocky Mountain mule deer, it is ironic that the wolves were removed from this national game refuge at a time when the excessive number of deer was a great concern to national forest administrators. According to the late D. I. Rasmussen, the last wolf in this part of northern Arizona was taken on the Paria Plateau about 1928.

NEW MEXICO

Wolves were widespread in New Mexico. Findley and others (1975) cite museum specimens and literature records for almost all counties west of the Pecos River. Even the Staked Plains had some wolves, and New Mexico is the only state to have what Goldman (1944) considered all five races of southwestern wolves. Knowledge of the distribution of wolves in this state comes mainly from the annual PARC reports of J. Stokely Ligon (1916 to 1924), his successors, and Vernon Bailey (1931).

As in Arizona, wolves west of the New Mexico plains were most prevalent in high mountain country capped with conifer forest. The literature shows wolves as especially common, or at least persistent, in the Mogollon Mountains and the adjacent Elk, Tularosa, Diablo and Pinos Altos mountains, in the Black Range, and in the Datil, Gallinas, San Mateo, Mount Taylor, Animas, and Sacramento mountains. Almost all the mountains higher than 6,000 feet with ponderosa pine forest had some wolves. Elsewhere wolves occasionally ranged through open glades next to cedar breaks, wooded ridges, and tablelands. These habitats were occupied northward in a broad front into Colorado. Only in the low desert areas of the state were wolves transient or absent.

Wolves had been essentially eliminated in New Mexico by the mid-1920s. Only in Hidalgo County's Animas, Peloncillo, and San Luis mountains did wolves persist into the 1930s—their constantly depleted ranks continually refurbished by new recruits crossing the Mexican border along long-established runways (Young and Goldman 1944). This is where government hunter Arnold Bayne continued to take wolves each year until the 1950s when the use of Compound 1080 eventually eliminated the trans-border stock. The last wolf "taken" in New Mexico was a carcass reported by Bayne (1977) from the Peloncillo Mountains in October 1970.

TRANS-PECOS TEXAS

Although wolves once roamed a large area of the Trans-Pecos, the only museum records are from the Guadalupe Mountains (1901), twenty miles southwest of Marfa in Presidio County (1942), Davis Mountains (1944), Cathedral Mountains (1970), and south of Longfellow near the junction of Terrell, Pecos and Brewster counties (1970) (Scudday 1977). Interestingly, the first two specimens were classified as the subspecies *monstrabilis*, the three later animals as *baileyi*. This led Scudday to suggest that the Mexican wolf was not native to the region and had wandered in from Mexico. It may also be instructive to note that the *baileyi* specimens were found the farthest southeast and were the ones most closely associated with Madrean evergreen woodland.

Literature references place wolves in the Davis and Glass mountains but not in the Chisos Mountains in Big Bend National Park. Wolves almost certainly occurred there, however, since some were taken near Terlingua (Stevens 1979). Wauer (1973) cites that the La Harmonia Company at Castolon, a long defunct town on the Rio Grande, processed and shipped east fifty wolf hides in 1925. Although these could have originated in the interior of Mexico, it seems reasonable to expect that at least some were obtained locally.

COAHUILA-SIERRA MADRE ORIENTAL

The former distribution of wolves in the outlying ranges of the Sierra Madre Oriental is uncertain. The only museum specimen from northeastern Mexico is one obtained by Lt. D. N. Couch, probably from naturalist Luis Berlandier's collection, housed in Matamoros, Tamaulipas. This location, in the tropics, is almost certainly not the origin of the animal (Bogan and Mehlhop 1980, McBride 1980).

Although Marsh (1937) reported wolves as common in the Sierra del Carmen vicinity, Taylor and others (1945), Baker (1956), and Leopold (1959) reported wolves scarce there. Other references to wolves in western Coahuila are proved by Baker (1956) and Leopold (1959) for the Sierra de las Cruces, Sierra de los Hecheros, Sierra del Pino, and Serranias de Burro. Both Baker (1956) and McBride (1980) refer to wolves on the desert plains southwest of Musquiz in the shadow of the Sierra Musquiz. McBride (1980) knew of wolves formerly occurring in the Sierra Rica, Chihuahua. These mountain ranges are all clothed in chaparral, Madrean evergreen woodland, and some pine forest. As elsewhere, the wolf was largely associated with temperate uplands and wooded habitats.

There are no records of wolves from eastern Coahuila, the Cerro San Luis Potosí in Nuevo León, eastern Zacatecas, or the Sierra Madre Oriental proper, but Dalquest (1953) reported wolves in the Mexican state of San Luis Potosí and examined one there. From the state of Veracruz there are several pre-World War I references and one specimen from Mount Orizaba. This last record is the only one from the Transvolcanic District and is the southernmost museum record. Never numerous in eastern and central Mexico, wolves are now almost certainly extinct everywhere in Mexico except in the Sierra Madre Occidental.

SIERRA MADRE OCCIDENTAL—CHIHUAHUA, DURANGO, SONORA, ZACATECAS

The Sierra Madre and its high outlying ranges and valleys, such as the Sierra del Nido, Sierra de las Tunas, Valle Santa Clara, and Valle Chuichuipa, have long been known as wolf strongholds. It was here, near Galeana, Chihuahua, that the specimen used to describe the Mexican wolf subspecies was collected. This long, blue ridge on northern Mexico's horizon represented the largest continuous area of wolf distribution in the Southwest. It was also from the northern limits of the Sierra Madre Occidental, in the San Luis and Guadalupe mountains, that wolves continued to invade Arizona and New Mexico long after resident wolves had been extirpated in the southwestern United States.

The wolf's wide range once included, and in small part remains, most of Chihuahua and Durango west of the Chihuahuan Desert and semidesert grasslands, extreme northwest Zacatecas, and the eastern edge of Sonora from 3,500 to 5,000 feet. In northeast Sonora, wolves are known to have occurred in the Sierra Pinitos; the Sierra Cibuta and surrounding hills, ridges, and peaks; and in the Sierra de los Ajos. Again, most records are in or near montane pine forests or evergreen woodlands (Brown and Lowe 1980). Wolves avoided steep barrancas and tropical-subtropical locales, preferring the high interior valleys, undulating ridges, and gentle slopes.

∽

1. These may have included coyotes. Wolves and coyotes were not always differentiated in early accounts. The tendency to call coyotes "wolves" in Texas and Plains states can also be confusing.

Bibliography

Allen, J. A. 1895. On a collection of mammals from Arizona and New Mexico made by Mr. W. W. Price, with field notes by the collector. Bull. Amer. Mus. Nat. Hist. 7(6):193–258.

Bailey, V. 1931. Mammals of New Mexico. *U.S.D.A. Bur. Biol. Surv. N. Amer. Fauna* 53:1–142.

Baird, S. F. 1859. *United States and Mexican Boundary Survey: Part II—Zoology of the Boundary.* Mammals, pp. 1–62. U.S.D.I., Washington, D.C.

Baker, R. H. 1956. Mammals of Coahuila, Mexico. *Univ. Kansas Publ., Mus. Nat. Hist.* 9:125–335.

Bartlett, J. R. 1854. *Personal Narrative of Explorations and Incidents.* 2 vols. New York.

Bayne, A. R. 1977. Personal communication to G. L. Nunley. In Nunley, G. L. 1977. *The Mexican Gray Wolf in New Mexico.* U.S. Fish and Wild. Serv. Rep. Albuquerque.

Bogan, M. A. and P. Mehlhop. 1980. Systematic relationships of gray wolves *(Canis lupus)* in southwestern North America. National Mus. of Natural History Report to the New Mexico Dept. of Game and Fish. *Endangered Species F.A. Report E:* 1–237.

Brown, D. E. and C. H. Lowe. 1980. Biotic Communities of the Southwest (Map). *U.S.D.A Forest Service, Rocky Mtn. Forest and Range Exper. Stat. Gen. Tech. Report RM-78.*

Conner, D. E. 1956. *Joseph Reddeford Walker and the Arizona Adventure.* Univ. of Oklahoma Press, Norman.

Coues, E. 1867. Notes on a collection of mammals from Arizona. *Proc. Acad. Sci. of Philadelphia.* 19:133–36.

Dalquest, W. W. 1953. Mammals of the Mexican state of San Luis Potosí. *Louisiana St. Univ. Studies, Biol. Sci. Ser.* 1:1–229.

Davis, G. P., Jr. 1973. Man and Wildlife in Arizona: The Presettlement Era, 1823–1864. M.S. Thesis. Dept. of Biol. Sci., Univ. of Arizona, Tucson.

Emory, W. H. 1848. *Notes of a Military Reconnaissance.* Washington, D.C.

Findley, J. S., A. H. Harris, D. E. Wilson, and C. Jones. 1975. *Mammals of New Mexico.* Univ. of New Mexico Press, Albuquerque.

Gish, D. M. 1978. *An Historical Look at the Mexican Gray Wolf (Canis lupus baileyi) in Early Arizona Territory and since Statehood.* U.S.D.I. Fish and Wildl. Serv. Rept.

Kennerly, C. B. R. 1856. Report on the zoology of the expedition. In *Reports of Exploration and Surveys, etc., 1853–1854*. Vol. 4. Expedition under Lt. A. W. Whipple, Corps of Topographical Engineers, upon the route near the 35th parallel. Washington, D.C.

Lange, K. I. 1960. Mammals of the Santa Catalina Mountains, Arizona. *Amer. Midl. Nat.* 64:436–58.

Leopold, A. S. 1959. *Wildlife of Mexico*. Univ. of California Press, Berkeley.

Ligon, J. S. 1916–1921 and 1924. Predatory animal control. New Mexico District. Annual Repts. U.S.D.A. Bur. Biol. Surv.

Lindsay, E. H. and N. T. Tessman. 1974. Cenozoic vertebrate localities and faunas in Arizona. *J. Ariz. Acad. Sci.* 9:3–24.

Marsh, E. G., Jr. 1937. Biological survey of the Santa Rosa and Del Carmen Mountains of northern Coahuila, Mexico. U.S.D.I. Nat. Park Serv. Report.

Martin, P. S. 1963. *The Last 10,000 Years*. Univ. of Arizona Press, Tucson.

Martin, P. S. and F. Plog. 1973. *The Archaeology of Arizona: A Study of the Southwest Region*. Amer. Mus. of Nat. Hist, Doubleday/Natural History Press, Garden City, N.Y. 391 pp.

McBride, R. T. 1978. *Status of the Gray Wolf (*Canis lupus baileyi*) in Mexico*. U.S.D.I. Fish and Wildl. Serv. Report.

———. 1980. The Mexican Wolf (*Canis lupus baileyi*). U.S.D.I. Fish and Wildl. Serv. Endangered Species Report 8:1-38.

McCullough, D. R. 1971. *The Tule Elk, Its History, Behavior and Ecology*. Univ. of California Press, Berkeley and Los Angeles.

Möllhausen, H. B. 1858. *Diary of a Journey from the Mississippi to the Coasts of the Pacific with a United States Government Expedition*. 2 vols. London.

Nentvig, J. 1763. *Rudo Ensayo*. Translation republished 1951. Arizona Silhouettes, Tucson.

Rasmussen, D. I. 1941. Biotic communities of Kaibab Plateau, Arizona. *Ecol. Monog.* 11:229–75.

Russo, J. P. 1964. The Kaibab North deer herd—its history, problems and management. *Ariz. Game and Fish Dept. Wildl. Bull.* 7:1–195.

Scudday, J. F. 1977. *The Mexican Gray Wolf in Texas*. U.S.D.I. Fish and Wildl. Serv. Report.

Sitgreaves, L. 1853. *Report of an Expedition down the Zuni and Colorado Rivers*. Robert Armstrong, Washington, D.C.

Stevens, J. T. 1979. Once abundant throughout the state, wolves are now almost gone. *Texas Parks and Wildl. Dept. Leaflet* 7000-45:1–3.

Taylor, W. P., W. B. McDougall, C. C. Presnall and K. P. Schmidt. 1945. *Preliminary Ecological Survey of the Northern Sierra del Carmen, Coahuila, Mexico*. Texas Coop. Wildl. Research Unit Report.

Tyler, D. 1964. *A Concise History of the Mormon Battalion in the Mexican War*. The Rio Grande Press, Chicago.

Wagoner, J. J. 1952. History of the cattle industry in southern Arizona, 1540–1940. *Univ. of Arizona Social Sci. Bull.* 20. Univ. of Arizona Press, Tucson.

Wauer, R. H. 1973. *Naturalist's Big Bend*. Peregrine Productions, Santa Fe.

Wheeler, G. H. 1875. *Report upon Geographical and Geological Explorations and Surveys West of the 100th Meridian*. Washington, D.C. Vol. 5:1–1019.

Young, S. P. and E. A. Goldman. 1944. *The Wolves of North America*. Amer. Wildl. Inst., Washington, D.C.

WOLF. *CANIS LUPUS*

||||||||||||||||||||||||||||||||||||||||||||||||||||||||||||||||||||||||||||

A. STARKER LEOPOLD
from *Wildlife of Mexico: The Game Birds and Mammals*
(1959)

*O*ther names.—Lobo; *Canis nubilus.*

Description.—Size of a large police dog, with broad heavy muzzle, wide-set eyes, and small, erect ears. (Even a small wolf is noticeably larger than a coyote and of heavier frame and build.) Forefeet large, leaving tracks 7 to 10 cm. across. Body grizzled brown or gray, not very different from that of the coyote. Shoulders and back darker than underparts. Measurements: head and body—1,000 to 1,200 mm.; tail—390 to 410 mm. Weight: 30 to 45 kg.

Range in Mexico.—Formerly throughout the temperate uplands, from Sonora and Tamaulipas south to Michoacán and Puebla. Wolves now exterminated in central uplands, and along eastern escarpment. The two remaining extensive blocks of occupied range are (1) the Sierra Madre Occidental, and (2) the arid mountains of western Coahuila and eastern Chihuahua. Additionally, Dalquest (1953) reports a population of wolves in western San Luis Potosí.

There can be no doubt that the wolf in its original abundance was the most formidable and destructive of livestock predators in Mexico. The other large carnivores, such as the mountain lion, jaguar, and grizzly bear, kill some stock, but animal for animal their depredations are minor compared with those of wolves. We can assume, therefore, that from the earliest days of Spanish settlement when domestic cattle, sheep, goats, burros, and horses were brought to this country, the wolves turned at least some of their attention from native game to the more vulnerable domestic herds and flocks, to the considerable detriment of the latter. Undoubtedly, also, the Spaniards took advantage of every opportunity and used every possible means to destroy the wolves. But in spite of persecution, wolves persisted throughout nearly all of their original range until fifty to seventy-five years ago, when technological improvements in firearms, traps, and poisons finally gave a conclusive advantage to the settlers. Now the range of the wolf is rapidly shrinking.

In the vicinity of Lake Pátzcuaro, Michoacán, the wolf was listed in the "Relacíon de Xiquilpan," written in 1579 (Barlow, 1944), and it was still present in 1884 according to León (1887). But in 1945 I could find no resident of the area who specifically remembered a wolf. Several old men knew vaguely that there had been wolves in past times. Similarly, at Los Reyes in western Michoacán a local hunter stated that he did not know the wolf but he had heard his father speak of it. Lumholtz (1902, vol. 2: 362) says that the wolf was exterminated in this area (Tancítaro) about 1870.

On the northern slope of Nevado de Toluca, Estado de México, E. W. Nelson found an elaborate pit trap for wolves which had been in use until about 1880. The following description of the trap is taken from Young and Goldman (1944: 288).

> This trap was made by digging a ringshaped trench about 20 feet deep, from 7 to 8 feet across the top, and tapering to a V at the bottom. The diameter of the circular trench across the outer walls was approximately 25 feet and the round, island-like center was 8 or 9 feet across. Both walls of the trench were carefully built from bottom to top with fairly smoothly-faced rock. To operate this trap, a young goat was staked on top of the round island in the middle, and poles loosely covered with branches and other vegetation were so laid across the trench that when a wolf tried to make his way to the bait, he would slip through and become helplessly wedged at the bottom of the pit. Such traps proved very effective in an area of heavy wolf infestation. Nelson was informed that the pits had not been used for more than 10 years previous to the time of his visit to this area in 1893.

Hans Gadow (1908) in his travels through central Mexico found wolves on the east slope of Mount Orizaba, Veracruz, about the beginning of this century.

In each of the accounts cited above, the wolf is carefully distinguished from the coyote, and I am satisfied that the records are valid. It is since the adoption of the breech-loading rifle and parallel improvements in other killing methods that wolves have disappeared in the southern reaches of the Mexican plateau.

In the sparsely settled uplands of northern Mexico, however, wolves still occupy large blocks of range. In some of the wilder parts of the Sierra Madre Occidental I found evidence of fairly large residual wolf populations in the recent past. Ten miles west of Colonia Pacheco, Chihuahua, we saw many tracks in 1937 and found remains of several deer at least some of which were wolf kills. However, this population is shrinking now. One hundred miles north of there, along the United States line, wolves regularly swing up from the Sierra Madre to raid the cattle herds in the Animas Valley and on other ranches near Cloverdale, New Mexico. The wolves in adjoining parts of northeastern Sonora are fewer, but a rancher near Casita complained to us in 1946 of losing some cattle to wolves. West and south of Durango City in the southern reaches of the Sierra I saw wolf tracks several times and heard of at least one cattle rancher who was seeking help in trapping wolves. As grazing and settlement continue to pinch down the wilderness areas of the Sierra Madre, however, the number of wolves and the range that they occupy will continue to shrink.

Reports of the abundance of wolves in Coahuila and eastern Chihuahua are conflicting. Marsh (1937) gives a lurid account of the ravages of "abundant" wolves on livestock in the region of the Sierra del Carmen, whereas Taylor *et al.* (1945) and Baker (1956) refer to the animal as uncommon in that area. In 1953 I spent a month in the Carmens and found no wolves at all. Eduardo López, a lifelong resident there, told me that a single wolf had come into the region in the late 1920's and preyed on cattle until about 1938, when it disappeared. Sr. López asserted, however, that there still are a few wolves to the south, and to the west in the Sierra Blanca along the Coahuila-Chihuahua border. Dalquest (1953) reports a thriving population south of there, in San Luis Potosí. It would seem, however, that although wolves may have been generally distributed in northern and central Mexico at one time, they were never abundant (Young and Goldman, 1944). The animals are scarce and scattered there now.

In winter, wolves are prone to hunt together in organized packs which are capable of inflicting big losses on livestock herds in one night. Originally, the wolf packs of the prairies attacked and pulled down bison—a task too great for a single animal to attempt. This pattern of group attack on a large prey animal works admirably on cattle, and there is no steer on the range strong enough or fleet enough to escape a band of wolves when he has been "cut out" or isolated from the main herd. As a rule, a wolf pack will make a new kill each night rather than return to an old carcass; this protects the animals, at least in part, from the traps and poison set out by ranchers. Young and Goldman (1944) cite many instances in which cattle-killing packs have operated successfully for long periods in the face of all-out warfare of stockmen and government trappers. But even the wariest individuals can be taken eventually by a clever and persistent trapper.

Not all wolves are stock killers. Cattle killing is a habit acquired by particular bands or individual wolves, and cattle losses often can be stopped by eliminating the individual killers without having to exterminate all the wolves in an area. Fascinating stories have been told of some of the most infamous wolves that have raided the cattle ranges of the West. Lobo, the "King of the Currumpaw Valley," New Mexico, whose biography is recorded by Ernest Thompson Seton, was one such animal.

The normal diet of the Mexican wolf consists mainly of deer but includes such other native mammals as peccaries, antelope, bighorn sheep, rabbits, and many of the rodents. At times wolves eat some plant foods, such as manzanita berries and other fruits, but this tendency is less marked than in the coyotes. In the Río Gavilán basin of northwestern Chihuahua we found many deer carcasses representing wolf kills, and one adult male wolf that we collected contained in its stomach a whole fawn—head, hoofs, and all—eaten in great chunks. Curiously, there was one extra ear, which had come from an adult deer, presumably the mother of the fawn. In her efforts to defend her young the doe must have leaped in too close. The bobbed-off ear was a record of her valor.

As the breeding season approaches, the packs break up into pairs, which seek their own dens for rearing their litters of young. Mating occurs in late winter, and the young are born after a sixty- to sixty-three-day gestation period, usually in March (Young and Goldman, p. 96). Litters range from 5 to 14 pups, averaging about 7. Until the whelps are a third grown they are kept in a den by the parents and come out only to feed and to romp in the sun for short periods. Most dens are in ground burrows; but wolves, like coyotes, sometimes use caves in the rocks, or hollow logs or stumps as den sites. The male is solicitous of the family and works as hard as the female to bring food for the growing young.

The den is abandoned when the young are about three months old, and thereafter the family hunts together, the parents teaching the young to do their own hunting. As winter approaches, family groups become the nuclei of winter packs, which outsiders or nonbreeding individuals may be permitted to join. Young wolves do not breed as yearlings; they become fully adult at the age of two years. While the adults are busy raising a new batch of pups, the yearlings forage a good deal on their own, often without much success. A young wolf that we took in July, 1948, along the Río Gavilán contained in its stomach only shreds of desiccated deer hide, stripped from the carcass of some long-dead animal. The period of emancipation from parental care is probably a difficult one.

The foregoing paragraphs have shown that wolves do extensive damage to domestic livestock. But what of their predation on game? At least some wolves live mostly on deer and smaller game such as rabbits and rodents. The wolves occupying the wilderness of the northern Sierra Madre Occidental must have lived entirely on game (mostly deer), since up to a few years ago there were virtually no cattle or other stock in the mountains. Yet deer were abundant. Under completely natural conditions, wolves and mountain lions seem to harvest merely the surplus or annual crop of deer, keeping the breeding herd at a reasonable level. In this sense, the population of the predator (wolf) is determined by the abundance and availability of the prey (deer), rather than vice versa. The deer in turn exist in numbers conforming to the carrying capacity of the range, as determined by supplies of food, cover, and water. Such a natural balance is advantageous to both the deer and the wolves in the long run, and it is erroneous to suppose that we must destroy the large predators in order to protect the game populations in wilderness areas.

On cattle range, it is usually necessary to kill wolves to prevent serious depredations on the vulnerable domestic animals. It may be necessary also to take some measures to restore vanishing game species, such as the antelope; for a few wolves along with coyotes seem to be preying on the remaining antelope in northern Chihuahua. But on the whole, keeping down the wolf population is not an important aspect of game management in Mexico.

As mentioned in the preceding chapter, there appears to be some degree of social intolerance between wolves and coyotes. To be sure, there are many areas where the two occur together on the same range, but I suspect that there are not as many coyotes on the wolf range as in similar areas where the wolves have been exterminated. Retaining a few wolves, then, may be one way to hold down excessive coyote populations.

Whatever the economic importance of the wolf may be in Mexico, it is one of the most interesting of the native mammals, and definite provision should be made to prevent its complete extermination. Setting aside a great national park or wilderness preserve in the northern Sierra Madre Occidental would be one of the best ways of maintaining at least a fragment of the shrinking population. The Mexican lobo is as much a part of the lore of the country as the feathered serpent, and we would be poor-spirited indeed if we could not find at least one place in Mexico where the wolf may persist, safe from the incessant warfare of the cattlemen.

Bibliography

Baker, R. H. 1956. Mammals of Coahuila, Mexico. *Univ. of Kansas Publ., Mus. Nat. Hist.* 9: 125–335.

Barlow, R. H. (ed.). 1944. Relacíon de Xiquilpan y su partido, 1579. Sobretiro de Tlalocán 1:278-306.

Dalquest, W. W. 1953. *Mammals of the Mexican State of San Luis Potosí.* Louisiana State Univ. Studies, Biol. Sci. Ser., No. 1.

Gadow, H. 1908. *Through Southern Mexico.* Witherby and Co., London. 527 pp.

León, N. 1887. *Historia geografía y estadística de la municipalidad de Quiroga en 1884.* Imprenta del Gobierno ó Cargo de José R. Bravo, Morelia.

Lumholtz, C. 1902. *Unknown Mexico.* Chas. Scribner's Sons, New York. 2 vols. 1,013 pp.

Marsh, E. G., Jr. 1937. Biological survey of the Santa Rosa and Del Carmen Mountains of northern Coahuila, Mexico. U.S. Nat. Park Serv., mimeo. rep.

Taylor, W. P., W. B. McDougall, C. C. Presnall, and K. P. Schmidt. 1945. Preliminary ecological survey of the northern Sierra del Carmen, Coahuila, Mexico. Texas Coop. Wildlife Res. Unit. mimeo.

Young, S. P. and E. A. Goldman. 1944. *The Wolves of North America.* Amer. Wildlife Inst., Washington, D.C.

TIMBER WOLF
(*CANIS LUPUS*)

BEN TINKER
from *Mexican Wilderness and Wildlife*
(1978)

*T*imber wolves once ranged south through the forested sierras on both the east and west coasts to mountains near the Valley of Mexico. Now their habitats on the west coast are sparsely distributed through Sierra Madre Occidental, where they occur in isolated areas in Sonora, Chihuahua, Durango, and Zacatecas. On the east coast their present habitats are in mountainous regions of Coahuila, Nuevo León, and San Luis Potosí. Although not plentiful in their present habitats, they leave their mark on the population of deer, peccaries, wild turkeys, and, occasionally, domestic flocks.

Today wolves are beasts of the forested mountains, but when both buffalo and antelope thronged the plains of northern Chihuahua wolves followed the Apache buffalo hunters and occupied the barren foothills near the plains. During the winter of 1938 a pack of wolves came down from Sierra Madre Occidental into the rolling country near Ascensión, Chihuahua, and preyed on the herds of antelope and cattle. In the spring they moved farther south, spending several days killing prairie dogs which infested a region near the prehistoric ruins of Casas Grandes. When the "dog towns" were cleaned out the wolves departed. They are not dangerous to man, but this pack created a reign of terror among the townspeople of Casas Grandes Viejo.

While mending a fence one of the vaqueros left his lunch on a boulder and returned to find it gone. He noted tracks where two wolves had cautiously circled about until one finally seized the lunch bag. He never found out whether they ate the red hot chili with the meat.

I have frequently seen wolves skulking through the timber but have never been fast enough "on the draw" to kill one. I had given up the idea when I secured two unexpectedly. This occurred during a trip when we were camped up on the headwaters of Río Yaqui in Sonora. The native guide had gone hunting and killed two whitetail bucks. Being quite a distance from camp and afoot, he hung them in an oak tree. Early next morning we went to bring them in and saw three wolves running around the tree, but the bucks were hanging too high. The wolves were so engrossed in leaping and running around the tree that I killed two and wounded the other, which we trailed without finding.

The specimens were adult males. The larger skin measured 5 feet 11 inches tip of nose to tip of tail and weighed 96 pounds. The skull measured: greatest length overall 11²/₁₆ inches, width across zygomatic arches 7²/₁₆ inches. The forepaws measured 4½ inches wide, 4¾ inches long; the hindpaws measured 3 inches wide, 4⅛ inches long. The other individual measured 5 feet 4 inches in length, weighing 81 pounds, with slight differences in other measurements.

The larger one compared in size to one I collected in the Endicott Mountains of northern Alaska. This big fellow bit off large green willow branches with its powerful jaws as it ran mortally wounded through the thicket. It was 6 feet long with heavy dark hair and weighed 102 pounds; sourdoughs called it a black wolf, which is a color phase of the gray wolf. I have never seen one like it in Mexico.

Recently while trout fishing on the upper reaches of the Liard River in Yukon Territory, I discovered a wolf was following my trail among the willows along the stream. Nearing an open spot it ran up the timbered canyonside, pausing once to look down at me, but the rifle was at camp.

Wolves are wary of humans but curious. A similar incident happened in Sonora. We had gone to move a bunch of steers which were in the mountains above the ranch. En route home I frequently heard a rustling sound in the oak thickets which flanked the trail for some distance. Every time I stopped to look and listen it ceased. Mounted, visibility was zero, so I dismounted and, "bellying down," saw a wolf standing in the thickets a few yards off the trail, with only its paws and legs visible. Sensing something was afoot it crouched for a moment and vanished.

Wolves are silent hunters except during the winter when we hear them howling and thus detect their presence on ridge crests and open meadows near the ranch. Mr. Ben Black, who has lived alone for many years at the old Lang ranch, says he often hears them during this season in the high timbered mesas in back of his house and sees others running atop the ancient earthen dam that spans a nearby valley. This dam was built by prehistoric people who terraced other areas in the sierras, but its purpose and history are unknown.

His ranch was a meeting place for cattle rustlers and gunmen when Wyatt Earp, Doc Holliday, and Curly Bill were making Tombstone famous. Señor Black digs out old soft-nosed bullets from the adobe house walls as he directs attention to many happenings during those lusty times.

Native hunters claim that when timber wolves mate they remain together until death separates them. There is no positive proof if this is a fact, but it is plausible and commonly believed. We have not been able to determine a definite mating season.

Timber wolves generally den up in caves or dig burrows under out-cropping rock ledges in secluded canyonsides where they whelp six to ten pups during early spring. At this time the female stays at home tending the youngsters while the male fetches any bird, rodent, or animal he can catch. When the pups are old enough they run with the parents.

Old dens are littered with bones of deer, peccaries, squirrels, and wild turkeys. As these animals and birds are plentiful in high regions of the Sierra Madre, we seldom find remains of livestock which wolves have killed, although rancheros on lower reaches of Ríos Yaqui and Mayo, where wildlife are scarce, frequently do.

Jim Anderson, a Mormon cattle rancher, who was my companion while trout fishing on a stream which flows into Río Aros, discovered two pups romping near a jutting ledge above the creek. We tied our horses and with a favorable wind detoured afoot to a higher point. Here we watched a litter of seven youngsters frolicking around their mother while she crouched outside the den. Such a sight was too interesting to last. A vagrant breeze or her keen eyes betrayed our whereabouts, and she hustled them inside the den. We returned to the horses in a quandary what to do about our find, which was solved by Jim's logical question.

"Whot ya gonna do ef ya' gits 'em?"

Timber wolves do not inhabit or range over any part of the Altar Desert in Sonora or Baja California, as these desert regions are remote from their habitats in the forested sierras.

WOLF BOY

||||||||||||||||||||||||||||||||||

ESTELA PORTILLO TRAMBLEY
from *Trini*
(1986)

(This is a brief excerpt from Estela Portillo Trambley's novel Trini. *Trini is a young Tarahumara Indian girl from the Sierra Madre mountains of Chihuahua, Mexico. Her mother has recently died. She is travelling with her father, José Mario, and her conservative aunt, Tía Pancha. They are moving to an area where the father can get work in the mines. After travelling through hostile Indian territory, they have arrived in the town of San Domingo where they are seeking a place to stay. The old woman Sebastiana takes them in and tells them a tale of what befell the son of Esteban when he encountered a loba in the Sierra Madre.)*

'm not rich!" assured the woman who stood before them in the dark, sweet-smelling little store. She was bending forward to get a good look at the tired strangers. Trini saw before her a small, thin woman with only one bleary blue eye. The other was staring glassiness, half-covered by a sagging lid. She was leaning on a mop inside a pail. A grainy dampness and the tang of lye soap exuded from the floor. "Esteban told you that? That old redbeard! He hasn't been right since the tragedy." She gave a huge heaving sigh, then she invited them to the room back of the store.

Behind the counter was a door covered with a dusty green curtain. She led them into what appeared to be the kitchen. "I'll get some food." She made the offer, then went about banging pots and pans.

Soon she had served them bowls of stew made of chicken and garbanzos. She brought in an armful of beer and opened each bottle on the kitchen table before handing it out. Tía Pancha frowned, taking the beer away from the children. Sebastiana stared at Tía Pancha for a second, then shrugged. She drank half a bottle of beer, gulping freely, before she asked José Mario, "So? The Indians didn't hang you, eh?"

While they ate the good stew, José Mario t   hir.
ney. Sebastiana listened intently, nodding her heac   eff
the time José Mario finished, Sebastiana had dru
Tía Pancha watching her disapprovingly. Sebastia
was very bleary. She looked around the table goo
a decision, then slapped her knees. "You can have   cig
and welcome."   son

"How much is the rent?" asked José Mario he
"Angelino's smiling in heaven because his l   wc
empty."   ric

"How much is the rent?" repeated José Mario   ma
"Rent, rent, who wants rent?" Sebastiana sat   Bu
and challenged José Mario with a slow, deep smi   gr
twinkling. Trini was getting used to the one eye. Sc   he
an's face, so eager in its interest, was alive with a
the eye unnoticeable. "It's your house!"   gr

Her statement was final and she made her way   H
another beer. She was shaking her head when she c   w
tell you about Esteban? Let me tell you about the r   an

Tía Pancha was full of interest. "You said a tra
That was Sebastiana's cue. She heaved anothei   ar
long drink from the bottle. "Poor man! He had   pu
would not believe. Handsome, talented, broke all   w
But full of pride. He paid for that." Sebastiana finis   sh

"How?" Trini's head was up from the table w   hi
children had half-fallen asleep.

"All the girls were after him, but he loved no
looked into her apron pockets and found a pack (w
matches. "Well," she continued as she lighted a cig   k
off into the hills, where the springs are. You saw then   m
into San Domingo."   w

Before the black mountains of the mines, a few
had been green hills, hills that had made Trini's hear
wide awake now. "We saw them!"

Tía Pancha motioned her to be quiet, as Sebasti
smoke of her cigarette and let it come out her nose.
happen on those hills..."

"What happened to the boy?" asked Trini impat
Sebastiana, taking her time, sat back, a foot acros
on hand, flicking ashes thoughtfully. "Well, he wer
one day, fell in a crevice, broke a leg. He lay there for
gry, in pain. Then one night he saw a pack of wolves

along the narrow path where he lay…" Sebastiana paused for
ct, her eyes reaching deep inside her for memories.

"What happened?" asked Trini excitedly.

"Stop interrupting, child," Tía Pancha scolded.

"He got back home safe and sound." Sebastiana lighted another
rette and sat forward, looking at one face, then another, waiting for
eone's urging. There was only waiting silence, so she continued:

"The wolves saved him! After that, when a full moon rose, he
ıld disappear into the hills again. One night a man from the bar-
was walking home late through the hills when he saw the boy
king love to a beautiful woman. He stopped to watch, naturally.
she saw him and ran away, leaving Esteban's son sitting on the
ss. Now the man, he might have been drunk, or maybe not, but
claims he saw the woman change into a wolf."

Sebastiana sat back in her chair and watched their disbelief with
at energy. "The boy returned to the village with a broken heart.
would never see his lady again. That didn't stop him though. He
nt back to the hills again and again, until one night he came home
I told his father he was leaving forever."

Sebastiana sighed and looked at José Mario's empty bottle. "Want
other beer?" He shook his head as she made herself comfortable,
tting her feet on an empty chair, lighting another cigarette. "The
man had come back, made love to him one last time, telling him
would never return—not as a woman, anyway. But she could turn
n into a wolf, that way they could stay together."

"He agreed?" Trini's voice was a near whisper.

"Of course," nodded Sebastiana with great wisdom. "That is the
y of love. Poor Esteban hasn't been well since." She slapped her
ee one more time and put her feet down from the chair. "I talk too
ich. You are tired. We go to Angelino's house." She led the way
th a lantern.

WOLF CUNNING

G. W. "DUB" EVANS
from *Slash Ranch Hounds*
(1951)

My hatred for wolves goes clear back to my early boyhood in Texas, and has been strengthened by countless experiences with them throughout my lifetime. Never once have I known a wolf to do anything to change my bad opinion of him; and, although I would very much regret the passing of bear and lions from these Southwestern mountains, I would shed no tears whatever over the death of the last lobo.

In my opinion, the lobo is the cruelest, most wanton killer of all of our Southwestern predators. Bear and lions do sometimes become stock killers, and both do sometimes kill wantonly, beyond the need for food. But such animals are the exceptions to the rule; whereas the opposite is true, in my opinion, of the lobo.

Years ago, when I was a boy in Texas, a lobo adopted as his home range the area immediately around our ranch headquarters. I think he chose this location at least partly because of my father's pack of hounds. I have seen many instances since then of wolves choosing a locality around a ranch headquarters where dogs are kept, partly no doubt because of the opportunities for food to be found around such a headquarters, but partly too, I think because the wolf delights in annoying and trying to kill the dogs. This particular lobo became an immediate threat to our stock, and he made our nights miserable by the way he stirred up and harassed our hounds. He would come in close to the house at night, arouse the hounds, get them to chase him a mile or so, then turn on them and chase them back—time after time and night after night, all to the tune of much barking and general uproar.

This is a favorite trick of wolves, one I have since seen repeated many times. Dogs in their own back yards are bold enough to chase a wolf; but they fear the wolf and, once they get out into the darkness and away from the familiar surroundings, that fear grows and, when the wolf turns, they will run from him. Often too, dogs will string out in such a chase and the wolf will turn and kill them one by one, as he catches them. Our Texas hounds in this particular instance had been wise enough to stick together and this wolf had not, so far, succeeded in killing one of them; but we knew that sooner or later this would happen or that the wolf would kill some of our stock, and we grew to hate him bitterly.

One night we heard the hounds take off after the wolf, and my brother, Joe, and I decided to slip out into a nearby arroyo and hide there in the hope of shooting the wolf when he chased the hounds back. We waited until the hounds came pounding back past us and, sure enough, there was the wolf close behind them, visible enough in the moonlight to make a target. Joe, being the older, had the rifle and he stood up to fire. The wolf turned swiftly at sight of us, but Joe's quick shot knocked him rolling. I have learned since that few wolf stories end so suddenly or so simply.

Cole Means tells of another very similar but less easily solved instance that occurred on the Means Y6 ranch. Here, too, a wolf took up headquarters near the ranch and proceeded practically to disrupt the work of the ranch. Every night he would come in and play this game of "you chase me and I'll chase you" with the hounds, and nearly every night he would kill stock. This went on for a considerable time, with sometimes as many as fifty men working on the problem of exterminating this one wolf. This wolf finally was killed, but at great expense both in stock killed and in man-hours.

Just a few stories out of my own experiences will show why I, and all cattlemen, hate wolves. A favorite wolf method of killing large animals is to hamstring the animals, breaking him down and making him completely helpless. Raw cowhide is extremely tough, and the heavy tendons in a full-grown steer's leg are even tougher, yet a lobo's sharp teeth and powerful neck and jaw muscles enable him to leap past a steer and cut through those tendons with no seeming effort. Once the animal is down and helpless, the wolf will gorge himself off the steer's body, sometimes not even taking the trouble to kill the animal first. I have seen these hamstrung, helpless animals still living after wolves had eaten great chunks out of them. I remember one night hearing an animal moaning as if in great distress. We could not get to her in the darkness but, next morning, found a fine heifer, hamstrung still alive and suffering in spite of the fact that a wolf had eaten at least twenty pounds of flesh off her body. A few incidents like this will teach anyone to hate wolves.

I have a painful memory, too, of finding, in one corner of a small pasture where the wolf had trapped them, eleven ready-for-market steers, some hamstrung and waiting to be shot, some already dead.

This was the work of a single lobo, and the wolf had eaten from only one carcass. The rest of the slaughter had been merely to satisfy the beast's lust for killing.

Incidents like these, repeated many times in my own personal experience, may give the reader some idea why I hate wolves and why cattlemen have repeatedly offered large rewards, sometimes up to $5,000, for the destruction of a single lobo.

Hound men have still other reasons for hating wolves, as I mentioned earlier. I well remember one fine pack of trained hounds that was ruined on one chase after one lobo. This pack belonged to my brother, Joe Evans, and represented generations of breeding and years of careful training. The pack strung out on a hot but long trail—long because the lobo is fast and will keep ahead of hounds for a long distance. The wolf turned finally and, one by one, killed the lead hounds. Naturally, the best hounds in the pack were in the lead. When Joe rode up and found his best hounds dead or dying, he swore never to run wolves again. Joe and his family loved those hounds, and losing them was almost as painful as would have been the loss of human friends.

A person not familiar with wolves might wonder why dogs, even strong trained hounds, unafraid of either bear or lion, should be so easily killed by a wolf. After all, the wolf is only another kind of dog, and not the biggest of the dog family either. Yet he is death to dogs. I have never seen a dog that would stand a chance in a fight with a lobo. Neighbors of ours once owned one of the biggest, one of the most vicious dogs I have ever seen; so big and vicious that he had to be kept chained constantly to keep him from killing other dogs and injuring people. He was truly a gigantic animal and about as dangerous a fighter as one could imagine. We took this dog to a ranch where a lobo was making regular visits and one night, hearing the lobo outside, turned the big dog loose. He charged out eagerly enough, and met the wolf. We heard the sounds of that meeting, but not for long. I don't know what the lobo did, but whatever it was cured the dog of any desire to fight him. The big dog turned tail and ran, not stopping at the ranch at all but fleeing miles across country to his own home and the safety of his own pen and chain. The lobo was unhurt and continued his depredations.

I recently read an article in which the writer defended wolves, claiming that they were brave, gallant animals, that their killing of other animals was no worse than that of any other predator, no worse than that of the human hunter "who kills for sport," and that the wolf was a necessary part of Nature's plan for the control of wildlife populations, since the wolf "kills only the weak, sick or crippled" and so tends to strengthen and improve existing supplies of game animals such as deer, antelope, sheep, etc.

I have no patience whatever with such sentimentality; can only believe that the writer knows nothing whatever about the actual habits of the wolves. It is absolutely untrue that the wolf kills "only the weak, sick, or crippled," whether of game animals or of domestic stock. He will kill such animals, yes; but he will also kill any other animal he happens to feel like killing, regardless of size, health, or value. The writer's contention that the wolf is necessary to maintain a natural balance in the deer and antelope herds, that without him deer and antelope would either die out or become tame as sheep, is simply childish. In the area with which I am most familiar, there have been no wolves at all for many years; yet the area is well populated with deer and antelope, and I could prove by the testimony of countless hunters who have walked or ridden these mountains in search of game that neither the deer nor the antelope are "tame."

It is true that other predators kill game animals, and a few individual lions and bear do become stock killers; but these animals rarely kill beyond the need of their own hunger. Sometimes they do, but not often. On the other hand, the lobo is a butcher, killing at every opportunity whether he is hungry or not.

The comparison of the lobo with the human hunter also is childish, in my opinion. Even if we grant that the human hunter also "kills for sport," game laws today control and guide his killing toward the beneficial control of game populations and limit it to the degree needed for that purpose. But you can't limit a lobo to one deer a season; nor can you tell him, "This year you can kill only a doe, because does are too numerous!"

Too, the hunter actually provides, through his license fees, the money without the benefits of which game of all kinds would have long since ceased to exist in this country. The wolf kills aimlessly, needlessly, and heartlessly without contributing anything at all. He has been praised for his stubborn survival against the centuries-long and world-wide war man has waged against him; but, to me, this survival is only an evidence of his cunning and ruthless courage. The very fact that man has, throughout the world and from earliest times, hated and waged relentless war against him, seems to me to be far more telling evidence on the opposite side of the picture. Such general hatred must be, and is, deserved. Granted that the wolf is brave, and granted that courage is an admirable quality, even courage becomes less than admirable when it is used, as in the case of the lobo, only for self preservation and wanton murder.

I have kept my hounds off wolf trails whenever possible, but there was one time when, using every possible precaution, I did encourage them to help toward the extermination of wolves in this area. During the work of clearing the wild cattle off Black Mountain, the hounds one day jumped and ran down a lobo pup. Figuring that other pups of the same litter would be in the vicinity, we let the hounds work and soon found the trail of a full grown wolf, probably the mother. We called the hounds in immediately, following the wolf's trail to where she had topped out of a canyon. Knowing that the hounds would never cross the canyon except on the trail of the wolf, we put a man at that point to stop them if such an attempt were made. I knew that, if the hounds got away from us on the trail of a full-grown lobo, the wolf would eventually turn and kill some of them, and I took every precaution to keep this from happening.

We then went back and used the hounds to trail and run down five more lobo pups. These pups, dead, were turned over to the Government hunter then working in the district.

A Government hunter-trapper named Ritchie did fine work toward the final extermination of lobos in this area. One by one he weeded them out until, finally, only one wolf was left. This was a female, and she was smart with the cunning of long experience. Mr. Ritchie worked long and hard to kill her and once did catch her in a trap; but a small stone caught in the trap and prevented its jaws from closing tightly, so that the wolf was able to, and did, shake the trap off.

After this experience this wolf would not approach even the most carefully laid traps, and of course no man could come within gun range of her. Her sex made her particularly dangerous, since she would certainly attract males into the country to mate with her, and her pups might well repopulate the area. As a matter of fact, well after it had been established that she was the sole survivor in the area, Mr. Ritchie did catch and kill a male wolf apparently drawn in from some other section of the country by this female. But as for the female herself, Mr. Ritchie used every lure and every trick of trap-setting he knew but finally admitted defeat and suggested that another hunter be sent against her. He felt that this wolf knew his scent and that of his mounts, as well as all his lures and tricks, too well for him ever to catch her, and that another hunter might have better success.

Albert Pickens was the man chosen for the job, and Albert spent two or three months in the area without setting a trap, studying this wolf's tracks, habits, and the reports of her doings brought to him by the ranchers and cowboys who were also on the alert for any sign of her. Albert patiently tried every scent lure he knew or which was suggested to him, leaving the various scents on bushes and rocks and then going back to search for tracks to see whether or not the wolf had been drawn to the spot, but never once did he find that she had been lured to where a trap would have caught her had a trap been set. Apparently she was just too wary of all scents to be drawn to any that might have been laid by man. During this period, Albert did kill another male wolf attracted to the area by the female; but this merely renewed the possibility that she might soon birth a new litter.

One day Albert, on horseback, followed the wolf's tracks to where she had stooled. Albert got a long stick off a nearby tree and, without dismounting and leaving his body scent on any spot of ground or any object that would be left there, managed to move the dung a few feet to one side of its original position. He then rode away.

The next day he went back to the spot and saw where the wolf had returned, examined the place, and finally circled to find and examine the dung in its new position.

Days later, Albert succeeded in finding another similar deposit. This time, he moved off to one side a little distance, dropped a piece of canvas and dismounted onto the canvas so as not to leave scent or sign, and, using every possible precaution, set two traps a few feet to one side of the stool. He did not move the dung at this time but let several days pass so that time and wind and weather might wipe out any trace of scent he might have left in the immediate vicinity of the traps.

Next, he rode back to this place some days later and, as he had done the first time, without dismounting at all, using a long stick, he moved the dung over between the two traps.

If all this seems like undue precaution, bear in mind that all other tricks known to trappers had failed, whereas this one worked. The next day, Albert went back to his set and found tracks showing where the wolf had returned, noticed the moving of the dung, went (as she had done safely before) to examine it in its new position, and had been caught in both traps. The traps were attached to drags, of course, because a wolf caught in a fixed trap will gnaw off its feet to get free. Albert followed the tracks of the wolf and the furrows left by the traps and drags and soon came upon the wolf in a thicket where the drags caught and stopped her.

That was the end of the lobos in this area. This happened in the early '20's, and no lobo has taken up residence in this locality since.

Since writing the above, I have received a letter from my brother, Joe, who has read the same article defending wolves which I referred to earlier in this chapter. Joe was so indignant about that article that he wrote several pages on the subject, some of which I quote:

> This article merely proves to me that the writer never raised sheep or cattle for lobos to kill! There were only a limited number of bear that killed stock, as they lived mostly on acorns, pinons, and berries. The mountain lions fed principally on deer or antelope, were easy to control because they could be caught with hounds. They would usually kill one deer or antelope and go back to the carcass day after day until it was eaten up. But the lobo wolf lived on cattle whenever possible because they were easier to catch than deer or antelope, and would kill a fresh yearling about every three days. Think how much this would amount to, at the present price of beef!

Joe reiterates my own remarks about the wolf killing for sport, and reminds me of the incident already mentioned of the lone lobo killing eleven ready-for-market yearlings in one night. He adds:

> The slaughter of lobos was not limited to yearlings, either. And it is not true that he killed only the weak, sick, or crippled animals, whether beef or wild game. I remember seeing a grown bull, about as far from being a weak, sick, or crippled animal as you could imagine, which was cut down by lobos and eaten off of while he was still alive.... This writer's idea of preserving the lobo is no more sensible than it would be to pet a rattlesnake or coddle a bandit or rapist who was endangering the lives of your loved ones or the sanctity of your home. If this writer had ever shed tears, as I did, over the torn and bleeding body of a well-loved hound as I carried him in my arms back to the ranch to die after an encounter with a lobo, he would sing a different tune! To kill the lobo wherever you find him is to render a service to mankind and to all wildlife.

I agree with Joe, and want to add here that the Fish and Wildlife Service (formerly The Biological Survey) has rendered an invaluable service to the livestock and game interests of the Southwest by the determined warfare they have carried on against the lobo. I and all the stockmen of my acquaintance, as well as the hunters, commend them for it.

THINKING LIKE A MOUNTAIN

ALDO LEOPOLD
from *A Sand County Almanac*
(1949)

A deep chesty bawl echoes from rimrock to rimrock, rolls down the mountain, and fades into the far blackness of the night. It is an outburst of wild defiant sorrow, and of contempt for all the adversities of the world.

Every living thing (and perhaps many a dead one as well) pays heed to that call. To the deer it is a reminder of the way of all flesh, to the pine a forecast of midnight scuffles and of blood upon the snow, to the coyote a promise of gleanings to come, to the cowman a threat of red ink at the bank, to the hunter a challenge of fang against bullet. Yet behind these obvious and immediate hopes and fears there lies a deeper meaning, known only to the mountain itself. Only the mountain has lived long enough to listen objectively to the howl of a wolf.

Those unable to decipher the hidden meaning know nevertheless that it is there, for it is felt in all wolf country, and distinguishes that country from all other land. It tingles in the spine of all who hear wolves by night, or who scan their tracks by day. Even without sight or sound of wolf, it is implicit in a hundred small events, the midnight whinny of a pack horse, the rattle of rolling rocks, the bound of a fleeing deer, the way shadows lie under the spruces. Only the ineducable tyro can fail to sense the presence or absence of wolves, or the fact that mountains have a secret opinion about them.

My own convictions on this score date from the day I saw a wolf die. We were eating lunch on a high rimrock, at the foot of which a turbulent river elbowed its way. We saw what we thought was a doe fording the torrent, her breast awash in white water. When she climbed the bank toward us and shook out her tail, we realized our error: it was a wolf. A half-dozen others, evidently grown pups, sprang from the willows and all joined in a welcoming mêlée of wagging tails and playful maulings. What was literally a pile of wolves writhed and tumbled in the center of an open flat at the foot of our rimrock.

In those days we had never heard of passing up a chance to kill a wolf. In a second we were pumping lead into the pack, but with more excitement than accuracy: how to aim a steep downhill shot is always confusing. When our rifles were empty, the old wolf was down, and a pup was dragging a leg into impassable slide-rocks.

We reached the old wolf in time to watch a fierce green fire dying in her eyes. I realized then, and have known ever since, that there was something new to me in those eyes—something known only to her and to the mountain. I was young then, and full of trigger-itch; I thought that because fewer wolves meant more deer, that no wolves would mean a hunters' paradise. But after seeing the green fire die, I sensed that neither the wolf nor the mountain agreed with such a view.

Since then I have lived to see state after state extirpate its wolves. I have watched the face of many a newly wolfless mountain, and seen the south-facing slopes wrinkle with a maze of new deer trails. I have seen every edible bush and seedling browsed, first to anaemic desuetude, and then to death. I have seen every edible tree defoliated to the height of a saddlehorn. Such a mountain looks as if someone had given God a new pruning sheers, and forbidden him all other exercise. In the end the starved bones of the hoped-for deer herd, dead of its own too-much, bleach with the bones of the dead sage, or molder under the high-lined junipers.

I now suspect that just as a deer herd lives in mortal fear of its wolves, so does a mountain live in mortal fear of its deer. And perhaps with better cause, for while a buck pulled down by wolves can be replaced in two or three years, a range pulled down by too many deer may fail of replacement in as many decades.

So also with cows. The cowman who cleans his range of wolves does not realize that he is taking over the wolf's job of trimming the herd to fit the range. He has not learned to think like a mountain. Hence we have dustbowls, and rivers washing the future into the sea.

We all strive for safety, prosperity, comfort, long life, and dullness. The deer strives with his supple legs, the cowman with trap and poison, the statesman with pen, the most of us with machines, votes, and dollars, but it all comes to the same thing: peace in our time. A measure of success in this is all well enough, and perhaps is requisite to objective thinking, but too much safety seems to yield only danger in the long run. Perhaps this is the idea behind Thoreau's dictum: In wildness is the salvation of the world. Perhaps this is the hidden meaning in the howl of the wolf, long known among mountains, but seldom perceived among men.

And Back

THE MEXICAN WOLF
(*CANIS LUPUS BAILEYI*): A HISTORICAL
REVIEW AND OBSERVATIONS ON
ITS STATUS AND DISTRIBUTION

||||||||||||||||||||||||||||||||||||||||||||||||||||||||||||||||||||||||||||||||||||||||||

ROY T. McBRIDE
from *A Progress Report to the U.S. Fish and Wildlife Service*
edited by Curtis J. Carley and Sharon F. Wehrle
(1980)

INTRODUCTION

*T*he gray wolf (*Canis lupus*) unquestionably holds the title as the most important predator of livestock in the history of North America and Mexico. So unified have been predator control efforts of stockmen that the wolf has been extirpated over most of its former range in both countries. The following excerpt from a 1907 Department of Agriculture bulletin aptly expresses the official views of the U.S. Government regarding the gray wolf during that time (Bailey, 1907).

> The enormous losses suffered by stockmen of the western cattle ranges and the destruction of game on forest reserves, game preserves, and in national parks through the depredations of wolves have led to special investigations by the Biological Survey in cooperation with the Forest Service, to ascertain the best methods for destroying these pests. The results appear in the present report, which includes also field notes on the distribution, abundance, and breeding habits of wolves.
>
> The chief object of the report is to put in the hands of every hunter, trapper, forest ranger, and ranchman directions for trapping, poisoning, and hunting wolves and finding the dens of young. If these directions are followed it is believed that the wolves can be so reduced in number that their depredations will cease to be a serious menace to stock raising. Prime wolf skins

are worth from $4 to $6 each, enough to induce trappers and enterprising ranch boys to make an effort to secure them if a reasonable degree of success is assured. Stock owners need little encouragement to catch or kill wolves on their own ranges, and it is believed that the forest rangers will be able to keep them down on the forest reserves. Their complete extermination on the western range is not, however, to be expected in the near future, and it is only by constant and concerted effort that their numbers can be kept down sufficiently to prevent serious depredations.

Through private financing by livestock raisers of bounties and salaried wolf trappers, and assistance of the Federal government by hiring professional wolf hunters, the wolf has been extirpated from most of the United States. Rare stragglers occasionally drift into southwestern Texas (Scudday 1972) and southern New Mexico and Arizona from Chihuahua and Sonora, Mexico (Gish 1977), but these individuals are soon killed or trapped.

The Sierra Madre of Mexico, principally in the States of Chihuahua and Durango, hold the last remnant population of wolves in that country. It is the purpose of this survey to document the remaining distribution of wolves and estimate population numbers in the Republic of Mexico.

CLASSIFICATION AND HISTORICAL DISTRIBUTION

According to Young and Goldman (1944) the historical distribution of the Mexican Wolf included the Sierra Madre and adjoining tableland region of western Mexico, extending north to southwestern New Mexico (Hatch), and western Texas (Fort Davis). Wolves still live in the northern part of the Sierra Madre with the exact southern and eastern limits undetermined.

Goldman (1944) gives one record of *C. l. baileyi* for Texas, taken 16 miles west of Ft. Davis, Texas. Since 1944, two other wolves identified as *C. l. baileyi* have been killed in Brewster County, Texas (Scudday 1972). One other wolf killed in southwestern Texas in 1935 by Nelson Elliot (U.S. Fish and Wildlife Service) was determined to be *C. l. monstrabilis*. Because of a gap in specimen records, it will remain unclear as to which subspecies of wolf inhabited the Texas-Chihuahua border area. Apparently both subspecies overlapped in this region. Reference is also made of a specimen of *C. l. monstrabilis* taken from Matamoras, Tamaulipas (Goldman 1944).

Having traveled and hunted extensively in the state of Tamaulipas, I have never heard of the presence of wolves there, either in past or recent years, and due to the geography and climate of Tamaulipas, my supposition is that the wolf specimen was killed elsewhere and transported to Matamoras. The state of Tamaulipas is mostly subtropical coastland with dense jungle and ebony forests along the southern river basins and little habitat that resembles gray wolf range in Chihuahua and Durango.

The distribution of wolves in Mexico has a peculiar boundary between Chihuahua and Coahuila. Many parts of Coahuila have excellent wolf habitat, but the wolf apparently never occurred in the northern and eastern parts of the state. Being familiar with the mountainous portions of Coahuila, it is surprising that I have not heard of wolves other than southwest of Muzquiz, Coahuila on the eastern border of Chihuahua.

Until late 1929, wolves were common to the Trans-Pecos area of Texas. However, no record of them is reported in present day Big Bend National Park.

The subspecies of wolf that inhabited southwestern Texas (*C. l. monstrabilis*) was extirpated by the late 1920's. Since a specimen of this subspecies was killed in 1935 in southern Presidio County, not far from the border, it is possible that *C. l. monstrabilis* still occupied part of northern Chihuahua (Scudday, 1972). Wolves occupied the Sierra Ricas of northern Chihuahua until the late 1930's and early 1940's (Raphael Guerro, Ojinaga, Chihuahua, personal communication). Possibly, *C. l. baileyi* did not begin to invade the southwestern United States until the resident subspecies were removed and livestock placed on the range between the Mexican subspecies and those in the southwestern United States.

To determine the current status and distribution, a survey was conducted in the winter and spring of 1977. Due to limited time and budget, it was impossible to examine the entire historical range of the gray wolf in Mexico. However, wolves were still found to be present in certain isolated parts of their former range....

The survey indicated that at least twelve wolves were in the state of Durango and six in the state of Chihuahua by spring of 1977. To confirm this data, a total of seven wolves were taken from these combined areas in the fall of 1977 and early 1978....

From the basis of this information it is safe to say that widely scattered, extremely isolated pockets of wolves still exist in the Sierra Madre and some of its extensions. Due to the reproductive potential of wolves, the existing number of remaining wolves can and does fluctuate greatly, depending on denning success or, conversely, the success of control efforts. It is doubtful, though, that in 1978 more than 50 adult breeding pairs of wolves could be present in the entire Republic of Mexico.

PHYSICAL DESCRIPTION

C. l. baileyi is described by Goldman (1944) as being the smallest of the subspecies of wolves in North America. However, I once saw a small collection of wolf skulls from Minnesota and I had a typical C. l. baileyi with me at the time. With one exception the Mexican Wolf skull was broader, as long or longer in overall length, and much more massive in thickness in jawbone and nasal orbits. From comparisons of skulls it would appear that some Mexican Wolves are as large as or larger than some Eastern Timber wolves, at least as far as skulls are concerned. One notable feature of C. l. baileyi is the broad zygomata, and in the flesh, the Mexican Wolf has an impressive head with short thick muzzle and large nose pad. They have deep chest cavities, thick necks and forequarters. Mexican Wolves show a decided downward slope from the shoulders to the hindquarters....

Pelage is varied in each litter, yet wolves in some geographic areas differ considerably. Most wolves from Chihuahua seem to have a more grizzled color to the back and flank, whereas wolves from southern Durango have tawny or brindle colored fur along the flanks and upper parts....

The Mexican Wolf has longer fur along the ventral portion of the neck and frontal region along the tip of the shoulders. This mane, or "hackles," is raised when the wolf assumes a threat posture.

Trapped Mexican Wolves display a variety of responses when approached. Some lunge wildly at the traps in an effort to escape; others sulk or "cower" and many bark and rear forward in an aggressive manner, baring their teeth and growling deeply. Some wolves lay still in the traps with very little struggling to escape. Those with an aggressive attitude hold their tails stiffly, either straight out behind their backs or in a vertical position and often wag them slowly.

According to Dr. L. David Mech (personal communication) wolves in Minnesota are easy to handle in traps and show little or no aggression. But a high percentage of Mexican Wolves are defiant, and difficult to take from a trap alive. Adult Mexican Wolves are difficult to keep alive in captivity. Many refuse to eat or drink and it is my conclusion that for captive breeding purposes, young wolves or wolf pups have a better chance of survival after capture than do adult wolves.

METHODOLOGY

To survey wolf numbers in Mexico it was necessary to locate areas where wolves are still known to exist. Wolves are so closely tied to the cattle industry in Mexico that I pursued a rather peculiar course in locating some wolf populations. Banks make livestock loans in Mexico just as they do in the United States and cattle are usually supplied as collateral. The bank loan examiners make exhaustive trips to inspect cattle secured by loans. They hear many excuses for cattle shortages, some of which are anthrax, rustlers, and wolves.

Cattle buyers who travel in remote areas buying cattle, often from Indians deep in the Sierras, were an excellent source of information. Some of these cowmen are familiar with back-country areas and often hear of wolf and lion depredations. The Cattlemen's Association of each state is also an excellent place to learn of wolf problems. Every source of information was searched out and reliable leads were checked by personal inspection.

Due to the decline of natural prey, one might make the statement, "no cattle, no wolves." This will be discussed at length in prey and food habits.

Wolf tracks can be distinguished from dog tracks under most circumstances. Wolf tracks are very large, more elongated and narrow in comparison to those of a dog. Their toes point straight ahead, whereas on a dog, the two outside toes generally point slightly outward from the heel pad. Wolves' heel pads are usually larger than dogs' and overall, the toes are not spread as wide apart as they are on dogs. Reading of "sign" is an art to a hunter or trapper and even though at times anyone might be fooled, I feel it is safe to say that wolf tracks were not confused with dog tracks. Tracks of wolves were substantiated by searching for and finding other sign of wolves to verify the track, such as scent posts, scats, and kills.

DISCUSSION

Habitat

While wolves are found in a variety of habitats throughout their historic range, there are certain preferred habitats utilized by wolves. Since their principal prey is ungulates, wolves are generally found in the better browse and grasslands where their prey exists. While it might appear that wolves are attracted to certain vegetative associations, they are actually responding to the availability of prey. Today wolves inhabit elevations above 4,500 ft. above sea level where higher rainfall has created better grazing conditions for wolf prey. These areas contain broken sloping country suitable for hiding dens, plus timber and brush for cover. I once took two wolves in the northern Chihuahuan Desert, an adult pair that had been killing cattle in the arid ranch country northwest of La Ascencion, Chihuahua. I felt they would not have stayed in this type of habitat, but the rancher could not afford a wait-and-see policy. This area was not far south of the celebrated wolf run on the New Mexico and Arizona borders (Young 1944).

With the exception of the above cases, the remainder of my wolf experience was in the high montane, oak, and pine country of the Sierra Madre and its extensions. Altogether this is beautiful mountain country with good grama grass mesas and an abundance of springs and natural water, and the climate is ideally suited to cattle raising.

Breeding and Denning

Wolves pair in January and breed in February. They are very active in these months and particularly susceptible to traps. The gestation period is 63 days and pups generally are born in April and May. There has been some discussion about wolves mating for life, and although I have no information to document this, there have been occasions when I observed individual adult wolves that made no attempt to travel with other wolves during breeding season even though there seemed to be available unpaired wolves. However, the wolf population in Mexico is so decimated that the wolf's natural habits are under a great deal of stress and could account for some unusual behavior.

Wolf dens that I have observed in Mexico were dug out under rock ledges on the slopes of canyon walls or hills. Oak brush and mountain mahogany were dense and dens well hidden. Several holes were usually in close proximity. Both parents tend to the pups. There does not seem to be the same gregariousness displayed by *C. l. baileyi* as with northern wolves, possibly because the native prey was originally deer and did not require a large number of wolves to bring down. As wolves later adapted to cattle, the same was true.

Pups seem to be on their own by October and begin to travel away from their parents by December. The largest group of wolves

I ever tracked was five. Frequently three wolves would be together, often yearlings, probably littermates. Mated pairs remain together much of the time but separate at intervals for lengthy periods, only to pair up again.

During the rainy season in Durango, which usually beings in July, tracking condition become ideal in some terrain. Wolf dens are vulnerable at this time since the parents leave well-marked trails to the den. A careful wolf hunter can usually get a shot at one of the parents at the den since wolves are sometimes defensive, allowing a man to get unusually close. Pups are fairly large by this time; some will run into the den while others run off with the parents. In the event that a dog gets near a wolf den, it is almost sure death for the dog, regardless of size. Wolf parents are extremely aggressive, and when a dog nears the den, they will inevitably attack, often giving the hunter a shot at them....

Hybridization

One noteworthy fact is that the Mexican Wolf has apparently not been subject to hybridization such as have wolves in the north which have been crossbred to produce sled dogs. Also, the behavioral barrier that apparently separates wolves from coyotes is still intact in Mexico. An interesting relationship exists between coyotes and wolves in Mexico: the wolf seems to totally ignore the coyote, while the coyote takes great interest in where the wolf has been. I have frequently seen coyote tracks following wolf tracks in an opposite direction, probably intent on finding a kill. When a wolf is killing steadily in an area there is invariably a swarm of coyotes, ravens, and eagles taking advantage of the remains of kills.

I have seen captive wolves on several ranches in Mexico, and although dogs of all sizes were abundant around the ranch, I have not heard a reliable report of crossbreeding. I have seen fights take place between dogs and chained wolves.

One particular instance occurred on a ranch in northern Chihuahua. A female lobo, captured at the age of perhaps two months, had been chained for the remainder of her life. She was approximately three years old when I saw her and had been fed a sparse diet of leftover tortillas and beans. She had matured into a slender, emaciated condition. Her head and feet were normal size but her body was so underdeveloped that her front legs rubbed together. At best she couldn't have weighed 45 pounds. Her canines had been clipped off and she appeared to be in no condition for a fight.

On this same ranch there was a female German shepherd that gave birth to most of the pups on the ranch. One morning the German shepherd jumped on the chained wolf and forced her to the ground immediately; I thought it would easily kill the wolf. Since it seemed such an unfair fight I tried to intervene, but the cowboys insisted they be left alone. A great deal of blood began to appear on both animals and it soon became apparent that the wolf was disabling the dog by powerful bites with her jaw teeth on the dog's upper forelegs. When the cowboys saw that "Perla" was losing and in fact couldn't get loose, they roped and drew her from the fight.

The wolf leaped up, apparently unhurt, and began to run excitedly to the length of her chain. When I returned in the afternoon, I found the wolf still very excited and the dog severely crippled in both front legs. I worked on this ranch several months, and the dog had not recovered when I left.

Prey and Methods of Killing

As the human population expanded with ranching, logging, and mining, serious inroads were made on the natural prey species available to the wolf. White-tailed deer, antelope, and mule deer were rapidly depleted and the wolf turned to new species introduced by man. Burros, horses, and cattle were easy targets for wolves. Wolves are capable of killing the adults of these species but generally take the young. Burros, adults and young alike, are targets for wolves, but in the case of horses, colts are usually killed. Calves are not readily killed by wolves when they are still paired with their mothers, but when calves are weaned and separated, wolves effect serious hardships on ranches.

Wolves kill by pursuit and attack from the rear. Wolves frequently hunt alone but seem to prefer to travel and hunt together. Yearling calves are generally bitten inside the hind leg and in the rectum, often the tails are sheared off at the body. On two occasions I found large steers killed by biting under the throat, but damage was also done in the rear of the victims, along with deep lacerations in the nose. When weaned cattle are not available, wolves kill calves, but not with the frequency noted in the case of yearlings.

Yearling cattle are easily frightened by wolves and in addition to actual kills, losses can result from cattle stampeding through fences, leaving open wounds on the cattle. In an area with a heavy population of screwworm flies, which lay eggs in open wounds, substantial loss by screwworm infection can result.

Wolves in Mexico do not appear to be scavengers, nor do they appear to feed upon sick, wounded or crippled animals. Contrarily, the wolves feed upon and prefer top-of-the-line animals. When cattle are weaned, a percentage of young calves usually do not adjust easily, responding with much slower growth and generally poorer condition than the other calves. These animals, when being driven to the pen, usually drop to the rear and have to be pushed along, while the healthier calves get far ahead in the drive. The same occurs during attack by wolves. The cattle stampede and during the chase the "sanchos" (poor calves) drop to the rear and present easy targets for the wolves. However, the wolves pass by these cattle and take the better, heavier calves even though it is more of a struggle to kill them. At times large chunks are bitten from the steer's hindquarters or flanks and wolves do feed at times without killing the steer, although these steers invariably die.

Even though some stricken cattle were still alive the second night the wolves did not feed upon them but returned to catch another steer. At times wolves kill three to four animals in the same night but only feed on one. This habit makes them a hated enemy of the cattlemen.

Biting Power

An outstanding physical attribute of wolves is their tremendous biting power. The ability to bite through a steer's hide while on the run and subsequently jerk out large chunks of meat is a considerable accomplishment, made possible only by the wolf's remarkable jaw structure.

Wolves accomplish other incredible feats with their powerful jaws such as biting the trigger and trap pan from large traps such as the number 4½ Newhouse. While holding wolves captive it was difficult to keep a suitable watering pan available. The wolves could completely destroy galvanized buckets as well as enamel pots and pans. It was found that by burying cast iron skillets to ground level, wolves could not puncture these types of vessels. How they can grind and bite on the chains which hold them without breaking their teeth is hard to imagine, but little damage is evident after wolves have been chained a month or more.

Sense of Smell

Wolves have a keen sense of smell and utilize it for defense and hunting. An interesting incident occurred in Chihuahua where two wolves were being held captive on a large ranch southwest of Casas Grandes. These wolves were found as pups and were perhaps two years old. Their diet consisted of corn tortillas and beans, of which they were not given much. I began giving them trapped animals that had been accidentally caught in wolf traps. They enthusiastically ate coyote, coatimundi, bobcat, and javelina. The wolves evidently began to recognize me from the host of cowboys and fence builders that were constantly coming and going from the ranch headquarters. The cowboys told me that long before I would arrive in the afternoon, the wolves would begin to pace excitedly and after perhaps 20 minutes, the ranch dogs would also detect my approach and begin to bark. On every occasion the wolves detected my arrival long before the dogs. Because I occasionally had something for them to eat, the wolves displayed more excitement than the dogs and whether or not I was carrying any food on my saddle, they reacted nonetheless. After my six month absence from this ranch the wolves obviously remembered me quite well and reacted in the same manner upon my arrival. The cowboys were impressed by the wolves' renewal of tail wagging and pacing and knew that I was returning after a long absence. This incident seems to demonstrate that wolves have excellent memories as well as an acute sense of smell.

Voice

The characteristic wolf howl has been described by numerous authors, but it is not the only noise that wolves can make. Trapped wolves have a short, deeply pitched baying bark, and can also growl deeply. However, the most commonly heard noise is the long howl which wolves frequently voice. Wolves seem to be fond of howling in the winter months. Howling serves to reunite separated wolves. When wolves howl close to ranch houses with dogs present, the reaction of the dogs is often comical. Dogs have deep respect for or even fear of wolves, and either bark excitedly when wolves howl or try to get under their owners' houses. My hounds took little interest in captive wolves that were tied in camp but would answer howls of distant wolves with a howl very similar to that of the wolves, a noise I never heard them make under any other circumstances.

I have timed one continuous howl for a length of 13 seconds. The howl varies little in pitch from beginning to end. The tone remains constant and when howling in a deep rocky canyon the volume seems extremely strong. Coyotes generally respond to howling wolves by barking and howling themselves, but the opposite is not true when coyotes howl first. The howling of wild wolves is probably the most exciting wilderness sound a human could ever experience, but one that is of rare occurrence in Mexico today.

Signposts

Wolves make long scratches in the dirt where they urinate. These scratches are often placed along the wolf's more frequented runways such as canyon bottoms, low gaps in mountains, and on the edges of forested mountain valleys.

Scratches are made by kicking the hind legs and pulling backwards with the forelegs. This leaves a mark about three feet in total length with deep toenail marks evident in some types of soil. Scratches are easy to identify and are excellent places for setting traps. Both sexes make these marks but they are definitely made more often by males, particularly in January and February during the breeding season. Sometimes urine is placed on a vertical object such as a prominent clump of grass, a low bush, or occasionally, large tree trunks. Wolves at times defecate on the sides of rocks near their trails and also in bushes that are only slightly lower than the wolves' hindquarters. They also respond to old wolf droppings along the runways by urinating on or near them and making the characteristic scratches nearby. It is not uncommon to find two or more scratches in one place, perhaps a half-dozen or more scratches of various ages. Wolf scratches are often found in the vicinity of their kills or near an old carcass that has already dried. At times, wolves wallow on dead objects such as old skunk hides or dry cowhide, making these hides excellent places to set traps.

Territoriality

Due to the scattered remnant of wolves, it is impossible to determine if territories that constitute segregated wolf home ranges still exist. Wolves can and do wander at will over enormous areas. Their favorite prey (cattle) exists in abundance wherever they roam, and at times wolves are driven long distances by human activities in their mountain habitat. A favorite wolf runway today may be the site of a sawmill tomorrow. Mines, logging, firewood cutting, goat herding, and constant deer hunting all contribute to disruption within the wolf's range. Consequently, wolves wander over large areas, constantly change routes, and sometimes never return to areas they once frequently used.

MANAGEMENT AND PRESERVATION
Control

Mexican Wolves first encountered extensive control measures in the states of Sonora and Chihuahua, where ideal grazing country for cattle was ideal wolf habitat as well. The early ranchers accepted wolf predation along with drought, rustlers, and anthrax. No cowman ever passed a chance to shoot a wolf, but traps and poison were virtually unheard of. Some bizarre methods were employed to control wolves but none were effective. In the 1930's and 1940's, Mexican cowmen ventured to the United States to buy bulls and American ranchers, attracted by low land prices, migrated into Mexico. These actions resulted in an exchange of information on control of wolves and the war began in earnest.

Originally wolves had the habit of returning to a kill to feed. Ranchers learned to lace these kills with strychnine, and although strychnine is an inferior control tool, it had great effect at first. Traps were set in canyons that served as travel ways for wolves and again, even though methods were crude, wolves were not trap-shy and many were taken. Dens, when found, were dug out and the pups destroyed. Some wolves, escaping from traps or a sub-lethal dose of strychnine, learned to avoid man and his devices. By the late 1950's, most of the wolf control program in Chihuahua and Sonora was in the "clean-up" stages. Individual wolves who escaped traps learned from their experiences, and gained local recognition for their ability to avoid traps.

In the 1950's, the U.S. Fish and Wildlife Service, in cooperation with the Pan American Sanitary Bureau, began a program to train ranchers and veterinarians in the use of Compound 1080 (sodium monofluoroacetate), an odorless, tasteless poison with an established reputation in the United States as an excellent control tool for coyotes. The introduction of Compound 1080 dealt the most severe blow to remaining wolf populations. Even adult wolves that avoided bait stations were not able to keep their young from feeding on them. Compound 1080 had a great part to play in the demise of the grizzly bear in Mexico as well.

In Durango and Zacatecas, wolf control commenced later than in Chihuahua and Sonora. Most of the high mountains of Durango were first logged for pine and ranching came later. With the arrival of cattle came the inevitable conflict with wolves. Ranchers purchased traps in the United States, and offered bounties for wolves. The most effective wolf trapping method was the blind trap set in known wolf runways. What the cowboy didn't know about the fine art of wolf trapping, he made up for with an excellent knowledge of wolf habits. A crudely set trap, poorly concealed and dirty with rust and blood would often set for months in a narrow mountain trail. Wind would cover the traps with leaves, rains would wash away the foreign odors, and eventually a wolf would step over a log or rock in the trail, and be caught fast in a trap. The few wolves that survived these early efforts displayed remarkable intelligence and some even won the respect, if not the admiration, of their adversaries. Following is an account of one such wolf that defied concentrated efforts to capture it. He certainly ranks with any of the notorious wolves of the United States.

"Las Margaritas" was the name given this particular wolf. He operated over a large territory along the Zacatecas-Durango border, and during the late 1960's began killing yearling steers and heifers at a ranch named Las Margaritas. The wolf had two toes missing from its left front foot and his experience with traps left a memory that served him well. All efforts to poison or trap this wolf were futile and in the spring of 1970 he moved northward to the Mazatlan-Durango Highway area where he began killing steers.

I was trapping in Durango and had heard about this wolf, but instead of having to go to Las Margaritas, he came to me. I was trying to catch a pair of wolves that were killing at El Carmen and an adjoining ejido, Augustine Melgar. I caught the female and the male left. Depredation started a few weeks later, and I was sure the male had returned, but I saw tracks in a trail and noticed the missing toes of Las Margaritas. During May, the wolf left, killed some cattle westward towards Llano Grande, and then disappeared. In June he returned to Santa Barbara and killed 18 more steers. The wolf seldom used the same trail twice and if he came into a pasture by a log road, he left by a cow trail.

I was sure I could catch Las Margaritas, but I couldn't get him near a trap. In July, he came down a log road and passed by a trap, winded it, turned back, and trotted up to the trap, scarcely missing the trigger with the gap caused by the missing toes. The wolf then left the road. This narrow escape seemed to have frightened him because he did not return until September, whereupon he killed 96 steers and yearling heifers in eight months on one ranch alone.

In October, I found sign of the wolf beside a logging road. I placed a trap at this spot. Two weeks later the wolf passed by the trap, advanced a few steps towards it, and then bolted out of the road.

He moved to a new area and resumed killing. In November, a pair of wolves showed up in the area and began killing in the same pasture that Las Margaritas was operating in. Several days after their arrival, I picked up tracks that the two wolves made before the dew. Margaritas' tracks were made after the pair. Finally the pair of wolves came to a trap and I caught the female. When Margaritas came to where the trap was pulled out of the ground he left the road and disappeared until December.

In late December, Margaritas began killing in a new pasture. Traps were set daily on travel routes of the wolf but the wolf seldom returned to a trail he had once used. Now convinced the wolf would not go to a baited site of any kind, I set three blind traps in a narrow cowtrail in the gap of a mountain. Two weeks passed and Margaritas came down a mountain divide and hit the cowtrail about 100 yards above the traps. Again, I felt confident I would have him caught. When he got about 15 feet from the first trap, he left the trail and went around the trap. Large live oaks were on either side of the trail and wind-blown leaves had hidden the traps beyond recognition. I had stepped from my horse to a steer hide while setting the traps and the dirt was removed by a sifter. The traps had even been boiled in oak leaves. Much care was taken to avoid disturbance of any sundry objects; the trap could have been born there and not been any better concealed. The wolf then returned to the trail and approached the second trap set on the other side of a pine tree that lay across the trail. Again he left the trail and went around the trap. As I neared the third trap I saw that the trap was gone but again the wolf had left the trail before getting to the trap site. I located the trap with a coyote in it.

The wolf left and began killing about 15 miles to the west. Almost a year had passed and I was now convinced that I would never catch this wolf. At times however, I had noticed where Margaritas had investigated a campfire along the road where log-truck drivers had stopped along the way to cook. I set a trap near a road that the wolf was sure to come down if it continued to kill in the area, built a fire over the trap and let it burn itself out. I placed a piece of dried skunk hide from an animal that had been run over months before in the logging road in the ashes.

On March 15 the wolf came down the road, winded the ashes and skunk hide and walked over to investigate. Margaritas was caught by the same crippled foot and the trap held. There was much celebration among the ranchers the following day. In eleven months of intensive effort and several thousand miles on horseback, I had managed to get the wolf near a trap only four times. Just how the wolf could tell the traps were there is something I cannot comprehend to this date.

Mexican Land Reform

Prior to the revolution of 1910, Mexico consisted mainly of large tracts of privately owned land. After the revolution, the constitution guaranteed the division of the land among the peasants. The result has been the conversion of large, thinly settled ranches into rural areas (called ejidos) with tremendous human population. The impact of the ejido on the wildlife and environment has been devastating. Trees are used for firewood, grass is consumed by herds of burros and horses, and wildlife is used as a food source whenever possible. Large families are the rule rather than the exception—birth control is practically nonexistent—and conservation is a luxury unheard of in most areas. The overall result on the environment and wildlife is unimaginable in an industrialized country like the United States.

Relatively few areas remain that are not altered by human encroachment. Even the luxury of setting aside areas such as national parks which would preserve large mammals, i.e. wolves, lions, jaguars, etc., cannot be afforded under the demands of the agrarian system that now exists.

Even though laws protecting wolves are in effect, they are seldom enforced. Therefore, unless some drastic type of reversal is seen in land reform and human population trends, the future of large mammals in Mexico is bleak.

Future

The subspecies *C. l. baileyi* faces imminent extinction under present conditions in Mexico. The reason for this extermination is clear; the only ingredients lacking are expertise and control equipment. In areas where poison is not available, resident farmers and ranchers use bizarre and cruel methods to kill wolves. There is no organized wolf control program in Mexico. Poison and trapping are done by individuals affected by wolf depredations. The source of Compound 1080 is unknown to me but it is made in Japan.

Since wolves conflict directly with the rural Mexican livestock industry, education, legislation, and/or law enforcement would have no effect in Mexico for the protection of wolves. It is also evident that Mexico's economy could not afford to set aside large sanctuaries that would preserve viable wolf populations. The conclusion that the gray wolf in Mexico will surely become extinct in a few years is based on the fact that 20 years ago wolves were abundant over widely scattered areas while today, in 90 percent of this area, the wolf no longer exists.

In 1977 Mexico and the United States agreed to live capture and hold for captive breeding wolves that are threatened by control methods. This program moved very slowly. Frequently, by the time wolf depredations were reported, the few wolves involved had already been poisoned or had left the area. Also as previously mentioned, not all wolves captured will live. Because wolves travel over such extensive areas it means that to capture them, the trapper must wait a month or more for wolves to return down their runways. It requires a great deal of time and expense to capture a small number of animals, yet no other option is available.

The Arizona-Sonora Desert Museum in Tucson, Arizona, and the Wild Canid Survival and Research Center in St. Louis, Missouri, are working cooperatively with the U.S. Fish and Wildlife Service to breed Mexican wolves in captivity. It has further been suggested that some facilities in California, New Mexico, Texas, and the Republic of Mexico may also be able to maintain captive wolves....

Reintroduction of wolves into the wild is the long-term objective of the captive breeding program. However, it is difficult to locate suitable areas without the inevitable conflict between wolves and people.

SUMMARY AND CONCLUSIONS

A review on the status of the Mexican Wolf in Mexico has determined that the *baileyi* subspecies is truly an endangered form of *Canis lupus*. While tremendous areas of suitable habitat still exist in Mexico and the United States, the wolf has been nearly eliminated by predator control efforts in both countries.

It has been determined that wolves prey primarily on domestic livestock, principally cattle, and so serious are these depredations that control is exercised in every area occupied by this species. Den hunting, traps, rifles, and poison are continually used in an effort to eliminate the wolf. Only widely scattered, small populations of wolves still exist with occasional stragglers occurring in former parts of the wolf's range.

The main pockets of wolves that are presently known occur in the states of Chihuahua and Durango, Mexico. I estimate a widely scattered population numbering approximately 15 wolves to be in a large area south-southwest of Durango, Durango. Much of this country is inaccessible by vehicle and some is Indian territory. Logging activity in the accessible areas moves the wolves constantly about in this rugged mountain area. Trapping is slow and difficult and at times little or no wolf sign is to be found, only to reappear months later. This is a breeding population of animals.

A second area harboring a small breeding population of wolves is north and west of Durango, Durango, and east of Tepehuanes. This area is also only partially accessible and the population consists of approximately six wolves. These animals are difficult to get to although a large rural population inhabits the area. Mining and logging are active industries.

A third area containing wolves is north of Chihuahua, Chihuahua, and east of Casas Grandes, Chihuahua. This was a breeding population but I currently know of only two adult wolves. The range of these animals is accessible by vehicle and horseback and they are currently depredating on cattle. They have been exposed to traps and poison.

A fourth area, which at times harbors wolves and still had wolves until 1977, is the Sierra del Nido of Chihuahua southward through the mountains surrounding the Santa Clara Valley of Chihuahua. I do not have an estimate of this population but it is probably less than six animals. Other areas producing reliable reports were not physically checked due to lack of time and funds, but assuming that these areas are similar to the above-mentioned localities, there is a high probability that some 50 wolves may still inhabit Mexico. None of these animals are immune to persecution and I have no practical suggestions that would insure their preservation in Mexico.

Aside from the capture and captive breeding, or the reintroduction of wolves into a protected area with suitable assurances to adjacent landowners, the Mexican Wolf has no chance for survival. This unique animal that once existed on natural prey in a vast wilderness ecosystem is now in direct conflict with the agricultural interests of a growing nation. The Mexican rancher can hardly be criticized for his attitude regarding the wolf as his viewpoint was shared by the American rancher as well. Only with a great deal of public interest and adequate funding can the wolf be preserved in any part of its historic range.

Bibliography

Bailey, Vernon. 1907. Wolves in relation to stock, game, and the national forest reserves. U.S. Dept. of Agriculture, Forest Service Bulletin 72, p. 5.

Gish, Dan. 1977. A historical review of the wolf in Arizona. U.S. Fish and Wildlife Service report. Typescript.

Goldman, E. A. 1944. Classification of wolves. Part II in S. P. Young and E. A. Goldman, *The Wolves of North America*. Amer. Wildl. Inst., Washington, D.C., pp. 389–636.

Guerro, Raphael. Personal communication to author.

Mech, Dave. Personal communication to author.

Scudday, J. F. 1972. Two recent records of gray wolves in west Texas. *J. of Mamm.* 53/3:598.

Young, S. P. 1944. History, life habits, economic status, and control. Part I in S. P. Young and E. A. Goldman, *The Wolves of North America*. Amer. Wildl. Inst., Washington, D.C., pp. 1–385.

MEXICAN WOLF RECOVERY PLAN (EXCERPTS)

llllllllllllllllllllllllllllllllllllllllll

NORMA AMES
Mexican Wolf Recovery Team
New Mexico Department of Game and Fish for United States
Department of the Interior, Fish and Wildlife Service
(1982)

INTRODUCTION

*T*he Mexican gray wolf (*Canis lupus baileyi*) has been described as smallest in size of the American subspecies of *Canis lupus* (Goldman 1944). McBride (1980) notes, however, that *baileyi* skulls are frequently as large as, or larger than, those of some specimens of *C. l. lycaon*, and the average of weights he records for *baileyi* exceeds the averages recorded by Pimlot *et al.* (1969) for *lycaon*. Such size overlap might be predicted from the demonstrated clines (Nowak 1973) in which size increases from south to north and from east to west of the range of *C. lupus*. Size is one aspect—an important aspect—of the known variability and adaptability of *C. lupus*, which once ranged over much of the Northern Hemisphere. In North America, it occurred throughout most of what is now the United States and Canada, north to the Arctic Ocean, and southward through northern Mexico and the highlands and plateau of central Mexico.

For *C. lupus*, 32 subspecies or geographic races have been recognized for the world (Mech 1970), 24 of these for North America (Hall and Kelson 1959). Two of these, *C. l. baileyi* and *C. l. monstrabilis*, were recognized for Mexico.

Monstrabilis is now considered extinct (Mech 1970). In 1960, Baker and Villa stated that *monstrabilis* was probably extinct in Mexico except in western San Luis Potosí, basing their opinion on Dalquest's 1953 report of wolves in that area. No further reports of wolves have come from that region (Nowak 1974), and McBride, in his surveys starting in 1974, detected no wolves in the historic range of *monstrabilis* in Mexico. The historic range of *monstrabilis* also included western Texas and southeastern New Mexico, but the last record of *monstrabilis* from this area is that of a wolf taken in 1942 south of Marfa in Presidio County, Texas (Scudday 1972).

Of *baileyi*, fewer than 50 specimens may remain in the wild (McBride 1980) plus a handful in captivity. These southern subspecies are of special scientific interest because of possible adaptations, however subtle, to the environmental and ecological conditions at the extreme southern limits of the species' range. Now, only *baileyi* remains as a living specimen. Many persons today feel that there are many other reasons, besides scientific knowledge, to prevent extinction of life forms, even large predators, including continuation of maximum genetic diversity and the intrinsic right of all forms to exist.

TAXONOMIC AND GEOGRAPHIC PURVIEW OF THE PLAN

Bogan and Mehlop (1980) found "no convincing evidence to support the recognition of *monstrabilis* as a subspecies separate from *baileyi*." In addition, they state: "Wolves formerly assigned to C. l. *mogollonensis* and C. l. *monstrabilis* seem best referred to C. l. *baileyi*." *Mogollonensis*, like *monstrabilis*, is considered to be extinct (Mech 1970).

Historical reviewers who wrote of *baileyi*, *monstrabilis*, and *mogollonensis* as separate subspecies recognized the adaptability and range expansions of *baileyi*. Scudday (1977) suggested that *baileyi* "was a late-comer to Texas, probably moving in as C. l. *monstrabilis* was eliminated in the Trans-Pecos region." Gish (1977) thought that *baileyi* increasingly moved into Arizona from Mexico and southwestern New Mexico as other subspecies were eliminated in Arizona. These indications of *baileyi*'s adaptability and range expansions within southwestern United States supports the biological possibility of reintroducing *baileyi* into those portions of the historic ranges of *monstrabilis* and *mogollonensis*, as well as *baileyi*...where suitable habitat may still remain. The Bogan and Mehlhop study would provide taxonomic justification for such reintroductions. Because suitable wolf release areas will be difficult to come by in southwestern North America, the team endorses adoption of the additional room provided by the Bogan and Mehlhop assessment. For that reason, information is provided below on the historic ranges of *monstrabilis* and *mogollonensis*, in addition to that of *baileyi*.

MAXIMUM HISTORIC RANGE AND POPULATION SIZE

Goldman (1944) records the former range of *baileyi* as: "Sierra Madre and adjoining tableland region of western Mexico, formerly extending north to southeastern Arizona (Fort Bowie), southwestern New Mexico (Hatch), and western Texas (Fort Davis), south to the Valley of Mexico."

Goldman (1944) gives the following for the former range of *monstrabilis*: "formerly southern and most of western Texas (apparently replaced by *baileyi* in extreme western part), southeastern New Mexico, and south into northeastern Mexico (Matamoros)." For *mogollonensis*, Goldman (1944) states: "Formerly the Mogollon Plateau region, extending nearly across central Arizona, and east through the Mogollon Mountains of central western New Mexico."

For recovery efforts, estimates of maximum historic populations of the endangered species are of use in indicating densities that might be ecologically possible for a re-established population if habitat were still available. Reliable figures of this type are unavailable for southwestern and Mexican wolves, and habitat and prey-base needs of any reintroduced groups of wolves must be based on recent studies of such factors. Mech (1970) notes that wolf densities in North America range from one per 12 to one per 250 square kilometers, the density being broadly related to ungulate abundance. Mech (in Jorgensen et al. 1970) also stated that "average densities of one wolf for 50 to 100 square miles are not uncommon throughout most of the species' range," the highest average density, one wolf per ten square miles, having been reported for Isle Royale and Algonquin Provincial Park, Ontario.

The matter of historic population size is raised here, however, to point out the following considerations. Subsisting on native prey species, wolf populations were always limited by the position of the wolf at the narrow top of the food pyramid. Conceivably, wolf numbers could increase locally and regionally as wolves preyed less on scattered, wolf-wise wild prey species and more on the more easily available herds of vulnerable livestock. It is important, however, not to accept unquestioningly the accounts of the 1800s and early 1900s that speak of huge numbers of wolves ravaging herds of livestock and game. Recent historical researchers (Gish 1977, Nunley 1977) have compiled totals of wolves taken during periods of intensive governmental wolf-control programs. The total recorded take indicates a much sparser number of wolves in the treated areas than the complaints of damage state or signify, even when one remembers that these figures do not reflect the additional numbers of wolves taken by ranchers, bounty-seekers and other private individuals.

In reviewing old accounts of southwestern wolf numbers, it is also important to keep in mind that the wolf is a wanderer and far-forager. A pack or an individual may travel through many square miles. The statement that "wolves were everywhere" could arise from the fact that one wolf or a few wolves were repeatedly seen at widely separated localities.

Even stockmen who complained of livestock losses to wolves sometimes recognized that their troubles were not caused by hordes of these predators. Scudday (1977) quotes from the observations of Judge O. W. Williams of life in western Texas in the late 1800s: "It is not that it [the wolf] causes any sudden, large loss [of livestock], but it is a constant, steady source of loss.... Yet these animals are not now and never have been numerous in our country.... Apparently in early times, nature did not allow for the wolf in the economy of this country [Pecos]. But when cattle were moved in...this condition was favorable to the appearance and increase of the lobo population." The realism of this relatively early assessment has important implications for the recovery effort.

POPULATION DECLINES AND RANGE REDUCTIONS— UNITED STATES

Both popular and technical books about wolves contain millions of words about the history of human efforts to reduce wolf numbers or to eliminate wolves entirely for the purpose of decreasing loss of livestock to wolf predation. There seems no need to burden these pages with a lengthy account, and one is inclined merely to insert: "List of books available free on request; send self-addressed, stamped envelope."

It might, however, be informative to add that campaigns against wolves have a dimension beyond mere control to prevent livestock loss, the dimension of "fear and loathing," to use the words of Mitchell's (1976) title, "Fear and Loathing in Wolf Country." Actions taken against a predator that causes loss of dollars and food and that competes with man for wild prey inevitably take on the emotional overtones of a crusade. People far removed from the scene of action, who will never own a cow or meet a wolf, are taught to abhor and fear the malefactor, and to applaud its death and even its suffering. Thus, when the federal government in 1915 entered the anti-wolf campaign in the United States and added men and equipment to those already deployed by ranchers, the move had the general support of taxpayers for both practical and emotional reasons. By the time wolf numbers were so drastically reduced that the survivors often bore individual names, the need to blot out those few survivors certainly stemmed as much from emotional, as from economic, reasons. Any recovery effort must still deal with the residues of that emotion.

In the United States, the wolf control efforts of the Bureau of Biological Survey of the Department of Agriculture were, under governmental reorganization, later transferred to the U.S. Fish and Wildlife Service of the Department of the Interior (Young 1946). Government agents brought effective technology to bear against wolves: steel leg-hold traps, poisons placed in baits, and the poison cyanide administered via "coyote-getters." Other time-honored techniques also continued to be used: denning, arsenic baits, and of course shooting, even roping and killing, when an adroit and appropriately equipped wolfer happened to meet a free wolf at close quarters. Removal of wolves was long stimulated by the offering of bounties by livestock associations, federal, state and local governments, as well as individual ranchers.

Factors other than antipredator programs also contributed to declines in wolf numbers at times. Gish (1977) records the effects of outbreaks of rabies and mange. Encroachment of human activities also caused loss of habitat, both to wolves and to their wild prey.

The records of wolves removed in antipredator efforts seldom identified kinds or subspecies of wolves. Wolves, in fact, were often lumped with coyotes in the records. Historical researchers, however, have been able to chronicle in more general terms the wolf reductions within the ranges of *baileyi, monstrabilis,* and *mogollonensis.* For the ranges within the United States, Gish (1977) has done this for Arizona, Nunley (1977) for New Mexico, and Scudday (1977) for Texas. For all three states, they record a rapid reduction in wolf numbers from 1915 through the early 1920s. The situation for southwestern United States is summed up in Gish's (1977) statement about operations in Arizona: "By the mid-1920s, the once million-dollar losses of livestock to resident wolves had been shrunken to a hit-and-run tactic of a very few scattered individual predators."

The key word in the statement is now "resident." The annual predatory animal control reports of the various district agents then begin to follow a pattern. For several years they record no wolves taken and declare that there are no wolves left in the state involved. Then, the series is broken with a report of yet another wolf or two taken in the state. This pattern is repeated through the 1930s and 1940s and, for some areas, the 1950s, with reports of wolves becoming increasingly rare.

The reservoir from which the "new" wolves came was in Mexico. Following the same routes across the international border that wolves had used for as long as man had noted and recorded the movements, single wolves or small packs ranged north into the United States, eating available livestock and game en route and, usually, returned to their home ranges in Mexico. Some sought and found new home ranges within the United States, at least until traps, poison or guns eliminated them or drove them elsewhere. It could be that these were usually young, often male, wolves seeking unoccupied ranges after annual reproduction increased pack sizes, if only temporarily, within their original ranges in Mexico. Because wolves remained in larger numbers in Mexico, at least until quite recently, and because some traveled the old traditional runways into the United States, occasional wolves continued to be reported and sometimes taken in Texas, New Mexico and Arizona until almost the present date.

The last record for western Texas (Scudday 1972) is that of two *baileyi* taken in 1970: a male shot December 5 on Cathedral Mountain Ranch, 17 miles south of Alpine in Brewster County, and another male found dead December 28 in a trap on the Joe Neal Brown Ranch where Brewster, Pecos and Terrell counties meet.

For Arizona, too, the reports continue until almost the present date. Nowak (1974) states that the Defenders of Wildlife organization knew of the presence of two wolves in the early 1970s in the vicinity of its holdings in Aravaipa Canyon, Graham County. He also mentions recent reports of wolves in an area northeast of Tucson. Frank Appleton of the Research Ranch at Elgin told team leader Ames in March 1973 that there was an active wolf den north of the Research Ranch in the Empire Hills at that time. In fall of 1972, Ross Carpenter of the U.S. Fish and Wildlife Service identified as wolf-caused a calf-kill and canid tracks found on the Alvin Browning Ranch in the Galiuro Mountains near the Pinal-Graham county line (Nowak, pers. comm.). Chuck Ames of the Coronado National Forest reported seeing a wolf in December 1973 on the Santa Rita Experimental Range, Pinal County (Nowak, pers. comm.).

In New Mexico also, the Last Wolf on Record merges confusedly with the reports of "wolf" sightings that continue to the present day. Many of these reports come from persons whose experience in such matters lends credence to their reports but, without a specimen in hand, it is difficult to certify the sightings as one of *Canis lupus*, much less of *C. l. baileyi.* A "wolf" was sighted south of Cloverdale, Hidalgo County, June 16, 1976 (pers. comm. to N. Ames, as are all otherwise-uncited reports in this paragraph). This is along one of the old wolf runways. In 1971, George Pendleton shot a "wolf" on the Cloverdale Ranch (Nowak, pers. comm.); specimen unavailable. A wolf skeleton was found on the Diamond A Ranch, Hidalgo County, in 1970 (Nowak, pers. comm.); specimen unavailable. Arnold Bayne did trap a wolf on this ranch in 1965 (Nowak, pers. comm.); specimen confirmed. In 1973, a canid was shot on the L-7 Ranch east of the Caballo Mountains and south of Highway 52, Sierra County. In 1975, W. K. Barker of the Bureau of Land Management sent a photograph of the animal to N. Ames. The animal could be a wolf, but the specimen is no longer available. Through the 1970s, sightings of large, wolflike canids in the Gila National Forest continued to be reported to the U.S. Forest Service; again, no specimens. "Wolves" were sighted near La Ventana, Sandoval County, in October 1973; this would be easy to ignore if it were not for the relative frequency with which Ames receives reports of "wolf" sightings from the Jemez Mountains and areas just to the north of them, often from apparently knowledgeable persons. A wolf was reported traveling through the Manzano Mountains near Torreon, Sandoval County, on December 17, 1973. When combined with the report of the escape of a captive wolf in the Manzanos about the same time, this record sheds light on a possible source of the "wolf" reports: escaped captive wolves, plus wolf-dog hybrids, many of which have been raised in New Mexico, and quite likely in Texas, Arizona, and Mexico.

The above reports have been included here to indicate that recovery efforts for the Mexican wolf should not dismiss out of hand the possibility that wolves may still occur within the southwestern United States. Even if surveys should not be deemed warranted to locate and protect any wolves surviving in these areas, surveys seem indicated for any areas into which wolves are to be released or would migrate to, if only to know possible sources of competition and hybridization.

POPULATION DECLINES AND RANGE REDUCTIONS— MEXICO

Mexican wolves have survived longer in Mexico than in the United States simply because human settlement, livestock, and predator removal came later to north-central Mexico than they did to wolf ranges in southwestern United States. Within Mexico, even in pre-

Columbian times, civilization claimed first the warmer, more easily cultivated lands that generally lie lower in latitude and altitude than the ranges of wolves in Mexico. In more recent times, however, cattle and other domestic livestock have been placed on the plateaus and highlands of north-central Mexico, and measures to control wolf numbers inevitably followed.

It was not until the 1930s and 1940s, however, that Mexican ranchers began to adopt the more effective wolf-control measures that were being used in the United States. When they did begin to use these traps and poisons, wolf numbers began to decline rapidly. In the 1950s, a program was initiated between the U.S. Fish and Wildlife Service and the Pan American Sanitary Bureau to train ranchers and veterinarians in the use of 1080 (McBride 1980; Leopold 1972). The program's avowed purpose was to control the spread of rabies (Nowak 1974). This disease had flared up in both cattle and wildlife north and south of the international border in 1945, spreading farther in 1946 and remaining widespread in subsequent years (Gish 1977). Baker and Villa (1960), however, point out that the cooperative program was initiated "at the repeated request of the livestock associations." McBride (1980) states that wolf control was applied in Durango and Zacatecas later than in Chihuahua and Sonora. Poison, traps, and other antipredator techniques severely decimated wolf populations wherever wolves remained. The process was often hastened by disorderly and excessive applications of 1080 that affected populations of predators and other wildlife in many areas. Morales (1970) tells of one area where "*se han cubierto extensiones de más de 170,000 hectáreas con 8.5 toneladas de carne, inyectada con 300 gramos de 1080, siendo que para esa superficie únicamente se require de 21 estaciones formadas con 945 kilogramos de carne inyectados con 168 gramos de 1080*"—in short, 8.5 tons of poisoned meat where even one ton would have achieved the same kill. This particular case occurred in Tamaulipas, but Morales indicates that uncontrolled application of 1080 was general in Mexico.

PRESENT STATUS OF WOLVES IN MEXICO

Today, individual ranchers continue to use poison, including 1080, and also traps and denning to remove wolves, even though the wolf is protected by law in Mexico (McBride 1980). In addition, large, thinly settled landholdings continue to be broken up and redistributed to peasants. The tremendous, and growing, human population of these rural areas cuts trees for firewood, overgrazes the land with burros and horses, and uses wildlife for food, and the present agrarian system makes preserves for large mammals an unaffordable luxury (McBride 1980; Leopold 1972). McBride feels that "education, legislation, and/or law enforcement would have no effect in Mexico for the protection of wolves." Recovery team member José Treviño senses the start of a favorable change in attitudes toward wildlife, especially at higher political levels, but only the future will tell the strength of the trend and the fruits it may bear.

...At the September 1980 meeting of the U.S.A.-Mexico Joint Committee on Wildlife Conservation, recovery team member José Treviño said he knew of perhaps as many as ten wolves in the wild in Mexico. In early 1981 Roy McBride investigated certain areas in northern Mexico that he thought offered the best chances for locating wolves for capture. He found none and came back to the United States discouraged about the prospects of finding more wolves (R. T. McBride, pers. comm.), although he planned to return to investigate other leads.

At the May 1981 meeting of the Mexican Wolf Recovery Team, José Treviño estimated that perhaps 30 wolves remained in the wild in Mexico and reviewed the most recent information he has gathered on the probable locations and sizes of the remaining groups. Treviño's summary indicates possible disappearance from some areas where McBride (1980) found indications of wolves' presence. It also indicates possible presence of wolves in some areas where wolves were not recorded by McBride. In the surveys, reports from ranchers are often the first clues to possible presence of wolves. Thus, few or no reports may come from an area characterized by lack of concern about or interest in wolves. This could account for the earlier lack of records....

LEGAL PROTECTION

Wolves are protected by law in all the areas within the historic ranges of the Mexican and southwestern subspecies. Dates of the protective legislation in the United States are: federal, May 1976; state, Arizona 1973, New Mexico, May 1976, Texas 1977. In Mexico in the past, seasons have sometimes been closed on wolves year-round throughout the Republic (e.g., 1967–68). In other years, seasons were open in individual states, with no restrictions on the number of wolves taken, according to the perceived need for wolf control. For example, in recent years, seasons have been open as follows: in Chihuahua and Sonora year-round in 1961–62; in Chihuahua, Sonora, Jalisco and

San Luis Potosí year-round in 1962–63; in Chihuahua and Zacatecas year-round in 1968–69, and the season was open May and June of 1971 in the entire Republic and in October and December of 1970 and January and March of 1971 in Chihuahua and Zacatecas. For 1971–72 and subsequent years, the U.S. Fish and Wildlife Service's listing of seasons in Mexico does not list the wolf and states that species not listed may be taken only under special permit from the Dirección General.

As the account in the preceding section indicates, law enforcement is least effective where the wolves remain in the wild today. Even within the United States, however, predator control directed against coyotes may endanger a wolf that may remain within or re-enter the United States. Governmental agencies responsible for predator control have restricted certain or all control measures in areas of the traditional wolf runways. The activities of private predator-takers, however, are not restricted in these areas.

REPRODUCTION AND PACK STRUCTURE

Although much has been published on the life history of *Canis lupus*, relatively little of the literature deals specifically with the Mexican subspecies, and some of that may have actually been derived by inference from what is known of northern subspecies. The available literature (e.g., Leopold 1972, McBride 1980) and records on captive animals (some of them summarized in Ames 1980) indicate reproduction of *baileyi* differs little, if at all, from that of other subspecies of *C. lupus*. They breed only once a year, and the normal gestation period is 63 days. Leopold says the Mexican wolf mates in late winter and whelps in March; McBride and Ames record mating in February and whelping in late April and May. Dens are usually ground burrows excavated in slopes where rocks will function to support the roof of the tunnel and burrow. The largest unborn litter recorded by McBride contained nine pups. Records of neonatal litters (e.g. McBride 1980, Ames 1980) show an average of 4 to 6 pups. Leopold's figure of litters of up to 14 is questionable. Various factors affect survival of neonatal pups, and the average one- to three-month litter is likely to contain four or five pups.

Both parents and other pack members, if present, will bring food to the young. McBride reports pups being on their own by October and traveling away from their parents by December. As indicated by McBride and elsewhere in this narrative, Mexican wolf packs may contain fewer individuals and be less cohesive in nature than is the case reported for northern subspecies of wolves.

Most authorities hold that wolves do not breed until their second year. Female Mexican wolves of the old ASDM-GR lineage for which good records are readily available (Ames 1980) bred for the first time, on the average, in their third year (second year—1, third year—3, fourth year—1). Age of sexual maturity of sires of this lineage is obscured by the fact that these sires were either unpaired until over three years of age or paired only with same age sisters. The one exception is a two-year-old male that sired a litter with his four-year-old dam. The availability of good nutrition under captive conditions has enabled female red wolves to breed successfully even as yearlings (C.J. Carley, pers. comm.), but it may be that most female Mexican wolves in the wild may not produce young until their third year. The red wolf captive breeding record augers well for proliferation in a captive propagation effort for Mexican wolves, but progeny of wolves released to the wild likely should not be counted on to reproduce until their second or third year.

PREY SPECIES

No recent field studies are available on the normal prey of Mexican wolves in the wild. McBride (1980) tells of wolves taking cattle, burros and horses, and refers to white-tailed and mule deer and antelope as natural prey. Bailey (1931) mentions only deer and cattle and says wolves prefer cattle. Leopold (1972) lists the following as natural prey of the Mexican wolf: deer, peccary, antelope, bighorn sheep, rabbits, many of the rodents, and occasionally some plant food such as berries and fruits.

WOLF RECOVERY PROGRAM BASED ON CAPTIVE BREEDING

Among researchers and managers of wolves, there is a considerable body of opinion that a wolf release stands little chance of reestablishing wolves in the wild unless it is of wild-caught wolves, preferably a socially cohesive group, held only a very short time in captivity before release. The Mexican wolf recovery program apparently cannot follow this course of action. The wolves that remain in the wild in Mexico are extremely few; their existence is already jeopardized; their scarcity and separation may make unlikely any further reproduction in the wild, and suitable, approved, protected release areas are yet to be found. McBride (1980) saw no evidence of wolf hybridization in Mexico, but earlier authors (recorded in Gish, 1977) mention occurrences of wolf-dog hybrids along the Mexico–United States border. Dilution of the remaining Mexican wolf gene pool by hybridization is at least possible as wolves become fewer and more scattered. The male wolf captured for the program in March 1980 was taken when he visited the ranch where he had a dog mate and a hybrid litter.

For these reasons, this recovery effort must start by taking wild wolves into protective custody and trying to increase their numbers in a captive breeding program. As the September 1980 meeting of the U.S.A.-Mexico Joint Committee on Wildlife Conservation, representatives of Fauna Silvestre agreed to the wild capture of as many as possible of the remaining wild wolves, both for the protection of the wolves and for their use in propagation efforts. Accordingly, in this plan "restoration in the wild" can be taken to mean restoration by means of releases of wolves from the captive breeding program to the wild....

To enhance the Mexican wolf recovery program's chances of success, the team feels that every effort should be made to minimize the undesirable conditioning that inevitable long-term holding and breeding in captivity is likely to produce. Facilities should be located and designed so that the management of the captive wolves is as much as possible like a transplant from the wild to the wild, and management should proceed with minimal human contact. The team feels the expense is warranted to establish and man one or more holding-breeding enclosures in a remote, natural area within the historic range of *baileyi*, *monstrabilis*, or *mogollonensis*.

The team would prefer to see Mexican wolves held and bred in such natural-area enclosures as opposed to zoological facilities in urban or similar situations with greater risks of disturbance of the wolves by human activities. This is no reflection on the expertise, character or interest of the personnel of such zoological facilities. Rather, it is a comment on the learning abilities of a sensitive, social animal that, once released, will be asked to succeed as a completely wild animal. It is a comment, too, on the wolf's ability to transmit some attitudes and experiences from one generation to the next.

Although the team makes such recommendations, it recognizes that their acceptance will be affected by the general availability of funds and by prior allotment of funds to recovery work for endangered species that face problems easier and less costly to solve. The guidelines for management and husbandry of captive Mexican wolves...were drawn up in recognition of the fact that the Mexican wolf breeding program has already started, and will probably continue, to be conducted in existing zoological facilities. This in no way lessens the team's recommendation for establishment of facilities more conducive to attainment of the plan's primary objective.

At the September 1980 Joint Committee meeting, the representatives of Fauna Silvestre indicated their interest in moving trapped wolves into a large enclosure in Mexico. Subsequently, landowners in certain areas have expressed interest in use of their land for wolf enclosures. Similar offers have been made in two cases in southeastern Arizona. In both Mexico and the United States, realization of an enclosure would require formal governmental authorization plus assured funding for construction, maintenance, personnel, and food and likely veterinary services for wolves. It is possible that funding would be available from private organizations, foundations and individuals to supplement that which could be provided by governmental agencies.

RESTORATION IN WILD VERSUS PRESERVATION IN CAPTIVITY

It has been suggested that extinction of the Mexican wolf might be prevented by propagation solely in captivity without attempts to restore wild populations by means of releases. The idea is attractive because it avoids the tremendous socioeconomic problems that restoration in the wild entails. We must therefore comment on this suggestion.

Team member Dennis Meritt, Jr., is assistant director of the Lincoln Park Zoological Gardens in Chicago and chairman of the Wildlife Conservation and Management Committee of the American Association of Zoological Parks and Aquariums. As such, he is well qualified to speak for zoos in general. He has stated that "long range, I do not believe zoos will maintain Mexican Wolves, if the release to the wild or re-establishment in the wild concept fails. We certainly would not here and I know other major institutions have similar thoughts" (letter of March 20, 1981, to Ames). He later commented that under the species survival programs in zoos, priorities necessarily had to be assigned to various species because of the lack of space and funds to accommodate all species in need of help. Because of the problems involved in wolf recovery, he felt few zoos would want to become deeply involved in wolf recovery programs.

If not established zoological institutions, then what about fenced enclosures similar to the proposed breeding enclosures in potential release areas for permanent holding of the wolves? Fenced enclosures, however large, are not equivalent to the wild, but conceivably they might ultimately have to be accepted as the means of preventing extinction of the Mexican wolf. Such an enclosure might closely approach a natural situation if it is an ecologically complete unit that continues to produce prey animals and water adequate for wolf survival with relatively little management by humans. If constant management and provisioning are necessary to supply food for the wolves, the area is in effect only a zoological park.

As the enclosed wolf group increases its numbers, the need for human management of the enclosed situation will grow accordingly. Also, the number of separate groups of wolves so maintained must be adequate to preclude the possibility of eventual development of inbreeding depression, and records of breeding must be kept and coordinated toward that same end. The problems of over-all responsibility for financing and managing might be as knotty as those of restoring wolves to the wild.

If Fauna Silvestre and the U.S. Fish and Wildlife Service elect to maintain populations of Mexican wolves in large enclosures, rather than attempt to reintroduce wolves to the wild from the captive propagation program, the team is willing to formulate recommendations on husbandry and maintenance programs for such enclosures. At this writing, however, the recovery plan is written with the optimistic approach that recovery, even for a large predator, means recovery in the wild. We agree with statements made at a 1975 workshop on wolf reintroductions (Henshaw 1979) to the effect that use of large enclosures confuses the right of certain individual wolves to exist with the right of the species or subspecies to exist. Moreover, if the Mexican wolf is alive in captivity but declared extinct in the wild without a reintroduction attempt, there is thereby removed a major reason for the preservation of large areas of habitat as natural ecosystems. Recovery of the Mexican wolf in some part of the wild is valuable in that it ensures continuity, not only of the wolf, but also of a wilderness ecosystem with all its animal and plant components.

HOLDING-BREEDING ENCLOSURES IN RELEASE AREAS

In preparation for wolf releases to the wild, the team recommends establishment of natural-area holding-breeding enclosures in areas ecologically suitable for releases of wolves, even though approval of releases in a particular area may not yet be obtained. The proposal is made with the thought that certain management steps for breeding enclosures so located may make it more likely that released wolves will not migrate from the release area.

Homing behavior has been reported for released wolves (Henshaw and Stephenson 1974) and for various other world canids (see list of references in Danner and Fisher 1972). These and, to a certain extent, the transplant of *C. l. lycaon* to Michigan and the first red wolf release on Bulls Island, all indicate that a wolf that is put down in unfamiliar territory may prefer to head for or try to find his former location where he knew his way around, knew where the lunch bucket was, and perhaps knew where his friends were, regardless of whether that location was a home range or a home pen. It is conceivable that the following scenario of on-site breeding might help solve this problem for the Mexican wolf recovery program, which must start with wolves bred in captivity:

A. Build an enclosure in selected, approved release area;

B. Settle breeding pair in enclosure, providing with food and water;

C. When pups are produced and reach weaning age, begin to provide carcasses of native prey as food;

D. As pups mature, begin to provide live native prey;

E. Remove parent pair to another breeding enclosure elsewhere, and

F. When young are adept at killing native prey, open enclosure.

Management of this operation should proceed with minimal human contact once the pups are born.

The scenario aims, of course, at inducing the released wolves to accept the area as home range. It has been suggested that scent-marking the release area's perimeter with urine from wolves other than those of the release group might further deter released wolves from departing the release area. The necessarily large size of release areas, however, predicates an enormously long perimeter and, consequently, such large amounts of urine and walking that the idea is included here only to show the team did consider it. Peters (1979) found that wolves traveling habitual routes used a raised leg urination every 450 meters. Peters (in Henshaw 1979) indicated he found no evidence that wolves automatically find scent posts aversive.

OTHER BEHAVIORAL FACTORS INFLUENCING EMIGRATION FROM RELEASE AREAS

Released wolves may also depart the release area because of the wolf's natural tendency to wander though large areas in search of prey and because of normal population increase and dispersal. In Mexican wolves, however, these factors may have dimensions that make wandering a more serious consideration in recovery efforts for Mexican wolves than for more northerly subspecies.

First, Mexican wolves' tendency to range far may be related to the fact that the biomass of native prey species may have always been spread somewhat more thinly over the drier habitats of Mexico and southwestern United States than is the case for moister northern habits. Secondly, we know little of what Mexican wolf pack structure might be in adequate habitat and free of persecution. This pack structure may differ somewhat from that of northern subspecies, again because of differences in kinds and concentrations of prey species, and again in ways that spread wolves more quickly over a larger area.

McBride has observed that Mexican wolves are found singly or in very small packs of two or three animals and never in the larger packs reported for wolf subspecies of Canada, Alaska and northern United States. Obviously, pack size, as a factor of survival, can vary with prey size, and these southerly wolves have had little need for large groups of cooperating hunters to bring down the relatively smaller ungulates of these southern latitudes. The recovery effort would perhaps be more wisely guided if we knew whether the lack of a *need for* large packs is accompanied by any genetic *predisposition against* formation of large packs. Such a predisposition would tend to hasten dispersal of reintroduced wolves—especially after successful reproduction—into new areas, possibly into human-wolf conflicts not likely in the original release area. A predisposition against formation of large packs could occur in wolves of desert habitats through its survival value for predators in areas of scanty prey base. Captive wolves maintained by team leader Ames are, according to Bogan and Mehlop (1980), of southern subspecies, with greater than 99 percent probability, and their behavior may therefore be indicative of that of southern subspecies, including *baileyi*. They apparently tend to reject wolves that may come to be perceived as excess breeding-age individuals and, because fences prevent the departure of the rejected individuals, to attack these individuals repeatedly and try to kill them. The conflict, in other words, has not been solved by establishment of re-ordered dominance relationships and tolerance of the dominated individuals, as has happened in some groups of captive wolves. Admittedly, close confinement exacerbates these conflicts, but the conflicts also stem from social behavior originating in the animals' genetic makeup. If such intolerance is at all genetically based in these southern subspecies, casting out of excess individuals and resultant population dispersal might occur more rapidly in released groups of these subspecies than might be the case for northern subspecies with relatively stronger tendencies to form larger packs.

All this is conjecture at this point. The recovery effort should, however, keep in mind the possible existence of such behavioral patterns and their implications for habitat use of released wolves. If an area proposed for wolf releases does not have a natural or artificial barrier to wolf movement, the area should perhaps be surrounded by zones of decreasing legal protection.

LEGAL PROTECTION FOR RELEASED WOLVES

The recovery effort should consider the use of flexible legal protective systems in order to enhance the acceptability of initial releases of wolves and of their continuing presence. One such system is the establishment of zones of varying degrees of protection, applied to the eastern timber wolf, *Canis lupus lycaon*, in Minnesota. Briefly, this entails a central area of complete protection, surrounded by a zone in which certain wolves or restricted numbers of wolves may be taken under permit or license, either solely for specific depredation control or, in some areas, for reduction of wolf numbers.

In southwestern North America, mountain ranges of potential value to wolf recovery attempts are scattered units separated by areas of lower potential. It must be realized, therefore, that here we may not be speaking of one large central zone of complete protection, but of a fragmented group of zones of complete protection surrounded by one or more zones in which depredating wolves may be taken.

The other system of flexible legal protection would require amendment of the Endangered Species Act to provide for an experimental population classification, as opposed to a reintroduced population, as considered now under the Act. The proposed experimental population classification would entail prerelease cooperative agreements and regulations for the management of the released wolves. For release in Mexico, governmental rulings to achieve similar ends are recommended.

RELEASE AREAS—HABITAT CONSIDERATIONS

Gish (1977) described southwestern wolf country as including areas from the chaparral-desert scrub country up through grasslands, and into the spruce-fir woodlands and noted that records are rare of wolves denning or establishing ranges in desert scrub below 3,000 feet. Leopold (1972) refers to former wolf habitat in Mexico as the temperate uplands. McBride (1980) says: "Today wolves inhabit elevations about 4,500 feet above sea level where rainfall has created better grazing conditions for wolf prey." For wolf recovery efforts, the nature of the habitat is significant in its potential for supporting suitable prey species, in existing use of the area for production of livestock and game, and, where potential conflicts exist, the extent to which compromises can be reached.

Several researchers have made predictions about the size of the area that a wolf pack would need for survival. At the 1975 workshop on wolf reintroduction (Henshaw 1979), Mech recommended a minimum area of 4,000 square miles, an area measuring 50 by 75 to 100 miles or about 40 miles in radius, for "establishing a reasonably viable, well-functioning, well-organized natural population of wolves which would interfere with man minimally."

The release area must be capable of producing a continuing supply of prey animals adequate to support the desired number of wolves. Fuller and Keith (1980) found the food requirements of the rather large wolves of northeastern Alberta to range from 0.12 to 0.15 kg prey/kg wolf/day. Mech (1970) found that the Isle Royale wolves consumed an average of about .17 pound of moose per pound of wolf per day in winter. He noted that this was two to four times the maintenance requirements that had been derived from studies of captive wolves. His thoughts on the fate of the extra calories indicate that the prey base should likely not be skimpy in re-establishment efforts: (1) wild wolves might spend more energy than was thought; (2) the wolves might be accumulating fat against possible hard times, and (3) digestion might be less efficient at high rates of food intake. The extra intake would also ensure a more adequate supply of nutrients, such as vitamins and minerals, that are often present in minute amounts.

Wolves in warmer climates likely need somewhat fewer calories. Computations of prey biomass needed to support released Mexican wolves, however, would have to figure in percentages "wasted" by wolves or "lost" to scavengers. Records are many (e.g., Mech 1970) of northern wolves thriftiness, of their staying with a kill unless disturbed and consuming it almost completely. Mexican wolves of recent decades have learned to eat one good meal from the yearling cattle killed, then depart to save their own skins. This recovery program may be lucky in its inability simply to trap and transplant Mexican wolves; the natural-area breeding-release scenario proposed may aid in reinstating a regime of thrifty consumption of native prey. As for use of wolves' kills by scavengers, quite likely coyotes are already present in most areas where releases of Mexican wolves might be considered. Scavenging of wolf kills by coyotes is therefore possible. It would remain to be seen whether the wolves would establish themselves in a territory and kill and drive off coyotes as has been recorded for northern wolves (Fuller and Keith 1981, Mech 1970, Seton 1929, Stenlund 1955, Young 1944).

In evaluating possible wolf release areas in Mexico and the southwestern United States, we must also remember that the ranges of this area, being relatively drier, support less prey food per square mile than do the moister northern habitats involved in the studies mentioned above. Moose must be translated into the smaller ungulates available here, and the availability of smaller prey that wolves would eat must also be considered. All this may mean the expenditure of more hunting energy per pound of food obtained because the units of prey are smaller and more scattered.

Despite the drier climate of southwestern North America, free water is available in the historic and present range of the Mexican wolf, and adequate amounts of free water must be accessible in any proposed release area, for both the wolf and its prey. Mech (1970) feels that wolves require considerable amounts of water, especially after gorging, and estimates a need of nearly two quarts a day for a 70- to 80-pound wolf. Team member Dr. Poglayen raised the question of whether wolves of more arid regions might be physiologically adapted to function with less water intake or with longer periods of water deprivation. The following observations indicate they are not. Team leader Ames provides water for captive southern wolves in 70-gallon hog waterers plus water in small pools. In winter, the latter freeze solid, becoming unavailable for drinking water, but small electric heaters prevent freezing of the water in the hog waterers. Evaporation is minimal because the waterers are covered. The frequency and amounts of water refills in winter, plus the numbers and sizes of wolves serviced allows for a rough estimate of daily water use per wolf and it proves to be very close to Mech's figure. More recently, Dr. Poglayen measured daily water use of a captive female southern wolf at the Arizona-Sonora Desert Museum, noting amounts used daily from the wolf's supply pail and allowing for evaporation indicated by a control pail placed in an adjoining unoccupied pen. Daytime temperatures during the ten-day period ranged from 96°F to 108°F. The wolf used a mean of 2,069 cc (2.19 quart) daily, and daily water intake ranged from 1,480 cc to 3,000 cc (1.56 to 3.17 quart).

A suitable release area would also include "broken sloping country suitable for hiding dens, plus timber and brush for cover" (McBride 1980).

Regardless of which wild prey species were eaten by Mexican wolves in the past, the recent diet of the remaining wild wolves of these southern subspecies has been livestock, primarily yearling cattle (McBride 1980). Even if the recovery effort teaches wolves that are candidates for release to enjoy a diet of native wild prey species, the wolf's ability to take cattle and its normal predilection to choose whatever prey is easiest to take must be borne in mind in the choice and management of release areas. Areas to be considered for initial releases of wolves should be, first, those with little or no existing use for livestock grazing and, secondly, those whose livestock allotments could be most easily and economically bought out or otherwise eliminated.

Particularly within the United States, big-game hunting has been a traditional use of habitat that might be considered ecologically suitable for releases of wolves. The recovery effort will have to address possible conflicts with the big-game hunting constituency. Educational efforts to promote understanding of, and sympathy for, wolves may lead to greater acceptance, by both hunters and the general public, of the idea of sharing the use of remaining habitat to prevent the extinction of these wolves. Possibly, also, the recovery effort should include the concept that re-establishment of adequate numbers of wolves might eventually warrant some controlled taking for sport and pelts. Part of the impetus for the early conservation movement came from game protective associations that wanted to prevent extinction of the sources of sport hunting and desirable meat and hides. Some today may also view the opportunity to take wolves and their pelts as a desirable product of appropriate management of the wildlife habitat and, taking this view, they may more readily accept re-establishment of wolves.

At present, deer numbers throughout much of southwestern United States are relatively low. This fact will undoubtedly cause more big-game hunters to oppose wolf releases than would be the case if deer were now as abundant here as they were in the 1950s and 1960s. Habitat management activities to benefit large ungulates are under way in the Southwest, however, and may be effective in increasing deer numbers. Some of these activities benefit other forms of wildlife as well. Agencies that manage lands and wildlife continue to provide waterings by well-drilling, development of springs, and provision of water impoundments and catchments. Vegetation is managed, where possible, to correct past damages of overgrazing and of reduction of habitat diversity and to improve the vigor and availability of forage plants. Techniques to manipulate vegetative cover include managed wildfires, prescribed burning, removal of undesired brush and harvests of mature trees, and seeding and planting of desired vegetation. These and other habitat-manipulation techniques should benefit deer populations and, thereby, also benefit released wolf groups.

Wolf releases should be considered only for large tracts of public lands. In the Rocky Mountains, public lands today face the possibility of major ecological changes for the sake of extraction of oil, gas, and strategic minerals and resultant increase in human population. This factor may further limit the choice of areas suitable for releases of wolves, both in Mexico and the United States.

Robinson (in Henshaw 1979) has pointed out that experience in Ontario and Minnesota indicate that wolves stand little chance of re-establishment in areas of high or moderate human population. He says that "somewhere between six and twelve persons per square mile is a critical threshold." Almost any area that might be considered as a release area in Mexico or the Southwest would meet this criterion.

Regulatory and policy mechanisms exist, at least within the United States, that would preclude releases of predators where they might jeopardize endangered prey species. The mobility of wolves, however, requires that extra attention be given, in selection of release areas, to the matter of possible impacts of wolf releases on any endangered prey species that might exist in a proposed release area....

PRIME OBJECTIVE OF RECOVERY PLAN

In formulating a recovery-plan objective for any subspecies of *C. lupus*, one must realistically view, not only the causes of the wolf's past endangerment, but also present trends toward ever-increasing human needs—whether real or perceived—for space and for the renewable and nonrenewable resources present or producible in wolf habitat. Having taken this realistic view, the Mexican Wolf Recovery Team sees no possibility for complete delisting of the Mexican wolf.

Section 4(g) of the Endangered Species Act of 1973 requires that recovery plans be developed and implemented "for the conservation and survival of endangered and threatened species...." The team feels that conserving and ensuring the survival of the Mexican wolf is the most that can be achieved today and has worded its prime objective accordingly: "To conserve and ensure the survival of *Canis lupus bai-*

leyi by maintaining a captive breeding program and re-establishing a viable, self-sustaining population of at least 100 Mexican wolves in the middle to high elevations of a 5,000-square-mile area within the Mexican wolf's historic range."

Bibliography

Ames, N. 1980. Mexican wolves in captivity: A review of the lineage originating in the 1960s at the Arizona-Sonora Desert Museum. Unpublished typescript.

Bailey, V. 1931. *Mammals of New Mexico.* North Amer. Fauna No. 53, Bur. Biol. Surv., Washington, D.C.

Baker, R. H., and B. Villa R. 1960. Distribución geográfica y población actuales del lobo gris en México. *Anal. Inst. Biol., Univ. Nac. México 30* (1–2):369–74.

Bogan, M. A., and P. Mehlop. 1980. *Systematic Relationships of Gray Wolves (Canis lupus) in Southwestern North America.* Natl. Fish and Wildl. Lab., Washington, and Univ. of New Mexico, Albuquerque.

Dalquest, W. W. 1953. Mammals of the Mexican state of San Luis Potosí. *Louisiana State Univ. Studies, Biol. Ser.* 1:1–229.

Danner, D. A., and A. R. Fisher. 1977. Evidence of homing by a coyote (*Canis latrans*). *Jour. Mammal.* 58(2):244–45.

Fuller, T. K., and L. B. Keith. 1980. Wolf population dynamics and prey relationships in northeastern Alberta. *Jour. Wildl. Manage.* 44(3):583–602.

———. 1981. Non-overlapping ranges of coyotes and wolves in northeastern Alberta. *Jour. Mammal.* 62(2):403–5.

Gish, D. M. (1977). An historical look at the Mexican gray wolf (*Canis lupus baileyi*) in early Arizona Territory and since statehood. Unpublished typescript. U.S. Fish and Wildlife Service.

Goldman, E. A. 1944. *The Wolves of North America,* Part II, Classification of wolves. The Amer. Wildl. Instit., Washington, D.C.

Hall, E. R., and K. R. Kelson. 1959. *The Mammals of North America.* The Ronald Press, New York.

Henshaw, R. E. 1979. Workshop: Reintroduction of wolves into the wild. In *The Behavior and Ecology of Wolves,* E. Klinghammer, ed. Garland STPM Press, New York.

Henshaw, R. E., and R. O. Stephenson. 1974. Homing in the gray wolf (*Canis lupus*). *Journ. Mammal.* 55(1):234–37.

Jorgenson, S. E., C. E. Faulkner, and L. D. Mech, eds. 1970. *Proceedings of a Symposium on Wolf Management in Selected Areas of North America.* U.S. Fish and Wildlife Service.

Leopold, A. S. 1972. *Wildlife of Mexico: The Game Birds and Mammals.* Univ. of California Press, Berkeley.

McBride, R. T. 1980. *The Mexican Wolf (Canis lupus baileyi): An Historical Review and Observations on its Status and Distribution.* U.S. Fish and Wildlife Service.

Mech, L. D. 1970. *The Wolf: The Ecology and Behavior of an Endangered Species.* Natural History Press, Garden City, N.Y.

Mitchell, J. G. 1976. Fear and loathing in wolf country. *Audubon* 78(3):20–39.

Morales, Z. Carlos. 1970. Control de fauna perjudicial. Dirección General de la Fauna Silvestre. Typescript.

Nowak, R. M. 1973. North American Quaternary *Canis*. Ph.D. dissertation, Univ. of Kansas, Lawrence.

———. 1974. The gray wolf in North America: A preliminary report. Typescript. N.Y. Zool. Soc. and the U.S. Bur. of Sport Fish. and Wildl.

Nunley, G. L. 1977. The Mexican gray wolf in New Mexico. Unpublished typescript. U.S. Fish and Wildlife Service.

Peters, R. 1979. Mental maps in wolf territoriality. In *The Behavior and Ecology of Wolves*, E. Klinghammer, ed. Garland STPM Press, New York.

Pimlott, D. H., J. A. Shannon, and G. B. Kolenosky. 1969. *The Ecology of the Timber Wolf in Algonquin Provincial Park*. Ontario Dept. of Lands and Forests.

Platz, C. C., and S. W. J. Seager. 1977. Successful pregnancies with concentrated frozen canine semen. *Lab. Anim. Sci.* 27(6):1013–16.

Scudday, J. F. 1972. Two recent records of gray wolves in west Texas. *Journ. Mammal.* 53(3):598.

———. 1977. The Mexican Gray Wolf in Texas. Unpublished typescript. U.S. Fish and Wildlife Service.

Seager, S. W. J., C. C. Platz Jr., and W. Hodge. 1975. Successful pregnancy using frozen semen in the wolf (*Canis lupus irremotus*). *Int. Zoo Yearbook* 15:140–43.

Seton, E. T. 1929. *Lives of Game Animals*, Vol. I, Part 1. Doubleday, Doran and Co., New York.

Stenlund, M. H. 1955. A field study of the timber wolf (*Canis lupus*) on the Superior National Forest, Minnesota. Minn. Dept. Conserv. Tech. Bull.

Woody, Jack. 1979. Minutes of Mexican wolf workshop. U.S. Fish and Wildlife Service.

Young, S. P. 1944. *The Wolves of North America*, Part I, Their history, habits, economic status, and control. The Amer. Wildl. Instit., Washington, D.C.

———. 1946. *The Wolf in North American History*. Caxton Printers, Idaho.

REINTRODUCING THE MISSING PARTS: THE EXPERIMENTAL POPULATION PROVISIONS OF THE ENDANGERED SPECIES ACT

DALE D. GOBLE

(2001)

> *If the land mechanism as a whole is good, then every part is good, whether we understand it or not. If the biota, in the course of aeons, has built something we like but do not understand, then who but a fool would discard seemingly useless parts? To keep every cog and wheel is the first precaution of intelligent tinkering.*
>
> —ALDO LEOPOLD, "CONSERVATION," IN *Round River* (1953)

The goal of the Endangered Species Act is to save all the parts—a goal that is embodied in the Act's requirement that the federal government "conserve" listed species. The ESA's conservation mandate includes not only an obligation to do no harm, but also an affirmative duty to use "all methods and procedures which are necessary to bring any [listed] species to the point at which the measures provided in this Act are no longer necessary."[1] Unfortunately, the ESA is remedial: rather than describing a procedure for an intelligent tinkerer approaching an undisturbed biotic community, the Act was adopted in response to the often-dramatic changes that had already occurred—changes that have pushed some members of the community into extinction and others to the brink. Saving all the parts is a rescue mission that often requires restoring species to communities. The drafters of the ESA recognized this fact and included among the Act's "methods and procedures" for recovering species the authority to transplant members of listed species into habitat from which they have been extirpated.

Reintroductions serve a variety of conservation objectives.[2] They can reduce the risks that small populations face from what biologists call stochastic events—the random disasters of the world. A hurricane or an oil spill, for example, might extirpate a species with a restricted range; a geographically separate population provides a bit of insurance against such catastrophes. More critically, there are species that have been entirely extirpated in the wild; they continue to exist only in the confines of captive breeding and rearing programs. Black-footed ferrets, red wolves, California condors, Guam rails—and Mexican wolves—have all escaped extinction only as captive populations. For such species, reintroduction is the only hope for an existence outside the endless pacing of cages.

Despite the biological benefits of reintroduction, it has often faced significant opposition. In some cases, this is due to the fear of landowners that land-use restrictions will accompany the reintroduced individuals. In other situations—particularly with the reintroduction of wolves—there has been a fear that the transplanted animals present risks to domestic and big game animals. To overcome such opposition, wildlife managers and conservation groups proposed the "experimental population" idea to Congress in 1982. Sponsors of the legislation hoped that federal agencies, state officials, and private landowners would be willing to "host" populations of listed species if they were assured that doing so would neither restrict their land-management options nor lead to significant economic losses. Proponents of the experimental population concept argued that it would help to overcome utilitarian objections to reintroductions by reducing the protection accorded the reintroduced, "experimental" population.[3] To understand how the experimental population designation reduces the restrictions applicable to listed species, it is helpful to examine the basic provisions of the ESA.

⟿

The ESA—like most statutes—operates by creating categories and specifying the legal results that are to flow from inclusion within those categories. The major categories in the ESA are "endangered," "threatened," and "proposed to be listed." The legal results that follow from placing a species into one of these categories are contained in the Act's management requirements. There are two primary mandates.

The first is the "consultation requirement." Any federal agency that proposes to do something that might place a listed species or its critical habitat at risk, is required to consult with one of two federal wildlife management agencies—the Fish and Wildlife Service or the National Marine Fisheries Service.[4] If the consultation process leads the wildlife agency to conclude that the proposed action will jeopardize the species, the action agency is prohibited from proceeding unless the proposal can be modified to protect the listed species. Since the issuance of a permit by a federal agency to a private person or entity is a federal action, a substantial amount of private activity is also swept within the consultation requirement. Consultation accounts for some of the hostility to reintroducing listed species since it raises the specter of costly delays and restrictions on habitat-modifying actions.

The second management requirement is the prohibition against "taking" a listed species. The Act broadly defines "take" as "harass, harm, pursue, hunt, shoot, wound, kill, trap, capture, or collect, or to attempt to engage in any such conduct."[5] The breadth of this definition is reflected in a statement in the congressional report on the meaning of the term: "It includes harassment, whether intentional or not. This would allow, for example, the Secretary to regulate the activities of birdwatchers where the effect of those activities might disturb the birds and make it difficult to hatch or raise their young."[6] As Congress noted, a wide range of activities fall within the proscription—a fact that accounts for much of the hostility to reintroduction since unintentional acts may take a listed species—and the taking prohibition is backed up by substantial criminal and civil penalties.

In an effort to reduce the effects of the consultation requirement and the taking prohibition, proponents of reintroduction urged Congress to create a new statutory classification—the "experimental population." Their objective was to minimize the effect of the consultation requirement and the taking prohibition by giving the wildlife management agency the authority to shift members of the experimental population among the ESA's other three statutory classifications—"endangered," "threatened," and "proposed to be listed." That is, the new "experimental population" category acts like a wild card that permits the wildlife agency to treat a species that is listed as endangered as though it were either threatened or proposed to be listed. This permits the agency to take advantage of differences in the treatment accorded species in the different classifications.

The consultation requirement, for example, applies only to species that are listed as either endangered or threatened. When an agency proposes an action that might affect a species that is proposed to be listed, the agency is required only to confer—a much less formal and time-consuming process, and one that is also far less restrictive since the action agency is not required to "insure" that its actions will not jeopardize the species. Thus, while an informal conference may lead to recommendations from the wildlife management agency, it does not stop the proposed action. An experimental population is treated as though it were composed of a species that is proposed to be listed and thus is subject only to the conference requirement.

Similarly, an experimental population is treated as a species that is "threatened" for the taking prohibition. The ESA also creates a two-tiered scheme for the application of the taking prohibition: if a species is listed as endangered, the taking prohibition is applied to members of the species by the Act itself; if a species is listed as threatened, on the other hand, the wildlife managing agency has flexibility in determining whether and how the prohibition will be applied. It may, for example, allow the taking of a listed species in certain situations—such as when a member of the reintroduced population is attacking domestic animals.

Finally, there is additional flexibility because the Act specifies that critical habitat is not to be designated for an experimental population.[7] This exemption removes the restrictions that the Act imposes on actions adversely modifying critical habitat. As with the removal of the consultation requirement, the lack of a designated critical habitat reduces the restrictions on land uses.

Thus, for most experimental populations,[8] there are no consultation requirements: actions authorized, funded, or carried out by a federal agency—including private actions requiring federal permits—can proceed without delay while the action agency "confers" with the wildlife management agency. Similarly, the wildlife agency has broad discretion to authorize taking that would be prohibited for species otherwise listed as endangered. Finally, since no critical habitat is designated for the population, the Act's restrictions on habitat-altering actions are also absent. The experimental population classification substantially reduces the stringency of the Act's requirements.

❦

The amendments authorizing the experimental population classification also reflected the potential for controversy that reintroductions often produce. Congress imposed public notice and participation requirements as a prerequisite to the release of any experimental population. An experimental population can be reintroduced only after the wildlife management agency has published notice of the proposed action, provided an opportunity for public comment on the proposal, and published the final rule that includes a statement of explaining the reasons for the agency's decision.[9] In addition to ensuring public comment on the proposal, the use of these rulemaking procedures is intended (in the words of the congressional report on the 1982 amendments) "to provide a vehicle for the development of special regulations for each experimental population that will address the particular needs of that population."[10]

The process leading to the reintroduction of the Mexican wolf was even more complex than the formal statutory provisions would suggest. Indeed, the process required more than fifteen years to complete.

The Mexican gray wolf (*Canis lupus baileyi*) was listed as an endangered species in April 1976.[11] Recovery planning for the species[12] produced a *Mexican Wolf Recovery Plan* that was adopted by the United States Fish and Wildlife Service (FWS) and the Mexican Dirección General de la Fauna Silvestre in 1982. The recovery plan concluded that the species had been extirpated in the wild and called for the reintroduction of individuals from captive breeding populations maintained by the two governments.[13] Ten years later, FWS issued a notice of intent to prepare an environmental impact statement (EIS) on a proposed reintroduction of an experimental population of wolves.[14] Following several public meetings to determine the issues that the EIS should address, a draft impact statement was released for public comment in June, 1995[15] after a lawsuit by several conservation groups forced FWS to proceed with planning for reintroduction.[16] The draft EIS triggered an extensive round of 27 public meetings and 3 public hearings; nearly 18,000 people commented either at a public event or in writing. On May 1, 1996, FWS published a proposed regulation on the release of an experimental population of Mexican wolves.[17] Four public meetings and hearings were held on the proposed regulation. On April 3, 1997, the Department of the Interior issued its decision to implement the preferred alternative in the EIS and to reintroduce captive-bred wolves into eastern Arizona.[18]

The regulation authorizing the reintroduction of the experimental population regulation determined that the reintroduced animals were a "nonessential experimental population." This designation justified the FWS decision to allow individuals to take wolves under a variety of circumstances. For example, a person may take a wolf as a result of unavoidable and unintentional conduct such as driving an automobile, trapping, or recreating; wolves may be harassed when they come within 500 yards of people, buildings, pets, or livestock; owners of livestock are permitted to kill wolves that are attacking livestock.[19]

The lengthy public process that led to the reintroduction of Mexican wolves went as Congress intended. It prepared the way for the release of a group of animals under legal rules that minimized the effect of those animals on people living and recreating in the release area: land use activities that require federal permits may proceed without consultation even if the activities are likely to have a negative effect on the wolves. Individuals may engage in a full range of activities without fear that those activities may unintentionally take a listed species. The economic interests of livestock owners are protected by permission to kill wolves attacking their livestock. Although some inconvenience may remain, the legendary restrictions of the mythic ESA are absent. The congressional mandate that the federal government use "all methods and procedures which are necessary to bring any [listed] species to the point at which the measures provided in this Act are no longer necessary" has led to the first wild populations of Mexican wolves in the United States in at least the last thirty years.

⁓

The experimental population provisions of the ESA are intended to reduce the pragmatic opposition to reintroducing endangered species into areas of their former habitat from which they have been extirpated. The provisions seek to minimize the effect of the reintroduced animals on economic and recreational activities by reducing or eliminating the protection that the Act accords such species.

But opposition to the reintroduction of wolves also has an emotional component that is little effected by the concrete statutory provisions. This is particularly true of wolves, a species with a unique mythical stature. For many people, the wolf is an instrument of balance, an animal that weeds out the sick and old while providing for its close-knit family group. For others, it remains the wolf at the door, a ruthless killer—the symbol of all that is unreclaimably wild. Wolves, in short, seem to encapsulate our contending visions of the place of humans in nature. For those who view nature as a utilitarian storehouse, the reintroduction of the extirpated species is at best to be a nuisance, at worst a disaster—and at a minimum a step backwards that calls into question the hard work of their ancestors in reclaiming the land and making it a garden. For those who view humans as a part of a natural community, reintroduction is a step toward the wholeness that Aldo Leopold grasped in his epiphany by the side of a dying wolf—the epiphany that led to his "first precaution of intelligent tinkering": save "every cog and wheel."

The 1982 amendments to the ESA could address the utilitarian concerns by reducing land-use restrictions; the amendments could do nothing directly to reduce the symbolic dispute.

Notes

1. The Endangered Species Act (ESA) is codified at volume 16 of the United States Code sections 1531 to 1544. The definition of "conserve" is at 16 U.S.C. § 1532(3).

2. On the use of reintroduction as a recovery tool, see B. Griffith, J. M. Scott, J. W. Carpenter, & C. Reed, Translocation as a Species Conservation Tool: Status and Strategy, *Science* 245 (1989):477.

3. The term "experimental population" is defined by the Act as "any population (including offspring arising solely therefrom) authorized by the Secretary for release…but only when, and at such times as, the population is wholly separate geographically from nonexperimental populations of the same species." 16 U.S.C. § 1539(j)(1). This definition imposes two limitations: To be an "experimental" population the release of the population must have been authorized by the Secretary *and* the population must be separate from other, nonexperimental populations.

4. The National Marine Fisheries Service (in the Department of Commerce) has responsibility for marine and anadromous species; the Fish and Wildlife Service (in the Department of the Interior) is responsible for all other species.

5. 16 U.S.C. § 1532(19).

6. H.R. Rep. No. 412, 93d Cong., 1st Sess. 11 (1973).

7. 16 U.S.C. § 1539(j)(2)(C)(ii).

8. When an experimental population is found on a national wildlife refuge or a national park, it is not subject to the reduced protection.

9. Formally, the amendments required that the decisionmaking leading to the release of an experimental population be structured through the promulgation of a regulation under the Administrative Procedure Act. 5 U.S.C. § 553.

10. H.R. Conf. Rep. No. 835, 97th Cong., 2d Sess. 34 (1982).

11. 41 Fed. Reg. 17,742 (Apr. 28, 1976).

12. The ESA envisions a linear process in which recovery planning plays a central role: a species is listed as endangered or threatened; the wildlife managing agency prepares a recovery plan for the species that specifies how the threat to the species' continued existence will be removed and mitigated; the plan is implemented and the species recovers to the point that it no longer requires protection under the ESA. On recovery plan requirements, see 16 U.S.C. § 1533(f).

13. Mexican Wolf Recovery Team, Mexican Wolf Recovery Plan (Sept. 15, 1982).

14. 57 Fed. Reg. 14,427 (Apr. 20, 1992).

15. 60 Fed. Reg. 33,224 (June 27, 1995).

16. "Lawsuit brings Mexican wolf back," *Idaho Daily Statesman*, May 23, 1993, at 4F.

17. 61 Fed. Reg. 19,237 (May 1, 1996).

18. 62 Fed. Reg. 15,915 (Apr. 3, 1991).

19. 63 Fed. Reg. 1752 (Jan. 12, 1998).

A TALE OF TWO WOLVES

||||||||||||||||||||||||||||||||||||||||||||||||||||||||||||||||||||||||||||||||||||||||||

David E. Brown

(1992)

*My hatred for wolves goes clear back to my early boyhood days
in Texas, and has been strengthened by countless experiences
with them throughout my lifetime. Never once have I known a
wolf to do anything to change my opinion of him; and although I
would very much regret the passing of bear and lions from these
Southwestern mountains, I would shed no tears whatever over
the death of the last lobo.*

— Dub Evans, *Slash Ranch Hounds*, 1951

A winter night in 1965 comes readily to mind. It was then
that another wildlife manager and I heard a wolf howl from
the northeast corner of the Papago Indian Reservation. Not
only was the animals' eerie cry to remain etched in our minds, and
make one of the hundred such camps extraordinary, we sensed that
we would never hear its like again—not in Arizona anyway.

For we were not the only ones who heard the howling. Local
ranchmen heard it too, and had found other evidence of a wolf's
presence. The next day, predator control agents arrived with traps
and "getters." Although no wolf carcass was ever found, the howls
and reports abruptly ceased. Some thought one of the cyanide-loaded
getters had gotten him, or since this was not wolf country, that the
animal had moved on. Whatever its fate, the animal was never heard
from again.

While I heard no more wolves in the succeeding years, I was to
hear plenty about wolves. In 1976 the Mexican wolf was declared
an "endangered species" by the U.S. Fish and Wildlife Service—by
then a largely academic classification as the *lobo* had been extirpated
within the boundaries of the United States. The last Mexican wolf
reported from Texas and New Mexico had been killed in 1970. No
wolf had been born in the wild in Arizona since 1944. The last Mexican wolf "holdouts" in Mexico were being eliminated in Durango
and Chihuahua by an American trapper named Roy McBride. The

only reports of a *lobo* in the U.S. were vague accounts of a wanderer from Mexico taking up residency in the upper Arivaipa Canyon area in Arizona's Sulphur Springs Valley—"rumors" that were soon replaced by stories of a "wolf" quietly taken by a private trapper for a reputed bounty of $500 put up by local stockmen.

Like most Arizonans I forgot about wolves.

Then, one day while browsing through the Arizona Game and Fish Department's library, I came upon four reports commissioned by the U.S. Fish and Wildlife Service on the history and status of the Mexican wolf. These accounts, prepared by Dan Gish for Arizona, Gary Nunley for New Mexico, James Scudday for Texas, and Roy T. McBride for Mexico, read like a fascinating novel. They document a 50-year campaign against the wolf in the Southwest, a war that was won only with the aid and total commitment of the U.S. government. Getting rid of the wolf was not the result of accidental overkill brought about by overzealous ranchers, but the successful conclusion of a well-considered strategy. Published as *The Wolf in the Southwest*, these accounts made a fitting obituary for the region's most hated and respected predator.

But not everyone accepted the wolf's final demise. In 1977 the U.S. Fish and Wildlife Service contracted with Roy McBride to supply the agency with some of the last wild-trapped *lobos* for breeding stock. Several wolves were captured, and captive breeding programs were instituted at the Arizona-Sonora Desert Museum and the St. Louis Zoo. A "Mexican Wolf Recovery Plan" was drafted, and eventually approved. The hope was that somehow, sometime, somewhere a *refugium* for the Mexican wolf would be found within the animal's historical range in the United States.

But such a hope has yet to materialize. Reintroducing an endangered predator is infinitely more difficult than preserving one. Now, more than ten years after the initiation of the captive-breeding program, no wolves have yet been released. Despite the Mexican wolf being a federally endangered species, and mandated by Congress to be a U.S. Fish and Wildlife responsibility, the agency has decided that it must have the state's permission prior to reintroducing the wolf to any area from which the same agency had previously eliminated the animal.

For obvious political reasons, none of the three states having potential release sites suggested a wolf reintroduction site. Nor are they likely to. The Texas legislature has even passed a law outlawing the reintroduction of wolves, and the only release site seriously considered in New Mexico—the arid, but ungrazed White Sands Missile Range—was withdrawn from consideration on the grounds that such a release would attract too much attention. No one has even proposed a release site in Arizona.

It thus appears that the restoration of a wild population of wolves to the Southwest is far in the future, if ever. The potential political opprobrium from a wolf reintroduction is just too great. Neither the U.S. Fish and Wildlife Service nor a federal land management agency is likely to endorse a specific reintroduction program, much less a state game and fish commission. The hatred of the stockmen for wolves is too intense, and their political outrage is too vociferous, for such a proposal to be sanctioned in the halls of Southwest state legislatures—the same legislatures that allow stockmen to remove any animal that poses a threat to livestock on private or public land. With no Southwest National Park or other suitable *lobo* habitat available that is livestock-free, I have resigned myself to hearing wolf howls only in my memory.

But something keeps nagging at me. How is it that such ancient countries as Greece, Italy, and Spain have wolves while America's Baby States do not? Why is it that the wolf has persisted through so many waves of Mediterranean civilizations into modern times? What is the status of wolves in these countries now? Are there any lessons to be learned that might be applicable to the Southwest?

I decided to go and take a look. In the spring of 1987 I went to Italy's Apennine Mountains and Abruzzi National Park; in the spring of 1989 I visited the Cantabrian Mountains and other Spanish *sierras*. Thanks to Franco Zunino, Italy's foremost brown bear biologist, and Tony Clevenger, who was studying bears in the Cantabrians, I got to meet wildlife biologists, university professors, public officials, villagers, farmers, shepherds, brown bears, and wolves.

What I saw was both familiar and surprising. Except for the presence of beech forest and other, more subtle floral differences, southern Europe's mountains had a Southwest flavor. Many of the oaks and other plants had a "familiar look" and several times I was hard pressed not to imagine that I was not in California, Chihuahua, or New Mexico. The European red deer is the same species as our elk, as is their brown bear and our grizzly. So are the wolves. And, while the farmers and shepherds expressed tolerance for bears, they detested the wolf with the same intensity as did their Southwest counterparts. The animals' unsavory dining habits and propensity to kill for fun are guaranteed to rile those whose life is spent in animal husbandry.

But centuries of battle with canine adversaries have resulted in a number of stock-raising techniques being practiced in Europe that are not seen in the Southwest. Although the attitude toward wolves in rural Italy and Spain is similar to that of Western stockmen, the procedures to deal with them are different. While Italian and Spanish wolves continue to be trapped, poisoned, burned-out, and shot as were their Southwest brethren, their domestic prey is looked after more judiciously.

I saw no cattle in the backcountry that were not attended by a cowherd. All of the cows come home to the barn at night, and no one would think of leaving cows and calves on the open range. Nor are cattle allowed to graze in the woods or in rough, brushy country. Guard dogs, some with spike collars to give them an advantage in a fight against wolves, accompany every herd of cattle, sheep, or goats.

Sheep are folded every night and guarded by shepherds as well as dogs. Large, unwieldy flocks must be rare—at least I did not see any. Surprisingly, much of the countries' rangeland looked better than comparable areas in Arizona and New Mexico despite having been used and abused for several hundred rather than 100 years. Livestock numbers and seasonal grazing patterns appear to have attained some sort of equilibrium with the capacity of the land to support them. And, as in rural America, the young people are moving to the cities; almost every village has fewer people now than 20 years ago. Some have been abandoned entirely.

As for *why* the wolf was able to survive in these countries and not in the Southwest, I now have no doubt. There was never a federal agency dedicated to the extermination of the wolf in Italy and Spain. Divided into principalities, autonomous regions, and provincial governments, these nations have never had a coordinated predator control program that, year after year, continued to field wolf trappers throughout the length and breadth of the country. With only local control efforts, the wolves could recoup their losses; areas cleared of wolves were soon repopulated by offspring of others raised in some other province.

Moreover, attitudes in the European countryside toward wolves appear to be changing. As villages shrink and vanish, new national parks and *cotas* are created and old ones expand. Livestock depredations on such lands are supposed to be compensated by governments which have a policy of maintaining some wolves as representatives of the nation's wildlife heritage. Should present trends continue, the hatred of wolves in the villages will gradually turn to acceptance, and may eventually even become appreciation.

Within Italy's Abruzzi National Park is the village of Civitella Alfedena with its large enclosure containing a dozen or so wolves for tourists to observe and photograph. Next to the enclosure is a two-story building devoted to exhibits on the wolf. Wolf traps, wolf posters, and all sorts of paraphernalia dealing with wolf lore are here for public display. (My favorite was a 19th-century poster of a pack of wolves attacking a snowbound train in the Alps, the passengers fighting off the animals from the roofs of the railroad cars.) The message is that Europe's most maligned animal need not remain man's enemy, and that if certain precautions are followed when grazing livestock and a modicum of tolerance is practiced, Italians will have wolves around for some time to come.

The educational display was effective. In a few minutes I learned more about the wolf in Europe than in 20 years of reading. By the large numbers of school children present, I strongly suspect that most Italians know more about wolves than the average American.

As for the future of the wolf in these countries, much depends on the effects of the Common Market. Should Italy's and Spain's agricultural and pastoral "efficiency" begin to rival Germany's and Switzerland's the wolf will be in serious trouble. If, however, these countries continue to expand their parks and wildlife areas (Italy now has two designated wilderness areas), and educate their public on the value of predators, the wolf's future should be secure. It would be a shame for these countries to lose the wolf now after he has withstood man's assault for centuries.

To return the wolf to the American Southwest will also involve a change in attitude, not so much by the wolf's old enemies who are in the wane, but by wildlife enthusiasts who have sought to maintain peace with the livestock industry. A new generation of conservationists needs to understand that the wolf and the grizzly are as much a part of their heritage as are elk, bighorn sheep, and mountain lions. Of what purpose are New Mexico's and Arizona's multitude of national forests, stellar collection of national parks, and great legacy of wilderness areas without the wolf and the grizzly? There is no reason why the citizens of Italy and Spain should enjoy more diverse fauna than the people of the American Southwest.

THE PHYSICS OF BEAUTY

SHARMAN APT RUSSELL
from *Kill the Cowboy*
(1993)

ot everyone is impressed when the wolf enters the room. The teachers are busy watching their students, keeping them quiet, worrying about loud noises. Some of the children are aware that this wolf, after all, has a name: Shaman. This is a named wolf, surely, really, not much more than a dog.

The wolf enters the room. His nails scrabble on the hard floor. He strains at the leash, lunging, eager, curious, excited, only slightly frantic. He has done this sort of thing since he was two weeks old. He has faced many rooms of people, and he will allow himself now to be touched and petted. He will allow his friends Pamela Brown and Kent Weber to parade him before a line of human faces and human scent. He is not a dog, and there are those in the room who know this immediately—who feel immediately the charge of knowledge like a luminous coil circling up their spine. This wolf is three times as strong as any dog his size. His head is larger to hold his larger brain; his jaws have twice the crushing power of a German shepherd; his eyes are set at a different angle; his legs are longer and more spindly; his paws are huge. This particular Northern Rocky Mountain timber wolf weighs about one hundred pounds and has a black coat that is highlighted subtly, to enhance signals that he uses in communication with other wolves. This is an animal born and raised in captivity that no one could say is wild. Still, he carries within him, in those yellow eyes and in that powerful body, all the genes of wildness and all the potential.

Pamela has prepared the audience. "Shaman will decide what to do," she tells them. "It's up to you how long he stays in here. If you are quiet and respectful, you can get to know him. If he is frightened, he'll drag Kent back out of the room."

In this auditorium, full of Pueblo Indian children of all ages, the students have a good sense of what it means to be quiet. The wolf brushes by a group of adolescent boys. They look at each other in obvious delight. The wolf returns to them, and they run their hands through his fur. Then they smell their hands—wolf smell. Shaman moves on to more children. More hands reach out to touch his luxuriant, miraculous coat. Like a wolverine's fur, Shaman's won't collect ice when he breathes against it in cold weather. The long outer guard hairs shed moisture and keep the dense underfur dry; by placing his muzzle and nose between his rear legs and wrapping his face in his tail, Shaman could sleep comfortably in the open at forty degrees below zero.

As the wolf moves about the room, some of the children look apprehensive. Wolves have forty-two teeth adapted to seize, tear, and crush. The incisors strip shreds of meat from bone. The upper premolar and a lower molar act like pruning shears to slice and snip through tough connective tissues and tendons. Wolves have tremendous upper-body strength, the better for bringing down large prey such as deer and elk. "Shaman is not a pet," Pamela has told this group again and again throughout the presentation. "Wolves and wolf hybrids do not make good pets."

A few of the children are upset by a movie they have just seen in which a wolf was shot by government trappers. One little girl frowns fiercely to keep from crying. The tendency to anthropomorphize animals makes sense when it comes to wolves. "Socially, we are a lot like wolves," Pam tells the children. "That's why dogs are our most popular pet, because they fit well into the human social structure." Wolves survive through group cooperation. The paramilitary description of a wolf pack, with its emphasis on dominance and hierarchy, is misleading. Wolves have complex and dynamic systems of interaction, family life, and entertainment. They sing. They celebrate. They love to play. In the wild, they romp with their pups and have games of tag. They hide behind bushes and jump out to scare each other. By necessity, they are alert and curious and intensely in the present. They remind us of how we must have been when we, too, hunted and gathered as a tribal society. For a child, the connection to wolves can be quite strong and personal. Naturally, children cry when they see wolves die.

Whatever their emotions—frightened, or sad, or delighted—by now everyone in the room is focused on Shaman. As the wolf follows his nose and interests, Pamela Brown throws out little comments. "Shaman is a ham," she says cheerfully to the school principal. "He knows how to work his audience." For a while Shaman goes under a table, threatening to bring down its cloth cover. Patiently, Kent Weber holds the leash. Shaman sniffs at a microphone. He stops beside a woman teacher.

"One of my favorite things about wolves," Pam says, "is that they are silent. They howl and they occasionally bark, but their vocalization is not as varied, say, as a coyote's. Wolves use body language instead. They use psychic communication. That's another thing that wolves have to teach us. You know almost everyone has had some kind of psychic experience. Usually, it's with your mother or your dog! Well, wolves use this special communication all the time, over many miles.

"Wolves are very timid," Pam reminds one boy who is giggling with a friend. "They are more scared of men than women. Most men are just too loud and scary and big. That's why wolves are rarely seen in the wild. Wolves are smart, too. They can't be trained to be a guard dog. At the first sign of trouble, they are the first to run!

"Like people, wolves have their own personalities," Pam turns to another child. "Shaman is here with you today because he is more sociable and passive than other wolves. I have to warn you about one thing, though. Shaman likes bubblegum. So be careful. Don't show him that you have any."

"Have you ever been bitten?" a girl asks.

"Oh, yeah," Pam says and rolls up her sleeve. "The only time I ever got bit was because of my own temper. People today have a lot of anger. But living with wolves has taught me to control my anger, to tone down my act. The wolf gave me plenty of warning. He growled and showed me that he didn't like what I was doing. I didn't pay enough attention. You can't have a big ego or try to throw your weight around with wolves. That doesn't work."

The children stare at the scar on Pam's forearm.

"Afterwards," Pam smiles, "that wolf would pull the bandage off my arm and gently lick the wound clean. We were always the best of friends."

At other school programs, and at shows for adults in churches and public halls, Pamela Brown and Kent Weber talk about wolves, bring in Shaman, show him off, and talk again after Shaman has returned to the van. The point being made is subtle. This is not a traveling zoo.

"What is happening to wolves," Pamela says, "is symbolic of what is happening to our environment. This program is about respect for all life. We are all connected in this world. Whatever happens to Brother or Sister Wolf will happen to us. We all have a place in the circle of nature."

Pam reminds her audience of America's early, pathological efforts to exterminate wolves. Today, Minnesota is the only state in the lower forty-eight that did not eradicate this species. Wisconsin is slowly and naturally being repopulated, as are Montana and Idaho. There are between 6,000 and 7,000 wolves in Alaska and as many as 50,000 in Canada. (In both areas, wolves are legally hunted and killed by helicopter and plane.) Italy may have 300 wolves and Poland has jumped to 1,000. No one knows what the population is worldwide.

Pamela Brown did not grow up in Canada or Alaska or in any place that had wolves. She grew up in the rural, northwest corner of New York. Although she spends a lot of time in schoolrooms now, she never liked school as a child and dropped out at the age of sixteen. She felt too confined. In the 1960s and 1970s, she lived in Manhattan, where she raised her daughter and worked in offices for lawyers and advertising agencies. "That," she says, "was a tremendous education!" By 1978, she was sharing a house in Connecticut with "other alternative people" and looking for something special to do with her life. One day, John Harris, who had been traveling about the country for nine years doing wolf education programs, came to visit with a wolf named Slick. There was an immediate rapport among the three of them: Pam, John, and Slick.

John Harris was raised in his family's wrecking yard in Hayward, California, where he rode with the Hell's Angels and became involved in the Native American movement. His work with wolves was eventually featured in national magazines and talk shows. John believed firmly that wolf education should not be entangled with politics, government grants, or big environmental organizations. He believed that teaching people about wolves required an unusual kind of commitment. It required a sense of freedom and honesty and directness. It had to be grassroots. It had to be uncorrupted. He and Pam were partners for seven years that included, in Pam's words, "thousands of programs, the political assassination of Slick, two trials, ongoing political harassment, and three more program wolves."

"You're the one," John Harris would say to Pamela Brown. "You're the one who can carry this on."

When John died in 1985, Pam moved to Santa Fe, New Mexico. At first, she carried on with a slide show instead of a wolf. Then she heard of a young man in Colorado who had inadvertently formed a wolf sanctuary; at that time, Mission Wolf had five wolves, abandoned by their owners, which Kent Weber kept in a two-acre enclosed pen. Kent wanted to get involved in wolf education. "If you're serious," Pam said sternly, "I'll book us a trip. But you'll need a van, and it'll have to have a strong cage in the back, and it'll have to be built a certain way, and it'll have to be dependable."

When Kent and his wife pulled up to Pam's house in four months, they had a van. An adult wolf named Lucas and a puppy called Shaman, as well as two big dogs, sat in the back.

For Pamela Brown, the future of the wolf lies in those hands that reach out to touch Shaman's fur. "I like teaching children," she says. "I like teenagers. I like wacky, off-the-wall people."

Traveling with a wolf also is a kick. "We modern humans are living at half-volume," Pam says. "We're in an apathetic, caged, domesticated state. But we can be turned up. When that wolf comes into the room, all the senses are alert. When you live around wolves, you get hooked on that kind of elevated state of consciousness. It's exhausting, of course. Because you also have to pay attention to people and to their interactions with the wolf. People have no sense of how to move or behave with a wild animal. I've seen parents walk up and offer their babies. This happens regularly!"

At least once a year, Pamela goes back east to family and friends. She takes her wolf program with her—the new video she helped produce or a documentary from the Canadian Film Board—traveling from upstate New York down to the Florida coastline. These shows are different from the ones she does in the West, where cowboys heckle her from the audience and ranchers try to stop her at the schoolroom door. In my own town of Silver City, when a representative from the New Mexico Livestock Association protested wolf education at a school board meeting, the superintendent promptly cancelled Pam's program. Later Pam herself cancelled all appearances in southern New Mexico because she feared for Shaman's life. Such things rarely happen in New York or Florida. Perhaps this is why Pam always returns to the West. The tension is here. The anger is here. The future will be decided here.

"I've done hundreds of shows in New Mexico and Arizona and Colorado and Texas," Pam says. "I don't mind when ranchers or other people try to intimidate me. That bounces right off. I keep in mind that I'm a grandmother. And my grandchildren will inherit this mess. I talk to my audience about personal responsibility. If you are going to let livestock loose on the public land, then you should do the job right. If sheep and cattle are guarded by herders or dogs, then depredations are rare.

"Wolf keeps us sharp. Wolf teaches us about the wisdom of natural selection. Without wolf, there's overpopulation of deer and rodents, overgrazing, and the eventual degradation of our grandchildren's land. For a long time now, humans have had this wonderful affair with the intellect. Now we have to get back into balance with nature. We have to restore some kind of harmony."

In the 1980s, it was Pam Brown who laid the groundwork for the struggle to reintroduce the most vulnerable of all wolf subspecies—the Mexican wolf. Wolves were never numerous in the Southwest; the historic carrying capacity of New Mexico was probably only about 1,500 animals. Under a vigorous predator control program, two southwestern subspecies quickly became extinct. In the United States, the last wild example of the third, *Canis lupus baileyi*, was killed in 1970—although a small population of *lobos* continued to exist in Mexico. In 1976, the Mexican wolf was listed under the Endangered Species Act, perhaps one of the most amazing pieces of legislation in the history of the world. The act mandates that an endangered species be not only protected but recovered as well. Accordingly, by 1980, six Mexican wolves were removed from the Sierra Madre of Mexico and placed in a breeding program. In 1982, the U.S. Fish and Wildlife Service, the agency in charge of conserving endangered species, approved the Mexican Wolf Recovery Plan. At that time, some fifty wolves were thought to remain in central Mexico, with a handful of animals in captivity.

The purpose of the recovery plan was to reestablish a viable, self-sustaining population of at least one hundred Mexican wolves within their historic range. That's what the report said. That's what the law said. That's what everyone, officially, said was going to happen.

In truth, when money to expand the breeding program was denied, the leader of the Mexican Wolf Recovery Team wrote to her colleagues: "As I understand it, limited FWS funds had to be committed to other projects because FWS sees no real hope for restoration of Mexican wolves anywhere in the wild."

Three years later, in 1986, the regional director of the Fish and Wildlife Service finally wrote game officials in Arizona, Texas, and New Mexico in search of a reintroduction site. Arizona noted blandly the problem of predation on livestock; Arizona had no sites to offer. Texas said that the Big Bend National Park and Guadalupe Mountains were suitable—although Texas had a law that made wolf reintroduction illegal. New Mexico suggested one site only, the White Sands Missile Range.

By now, most of the wild population of wolves in Mexico had been killed off, and there were less than thirty Mexican wolves in captive breeding pens.

A study of the four-thousand-square-mile missile range—essentially closed to public access and completely closed to cattle or sheep—was funded. The Fish and Wildlife Service assured the military that these endangered wolves would be an experimental population, legally killed if they wandered off the range or interfered with the defense of our country. Submitted in February 1988, the study concluded that the missile range could support some thirty-two Mexican wolves. Five months before that, however, the general at White Sands had already made up his mind. The decision against reintroduction probably was based on the military's reluctance to annoy the state's ranching community.

The regional director of the Fish and Wildlife Service issued this statement: "We have no sites. The wolf reintroduction program, as of now, is terminated."

Carol Martingdale was an anthropology student at the University of New Mexico. Years ago, she had run a farm of one hundred hogs and sixty goats in southern California. She had learned to live with predators and to respect them. Carol's premise is simple. "Wolves have a right to be here too." When she read that the Mexican wolf had been bureaucratically dumped, left to slowly die out in zoos and breeding pens—another extinction, another sputtered flame—she was shocked. She had one friend with a computer and one who did artwork. She spent a day tacking up fliers around the UNM campus. They were not radical. "Write to your congressman," Carol urged. "Help save the *lobo*."

Sue Larson, a local veterinarian, saw the flier. As a child, Sue had been horrified by road kills; long car drives with her parents were inordinately depressing. In veterinary school, she was called a "humaniatic" by other students, many of whom came from ranching backgrounds and saw animals in a more utilitarian light. Sue deprecates her emotional bond with other species, as she has been taught to do. "I know it sounds corny," she confesses and mimics a smarmy tone. "I became a vet because I *really liked* animals." When Sue speaks of wolves, however, she makes a point of being unsentimental. Wolves *will* start eating their prey before it is properly dead. Wounded or vulnerable wolves may be killed by their own pack. Parent wolves eat puppies that act diseased or strange.

"You have to have some romance about wolves to get involved in reintroduction," Sue concedes. "But on a practical level, you can't afford it."

Sue took a flier home and contacted Carol. So did others. Surprisingly soon, the Mexican Wolf Coalition held its first meeting. It was, by all accounts, an odd mix. There were biocentrics and anthropocentrics. There were representatives from Greenpeace and from the federal government, from the Audubon Society and from Earth First! For the next three years, this citizen's action group worked together to marshal public support for the Mexican wolf. Many of these people had seen Pam Brown's program. They all built on what she had done. In New Mexico, they confirmed what other national polls already showed: overwhelmingly, most Americans like the idea of wild wolves. At basketball games and meetings, using Sierra Club and Audubon mailing lists, the coalition passed around a petition. Do you want the *lobo* back? Some twenty-two thousand New Mexicans said yes.

Yes.

That was nice, but it wasn't really news. It didn't light a fire under the Fish and Wildlife Service. It didn't impress the Defense Department at all.

Lori Fish (who has asked that her real name not be used) and Dan Moore belonged to the Mexican Wolf Coalition. They also had ties to Earth First! They were then in their twenties, younger than most of the other coalition members. Longtime colleagues, they saw themselves as warriors—warriors and clowns. They are, today, in an awkward position. Their lives stretch ahead, middle-class Anglo-American lives, a road to success that is straight and paved and almost without speed limit. Their lives are full of opportunities and choices. Yet both Lori and Dan feel that almost anything they might choose would be a form of betrayal. They see...how consumerism and overpopulation drive the consumption of natural resources. They see the train wreck. They stand at a street corner and look around at the cacophony of metal and plastic and energy use, and they suddenly think, "Wow. How can we keep this up? How can we sustain this? *This is crazy.*"

The generation that came of age in the 1960s saw a flawed culture and tried, optimistically, to change that culture. The generation that came of age in the 1980s saw a flawed species, the entire human race out of control. How do you change that?

From such insight, Lori Fish and Dan Moore make the kind of decisions that Steve Johnson made twenty years ago, when decisions were easier. Will Lori have children? She says no. Will Dan? He talks in circles. (In part, he is being polite; he is, after all, talking to me—a mother.) Do they use a car? Lori lives on a piece of land that has no running water or electricity or telephone in a remote county where the population averages one person per square mile. She owns a car so that she can go to meetings like those held by the Mexican Wolf Coalition. Dan lives in Albuquerque and rides his bicycle. How do they make a living? Lori shrugs. She doesn't need much money. Dan has an odd assortment of part-time jobs, none of which completely please him. He mutters. What is right livelihood? What is right action?

How do they decide, I wonder, when to buy a new pair of shoes? How old must shoes get before they can be thrown away? What consumer pleasures are allowed? Can they eat at McDonald's? Can they go to a movie? (The cost of the most popular movie playing now would probably be enough to reintroduce the Mexican wolf and run the program—at about $400,000 a year—well into the twenty-first century. In America, the cost of reintroduction is something of a red herring.)

"All these diversions and temptations," Dan sighs. He is not completely serious. He is an intelligent, funny guy who finds refuge in self-mockery. "And the positive reinforcement is always in the wrong direction! It's a struggle to keep doing the right thing, to keep from being sucked back into the wrong thing."

"You gotta keep fighting," Lori says. "If you don't keep fighting, it'll just get worse. You gotta fight. And you gotta have a sense of humor."

At the beginning of 1990, both Dan and Lori believed that the Mexican Wolf Coalition was seriously lacking in these two qualities—in gumption and in humor. The conservative element in the coalition seemed to be in control, and the Mexican wolf was not much better off as a result. Dan and Lori were told to "wait, just wait." They were told that the general at White Sands was about to retire, that there were competing environmental agendas, that deals were being made behind the scenes. Defenders of Wildlife started its compensation fund for ranchers; the money would be paid directly to livestock owners suffering losses from reintroduced wolves. Everywhere, wolf advocates were trying hard to be reasonable. It was the Sir Galahad complex.

Lori went north to Montana to talk with the more radical Wolf Action Group. Dan went to Santa Fe to talk with Pamela Brown. They both came back feeling righteously litigious. In that mood, they decided to sue the secretary of the interior and the secretary of defense for failure to enforce the Endangered Species Act. (Under the act, all federal agencies are required to cooperate in carrying out endangered species programs.) They would force the government to support its own policy. They would take action because "We are the only ones with enough balls or, in my case, enough ovaries to go for it," said Lori Fish. "It's an example of grassroots volunteers leading the way."

Not everyone felt so ballsy. At a meeting of the Mexican Wolf Coalition, an environmental lawyer gave them the worst-case scenario. If they pursued this suit and lost, they might damage—even ruin!—the Endangered Species Act. It was a dangerous precedent. The Mexican Wolf Coalition got nervous. Dan and Lori got mad.

"What good is a law if you can't use it?" Lori asks. "If we can't enforce the Endangered Species Act, then we've already lost it."

On their own, Dan and Lori hired another lawyer and, with his help, got the Sierra Club, Environmental Defense Fund, National Audubon Society, and Wilderness Society involved. In the end, all these organizations, as well as the Mexican Wolf Coalition, joined the lawsuit. (The president of the coalition resigned.) Dan Moore and his friends took the petitions with their twenty-two thousand signatures and strung them on a ribbon thirty yards long. They presented this to the regional director of the Fish and Wildlife Service. It was a photo opportunity. It was a gift to newspaper writers who could employ puns such as "Wolf Advocates Howl in Protest!"

Later that summer, Dan, Lori, and forty other demonstrators literally howled in front of the downtown federal building in Albuquerque, throwing their heads back and cupping hands around their mouths for the sake of projection. (It is an absorbing fact that humans can mimic the sound of howling wolves enough so that wolves respond with curiosity and interest. Some hunters use this method to lure wolves to their deaths.) Lori Fish dressed as a black-robed judge, for the federal agencies at that time were trying to have the lawsuit dismissed by a U.S. district court. "Tell it to the judge!" the crowd kept chanting. "Out of the zoo in '92!"

The media loved it. "You don't have to be very outrageous in this society to be outrageous," Lori notes. "A few wolf howls. It doesn't mean much politically. But it keeps our spirits up."

Publicity, headlines, anger, wolf howls—a lawsuit! The Fish and Wildlife Service began to backpedal, and the Defense Department too cried out that they were, by gosh, they *were* considering wolf reintroduction at White Sands. The Endangered Species Act was being held up like a golden shield, a chalice, the grail itself—and the magic was working. The best case scenario was coming down the pipe.

During the time, Pamela Brown spent a day with the schoolchildren at the White Sands Missile Range. Not one was aware of the Mexican Wolf Recovery Program.

By 1992, Mexican wolves were not out of the zoo. But, as everyone agrees now, the lawsuit had been successful. Tumultuous public meetings were held ("I thought I was at a rodeo," Dan remembers), and the Fish and Wildlife Service began preparing an environmental impact statement for reintroduction of the Mexican wolf in the Southwest. Arizona found four sites to evaluate. Texas began studying Big Bend National Park. In 1993, environmental organizations agreed to dismiss the lawsuit if the government continued forward with the process of reintroduction.

Suddenly, however, breeding was the problem. There weren't enough new litters to increase the captive wolf population, and biologists wanted a pool of seventy-five to one hundred wolves before they would let any loose. Today, the release of an experimental group of Mexican wolves, either at White Sands or in the Blue Range of eastern Arizona, is not expected until at least 1995. Even that will not happen if more funds are not made available.

Carol Martingdale and Sue Larson and Lori Fish and Dan Moore are watching. They want to see the end of the race. They are also ready to pursue other interests. Carol is concerned with Native American rights; she talks about human diversity. "Why do we all have to be alike?" she wonders. "Bo-ring!" Like Steve MacDonald, Lori Fish is promoting land health in the national forests that make up her own backyard. Sue Larson would like to help other endangered species, less glamorous ones perhaps. Dan Moore now works with the Citizens for Alternatives to Radioactive Dumping; he is also a paralegal for two women lawyers who take on cases in police abuse, prison rights violations, and sexual harassment.

I ask them, each one, why they have fought so hard to help reintroduce the Mexican wolf. As they well know, there are many, perhaps more important environmental causes. The wolf, after all, is not an endangered species worldwide. And the Mexican wolf, although truly endangered, is only a subspecies. More subtly, the recovery plan for the Mexican wolf is extremely high tech. It is frankly repugnant. Before the animals are let loose, radioactive disks will be surgically placed in their stomachs so that orbiting satellites can track their scat. The released wolves will then be radio-collared, monitored, and controlled—that is, killed—if they misbehave. Any pups born in the wild also will be caught, measured, deparasitized, radio-collared, and fitted up with radioactive dye. This is humanity at its busiest. This is the irony of space satellites beaming in on a single pack of wolves living a carefully managed "life in the wild" on a military missile range.

There are those who wonder if this is what the modern environmentalist should be doing.

Dan just looks at me. *Who is this woman?*

"Oh man, the big existential question," he sighs. "You don't want to ask anything hard, do you? Well..." he gathers steam, "the way I see it is that from 1987 on, we got a 911 emergency call. If we hadn't responded, nothing would have happened. The Mexican wolf would have simply gone off the face of the earth, after being here for thousands and thousands of years. The idea of saving a species, even a subspecies, may seem arrogant. But who else was going to do it?"

"Wolves represent something," Lori says. "They are social like humans, but they are also wild. *Wild.* I just spent five days in jail for protesting a ski resort in Colorado. I thought about wolves—and about jaguars—the whole time. We used to have wild jaguars in Arizona and New Mexico. I felt just like a trapped wolf or jaguar in its zoo or breeding pen. I've been arrested. We've all been arrested."

"There are lots of reasons why," Carol speaks briskly. "Wolves are mystical. I've heard that one, and I agree. But it's not something I say to ranchers. For some people, you know, wolf reintroduction is just an ego trip, something to shove down the throat of the livestock industry. For me, I like the idea of an entire ecosystem. Predators like wolves belong in the Southwest."

"If we can be successful with the Mexican wolf," Sue Larson says, "with a species that we strove so hard to eradicate, then maybe we have a chance with other species. Maybe, too, we have a responsibility to make amends, to the species themselves, to *ourselves*. Maybe, ultimately, reintroducing the wolf is a selfish thing. Wolves are missing. It's a sadness to have them gone. We took a land of teeming wildlife and brought many animals to the point of extinction. *We have to do everything we can to reverse that trend.*"

"Lines are being drawn," Dan Moore agrees. "We can try and reinhabit the North American continent, repopulate some of its wildlife, change the way people travel and make their economy. Or we can have the total commoditization of everything. The dream or the nightmare."

As Lori says, wolves represent something.

This must come from the heart.

The Southwest would be a better place if thirty-two wolves lived at the White Sands Missile Range, killing deer and bearing pups in the pinon-juniper, oak and ponderosa pine forests of the San Andres and Oscuras mountains. The Southwest would be better still if forty more wolves hunted southeastern Arizona in the Galiuro and Pina-lenos, the Chiricahuas, and Atascosa mountains. The state of Texas would be improved if a pack of radio-collared *lobos* patterned Big Bend National Park with their scent markings and territorial signs. All Americans would feel better if we could agree to share our public land with one hundred Mexican wolves, a fraction of the wildness that once was here.

Either you think so or you don't.

THE FEDS

||||||||||||||||||||||||||||||||

RICK BASS
FROM *The New Wolves*
(1998)

*F*irst there's the law, which says plain and simple that the Mexican wolf is an endangered species and must be recovered, if possible: the attempt must be made.

Beneath and below that law, however, lie all the various invisible realities of our culture: the substructure of politics. Never mind the law, nor the fact that 79 percent of New Mexico residents support wolf reintroduction, as do 61 percent of Arizona residents. Certain moneyed interests have contributed heavily to certain governors and senators and representatives, so that the law has been bent to call the wolves "nonessential" and "experimental," which in theory is supposed to make the 15 percent, or 20 percent, or 34 percent of people who oppose them, depending on where you're doing the polling, not hate the wolves, or the idea of wolves, quite so much.

It's an amazing aspect of our democracy: how the money of so few can purchase such sweeping power—and how the furious passions of so few can similarly influence the law based solely upon the power of their anger or fear or, in some instances, hatred.

These minorities cannot prevent the law—the constructed law—of man, nor the more ordered, flowing laws of nature, from occurring and proceeding. They can only forestall, and momentarily divert, these laws.

The feds get sued by the environmentalists for breaking the law of the land when they cut too much timber or graze too many cattle or withhold the wolves from recovery; but they get sued also by the timber companies and ranchers for breaking the law of money—this afternoon's money—when they don't cut enough timber or graze enough cattle, or when they attempt to recover the wolves. As such, the feds are always between a rock and a hard spot, and you can see their nerves fraying, their tempers thinning: the siege mentality setting in, so that they—BLM and U.S. Forest Service officials—fragment, for self-preservation's sake, and become quasi-military, with their shared uniforms and the feeling of being under constant barrage. And you can understand their frustration: their true employers are the hearts and minds of the American people—the democratic majority—while the reality is that the ones who do the hiring and firing—their artificial employers—are the moneyed interests of the corporate minorities.

The disparity between these two forces conspires to shred agency officials into further fragments, until they forget how to act naturally. They are like caged animals, looking back and forth from one vocal constituent to one moneyed constituent, and rarely these days do they have time or even authority to look at the forests, or the range, or the grizzlies, or the wolves themselves—much less the time or authority to look at the future or the past. Science in our government is becoming extinct, as it lingers trapped too long between those two savage forces.

It has always been this way, but it seems that more than ever the situation is becoming untenable.

Dennis and I are at a Mexican food restaurant in Albuquerque with a couple of Fish and Wildlife Service folks—Dave Parsons and Wendy Brown, lead coordinator and assistant, respectively, for the reintroduction project—who have come up here on a Sunday, their day off, to fill us in on the recovery process from their perspective and to answer questions. They've gone to great lengths to answer, in print, almost every possible question that could ever be asked about Mexican wolves—chief among them the unanswerable "Can they adapt from the zoo to the wild?" Only time can answer that one.

The red wolves that have been introduced from captivity to the Carolinas are now into their second and third generations of successful offspring, so it can be done, though anyone who would extrapolate from North Carolina to Arizona must prepare for the unexpected. Dave and Wendy are scientists, but our conversations seem to veer from the very beginning toward politics and, having established that course, seem unable to break out of it. Perhaps it is all my fault: perhaps when they asked me what I wanted to talk about, I should have asked them about paw widths and lengths. I should have asked them about the wild-conditioning pens planned for the Sevilleta National Wildlife Refuge in New Mexico, from which some of the wolves will be selected for release into the wild (electric fencing, chain-link fences, gates buried four feet deep that rise ten feet high with no gap larger than two inches, and so on, and on.)

But politics seems the order of the day: politics and margaritas. In a nutshell:

Texas is out as a reintroduction site because of the strong antiwolf politics.

White Sands has a lot of mountain lions, which might prey on the city-soft wolves, and also has less water than does the Blue Range.

Arizona—the Blue Range—isn't Yellowstone, but it's clearly the best site from a biological standpoint. There's some squabbling going on between the game and fish commissions of Arizona and New Mexico, despite their constituents' support of wolf reintroduction— the Arizona Game and Fish Commission passed a resolution support- ing wolf reintroduction in New Mexico, and the New Mexico Game and Fish Commission passed a resolution supporting wolf reintro- duction in Arizona. (Also slightly complicating things from a politi- cal perspective, the Blue Range crosses over into New Mexico.)

It reminds me exactly of the recently designated Grand Staircase/ Escalante National Monument in southern Utah, 1.8 million acres of public land that the Republican legislature of Utah was trying to grab for the purpose of an immense low-grade coal mine. Never mind that over 70 percent of Utahns, and Americans, wanted the land kept as it was—the Utah Republicans, elected by the big corporations, went after it anyway. President Clinton came in, ignored the Utah senators and representatives, listened directly to the will of the people, and created, or rather preserved, that red desert for America in perpetu- ity. (And in so doing, I fear, possibly let himself off the hook of criti- cism for his failure to permanently protect forested public roadless areas in the Northwest—but that is another matter not yet linked to Mexican wolves.)

I mention to Dave and Wendy my fear that the United States is convoluting, is undergoing some horrible metamorphosis wherein the western half of the country—containing the remaining bulk of our natural resources—is fragmenting, being leveraged into some awful, ailing kind of puppet state, like Chechnya or Afghanistan, in which the people's desires are ignored to serve the larger corporate mega- liths. I confess that my fear is that the majority of western governors have ridden corporate donations to their current positions of power, outspending their opponents on TV and radio by margins of three to one, five to one, even ten to one; that the western Republican governors are now acting to liquidate anything on public lands that's not nailed down; and that it's the public's duty to future generations, to nail down what we can, and to turn the thieves and plunderers back.

Strong talk, for a Sunday. I get the feeling that even on their off day, it's best if Dave and Wendy don't pursue this discussion. There's a bit of a silence, after which they ask me what it's like in northern Montana: meaning not the politics, but the countryside. *Biology*; we ease back into it.

Except that they do offer this: governors "come and go," and the volatility of such political repositioning makes the feds' job much harder.

I start to comment that all death throes have a certain spasticity to them, but decide I've been dire enough; they need encouragement, not discouragement. I try to think of something biological. But then Dave and Wendy mention politics again—that even though the Draft Environmental Impact Statement was finished in 1995, they suspect it won't be until after the November '96 elections that the Final EIS comes out (this turned out to be the case); and that if wolf support-ers are serious about recovery efforts, they'd better get their pens and paper out and send in some letters, because the opponents of wolf reintroduction, though small in number, have been busy at the typewriter.

The air force, for instance, has written, fearful that wolves will interfere with their airspace over the national forests in a manner "not unlike the restrictions the spotted owl has placed."

The army has written, the Apaches have written. The game and fish commissioners have written—all with one form of opposition or another—as have the governors.

Where are the wolf's advocates? The grand total of respondents, on both sides, has been a measly 17,374, including the Arizona Wool Producers Association, the New Mexico Wool Growers, and the Blue River Cowbelles.

Hell, the Lava Soil and Water Conservation District is even against reintroduction, which really chaps my britches. (Wrote the LSWCD, "Let's support the Mexican wolf—in the Albuquerque Zoo, where the wolf enthusiasts can visit him all the time." The feds' laconic, courteous response? "Thank you for your comment.")

Wendy explains that the public opinion polls and surveys are showing us what we already know in our guts—the invisible thing we can feel in the air—that the people who are against reintroduction feel frightened and disconnected and hence insecure and angry.

"They don't hate the wolf specifically," she says. "They just view it as one more example of the loss of control in their lives." You can blame part of this invisible unease on corporate restlessness in the days of monopolies and mergers. Or you can blame it on something more spiritual and pervasive—on a trauma to the soul of the land itself, and our disconnected, semi-electronic relationship to it. In many ways the opponents of wolves seem so much like the wolves themselves that it is wildly ironic: though their numbers are small, they seem to retain a core fierceness that cannot be ignored—nor would you want to, for fear is one of the most primal emotions of any place. It's never going to go entirely away—not in a wild, healthy ecosystem.

Dennis tells us a story about Jerry Scoville and his first night down in the desert. Jerry had driven down from his home outside Seattle—a day and a night on the road—and was whipped. He wasn't going to be able to make it all the way into the Blue that night. He was out on some forever-stretch of prairie, it was dusk, so he pulled over onto the shoulder and leaned his seat back and rubbed his sandy eyes, watched the lurid sunset, and fell deep asleep for the night.

Jerry says he woke shortly after midnight to the cold steel of a revolver stuck in his ear.

"Just what do you think you're doing here?" a voice demanded.

It was no time for smart-aleck answers, such as "Sleeping," or "Visiting Arizona—the Sunshine State," or even "Well, actually at this moment, shitting my britches."

The gist of that shadowy conversation was that the countryman believed that the Washington State license plates on Jerry's car indicated that it was from Washington, D.C.; that the countryman had caught a spy, an infidel from that foreign land, napping within his territory.

Jerry had to show him his driver's license, with the street name and the town—"Seattle, Washington"—to convince him he wasn't a fed.

Jerry says he left out the part about how he was a biology professor working to restore the Mexican wolf to its native habitat. He was allowed to continue on his way. He was allowed to live.

Sure, a lot of it's hype. This really happened, and there's nothing hyperbolic about a pistol stuck in your ear—that's flat-line reality— and yet, in the reporting of it, the press gravitates toward the detailing of these sorts of extremes rather than chronicling the much larger biomass, or story-mass, of the events and emotions in the middle.

And yet these extremes, such as the pistol-waving *paisano*, the Unabomber, or militiamen, do need reporting, in addition to the main story. These extremes have sociologic power beyond symbolism, and power beyond the establishment of a story's physical outer boundaries and parameters.

Again, these stories from the fringes are like the wolves themselves: perhaps there are only ten or twelve of them out there, or a hundred or two hundred, but in their compressed isolation they have achieved, it seems, some kind of core density—a power—a fire of sorts, which will either finally smolder and blink out, or explode, fragmenting that middle ground around it, and in so doing giving birth to new philosophies, new ways of being....

Which, in the manner of geology, will always only seem like a new story to the fresh observer; though they have all already been told from the very beginning. There are no new stories in nature, only new observers.

Even among the thirty thousand ranchers who hold permits to graze cattle on public lands, 21 percent, or sixty-two hundred of them, support wolf reintroduction.

The mainstream numbers hardly ever get reported: the fact that Catron County, New Mexico, for instance—deep in the shadow of the wolf recovery area and home of the vitriolic "Wise Use" movement, a corporate-sponsored facade of grassroots activism for "states' rights"—is comprised of almost 50 percent nonnatives, and that most of those immigrants are refugees from the suburbs of California. You won't read either that over 50 percent of the residents in the Catron County area support wolf reintroduction. The only stories that make the wire concerning Catron County are the ones like Jerry's, or the stories about the crazy piss-ant local politicians, nutty county commissioners trying to drum up reelection support by shooting at helicopters or preaching about the Red, or Pink, or Yellow, or Green Menace. You can find this in Catron County, New Mexico, or Nye County, Nevada, or Lincoln County, Montana. You can find a few disillusioned, angry, justifiably bitter individuals—brittle but momentarily powerful in their isolation—in the last summoning of their rage. If you're not careful, the momentary power of these lone or loosely connected responses can fool you into thinking that this is how things really are. These responses can mask the greater attributes of a community—the hidden, permanent well-springs of hope; the willingness to help anyone down on his luck; the members' great friendliness and loyalty among themselves. Tenderness, goodness, is as prevalent in these communities as anywhere else in the country, and more so.

In Alpine, Arizona, Dennis and I had one small incident, in the gas station. We were visiting with the store owner, talking about hunting, and when asked why we were there, we told him about our hopes for the wolves. We had the usual conversation, well tempered and respectful but passionate, about government interference, government regulation, and the United Nations—"You guys are all right," the owner conceded, "you'll at least *listen*"—but then something strange happened: the name *Bruce Babbit* was mentioned, and the man's demeanor changed as if thrown by a switch. All reason and, it seemed, humanity, left him—his face went stiff—and he replied coldly, barely able to speak, so great was his hatred, that "the only problem with Bruce Babbit is that he is alive." And that was the end of that conversation.

A well-dressed man in a suit and black cowboy hat who'd been standing in the back of the store behind us, listening—he did not appear to have ever done a day's worth of physical labor in his life—picked up an ax, swung it lightly in our direction a few times, nodded to the store owner, and walked out with it, still swinging it like a baseball bat and smiling. "Gonna split some *wood*," he said mysteriously.

And on our way to a camping spot that night—we passed our turn—we realized an old white truck was following us, for when we turned around to go back to our turnoff, it did too, though it didn't follow us down to our campsite and was, I think, only another invisible kind of scent marking, a sort of subtle harassment or wolflike territoriality.

But that was just that one little spike of an incident—that one little burr. We also saw the mainstream of friendliness.

On Dennis's and my swing through Catron County, in our shiny red rented sport-utility vehicle that identified us so clearly as outsiders, it seemed that all the county's residents—none of them knowing who we were or what we were there for, only that we were from the outside—went out of their way to wave to us as they passed on the road: as if consciously trying to represent themselves accurately as friendly, not mean; as if hurt by the image the outside world was forming of them. Ten or twelve trucks in a row went past one morning, each giving that wave across the steering wheel.

Without doubt, the communities are being stretched thin by this century's end, as are the wolves. Environmentalists in the next century are going to have to go both ways instead of just one: we will have to be both fiercer and more tolerant—a tough position, but one that the situation demands. We must adapt or fail. We must take care of the wolves and yet concern ourselves, too, with the rest of the system—the increasingly huge society of man, that immense biomass in the middle—without compromising our beliefs and values.

The societal stresses of human economic and cultural transition, and economic recoveries, are well documented. The wolves will have their own stresses. Parvo virus, canine distemper, infectious canine hepatitis, leptospirosis, rabies—all are in greater concentrations now, due to domestic dogs, than they were the last time the Mexican wolves were out and about, free and at large.

Mites, ticks, fleas, heartworm, tapeworm, hookworm; any of a thousand stresses could accumulate upon them, here at century's end, to be one stress too many, and the wolves could disappear, could blink out. They could hybridize with coyotes, rather than killing the coyotes, and disappear in that manner—again, blinking out—for a few millennia.

Or they could find root-cracks of survivability and explode with dramatic success into the next century, the next cycle.

EL LOBO'S HOMECOMING

||||||||||||||||||||||||||||||||||||||||||||||||||||||||||||||||||||||||||||||||||||||||

JOAN MOODY
(1998)

*S*now lay two feet deep among the tall ponderosa pines of eastern Arizona's Blue Range Mountains. It was January 26, and dignitaries, reporters and interested citizens were gathered in the Apache National Forest to witness history being made—the return of Mexican wolves to an ancestral home from which their kind had been absent for more than a quarter of a century.

Quietly, the onlookers stood near a chainlink fence enclosing a third of an acre of woods close to the Campbell Blue River and the Arizona–New Mexico border. They watched as a dozen people led by Secretary of the Interior Bruce Babbitt carefully carried three shiny metal crates toward the pen, only the crunch of their boots and the clicking of cameras breaking the silence.

Shortly, Secretary Babbitt raised a sliding door on one of the crates. A few seconds later a tawny female wolf pup—Number 511 to biologists of the U.S. Fish and Wildlife Service (FWS)—burst out and bounded excitedly about the holding pen. Her mother soon joined her. Her warier father did not follow suit until later—after the spectators had left. But mother and daughter were enough. El Lobo was home on Arizona soil again.

This three-wolf family was the vanguard of 11 Mexican wolves brought by early February to planned release sites in the Apache Forest. The three wolves came from Sevilleta National Wildlife Refuge in New Mexico, a breeding facility where the young female had been born.

As of last January, only 175 Mexican wolves were known to exist, all born in captivity at one of 32 zoos and wildlife facilities in the United States and Mexico. A comparatively small subspecies of gray wolf, El Lobo (*Canis lupus baileyi*) is recovering thanks to a captive-breeding program that started 20 years ago with the capture of wolves in Mexico. Only five wolves were found then—the only known wild wolves west of Minnesota and south of Canada except for occasional transients crossing the Canadian border and a British

Columbia pack that started ranging into north-western Montana in the late 1970s to launch the recolonization that has since proceeded apace there.

"We are bringing back a species from the brink of extinction," declared Jamie Rappaport Clark, Fish and Wildlife Service director, as she joined Secretary Babbitt in helping to carry the first wolf crate into the holding pen. Unlike the wild Canadian gray wolves reintroduced in Yellowstone National Park starting in 1995, Number 511 and her parents face the challenge of learning to live in the wild for the first time. Nevertheless, they represent great hope for the future of their species.

The wolf bearers carried that hope with the crates—and symbolized a changing attitude toward predators in this generation. They included citizen environmental leaders and officials from state and federal agencies who noted before the reintroduction ceremony that although the government is now trying to bring the wolf back, it once established and paid for the very predator-control program that extirpated El Lobo from its age-old habitat.

Rancher Will Holder remarked that he was particularly glad to help carry the wolves because his grandfather participated in killing what some called the last wild wolf in Arizona. "Our family has started thinking about how we affect the environment since the wolves were removed," said Holder, a fourth-generation rancher.

Perhaps the most symbolic wolf carrier was Trish Stevenson, granddaughter of celebrated conservationist Aldo Leopold who, in his 1949 classic, *A Sand County Almanac*, described his personal epiphany as he watched the death of a wolf he shot in this same area almost 90 years ago. "We reached the wolf in time to watch a fierce green fire dying in her eyes," Leopold wrote in his now famous essay "Thinking Like a Mountain." "I realized then, and have known ever since, that there was something new to me in those eyes—something known only to her and the mountain. I was very young then and full of trigger itch; I thought that because fewer wolves meant more deer, that no wolves would mean hunters' paradise. But after seeing the green fire die, I sensed that neither the wolf nor the mountain agreed with such a view."

The wolf's death helped ultimately to transform Leopold's thinking, prompting him to abandon earlier beliefs and to develop a new philosophy of land and wildlife conservation. In the process, he changed from wolf hunter to wolf defender as well as an eloquent defender of all the values of wilderness.

"The Apache National Forest always held a special place in Leopold's heart," his granddaughter said. "It was the land of his first job, where he fully learned what wild country was and where the binding power between landscape and mind became an irrepressible factor in his life. The mountain and the wolf showed him something new, that the Earth is here not only for the use of people, but also that the Earth is a whole organism and richer for every cog and wheel that is part of it. The wolf reintroduction program is part of rebuilding the organism. My family is extremely proud to be part of this program today.... Thanks for returning the 'green fire' to the mountain."

"The reintroduction of wolves is history in the making," said Defenders of Wildlife President Rodger Schlickeisen after helping to carry a crate. "It's cultural history as well as conservation history. After centuries of trying to exterminate the wolf and nearly succeeding, this country in the past three years has made a remarkable turnaround. It's a sign that our society can learn from its mistakes. Saving every endangered species is important, but the wolf is special because it is a leading symbol of wild nature."

Bobbie Holaday, executive director of Preserve Arizona's Wolves, who has worked for many years to bring back the Mexican wolf, summed up the feelings of participants: "You couldn't put a price on the moment those wolves came out of those crates."

Secretary Babbitt thanked both Preserve Arizona's Wolves and Defenders of Wildlife for leadership in efforts to reintroduce wolves. "Government can't do all of this by itself," he said. "We owe a very large measure of gratitude to those who have so strongly backed the Mexican gray wolf effort in so many important ways. To borrow a phrase from John F. Kennedy, success does have a hundred fathers, and that is almost always the case in the American conservation movement."

Eight additional wolves were brought to other sites in the Apache Forest within days of the January 26 release. On January 29 FWS put a second pair from Sevilleta in a holding pen at Turkey Creek. On February 4 biologists brought a family of six wolves, including two young females and two young males, from Wolf Haven International near Olympia, Washington, to a site called Hawks Nest. Biologists hope the wolf pairs at the three sites will mate successfully and raise pups in the wild.

Despite their arrival from the West Coast during a heavy snowstorm, the Washington wolves seemed to adapt readily to their new Arizona home. Dave Parsons, FWS Mexican wolf recovery leader, reported on the Hawks Nest family's first day that "the wolves are reacting just fine. They've already begun establishing trails and feeding on deer and elk carcasses." The three groups of wolves were expected to remain in their pens for six to ten weeks under the constant watch of wolf guardians—experienced biologists and other professionals who set out road-killed deer and elk carcasses for the wolves and who will decide when they are ready for release. Three guardians—Kevin McHugh, Cadie Pruss and Dan Stark—work for Defenders of Wildlife.

So far, the guardians report that all is well with the wolves. McHugh observed in his journal: "I have heard the wolves howl. The Campbell Blue gang likes to howl about midnight. I always jump out of my bedroll and run outside. I stand there in my union suit, in the snow, and listen. Campbell Blue is the perfect natural amphitheater. It is in a deep valley, and the valley floor is clear and open. The howls roll down the valley and echo off the surrounding hillsides and reverberate; they sound almost amplified in the nighttime."

After release, the wolves will be able to roam through not only the Apache Forest but also the adjoining Gila National Forest in New Mexico, both ideal habitat with a generous supply of deer, elk and other prey. The Gila Wilderness, established at Aldo Leopold's instigation and the first in the nation, and the Aldo Leopold Wilderness named in his honor are both in the 7,000-square-mile Blue Range Wolf Recovery Area, twice the size of Yellowstone National Park.

The goal of the reintroduction plan is a self-sustaining wild population of at least 100 Mexican wolves by year 2006. Additional wolves might be released in the Army's White Sands Missile Range in New Mexico. Defenders Southwest Representative Craig Miller is working with Texas and Mexican officials and citizen groups to lay the groundwork for further reintroduction in historic wolf range.

The Turner Endangered Species Fund recently built a wolf management facility on media mogul Ted Turner's Ladder Ranch near Truth or Consequences, New Mexico, where wolves arrived last December. "The Turner fund is fortunate to have the expertise of Mike Phillips, who coordinated Yellowstone wolf reintroduction for the National Park Service and red wolf reintroduction for the Fish and Wildlife Service," Miller says. "Eventually, Ladder Ranch wolves are expected to be released in Apache or at White Sands if that area is used. The degree of cooperation among private, state, federal and international wolf supporters is very encouraging."

Released wolves will be managed as a "nonessential, experimental" population, a designation that gives agencies management flexibility that in other areas has lead to lower human-caused wolf mortality. Wolves that prey on livestock can be removed. As it has been doing in the northern Rockies, Defenders of Wildlife will reimburse southwestern ranchers at fair market value for any livestock lost to wolves. Such losses are expected to be relatively small because wolves prefer to prey on wild ungulates such as elk and deer. FWS predicts livestock losses under a worst-case scenario at only a fifth of one percent. Defenders maintains a $100,000 Wolf Compensation Trust from which the reimbursements are paid. Since 1987, total expenditures in the northern Rockies have come to only $58,934 to 56 ranchers for 268 livestock.

"As ranchers see that losses of livestock are nowhere near as high as they feared and that we will put our money where our mouth is, acceptance of the program will increase," Miller predicts. In addition, Will and Jan Holder and other ranchers are working with Defenders on a program to encourage acceptance of wolves by helping ranchers who manage their land in a predator-friendly way to certify their beef as Wolf Country Beef. In some markets this designation will give the meat a competitive advantage.

The Mexican wolf program is the third wolf reintroduction effort in the United States. Seventy-one captive-bred red wolves, a southeastern species that also had been extirpated in the wild, were released in northeastern North Carolina starting in 1987, and 37 were released in Great Smoky Mountains National Park in eastern Tennessee beginning in 1991. Sixty-six gray wolves were reintroduced in Yellowstone National Park and central Idaho in 1995 and 1996, the beginning of packs that now total some 160.

"This is a triumph of the Endangered Species Act, the landmark conservation law through which Americans, as stewards, protect and restore the whole of God's creation," said Secretary Babbitt.

ROAD TRIP WITH
MEXICAN WOLVES

||||||||||||||||||||||||||||||||||||||||||||||||||||||||||||||||||||||||

JANE SUSAN MacCARTER
(1998)

*(The opinions expressed in this essay are those of the author and
do not reflect the views or policies of her employer, the New
Mexico Department of Game and Fish.)*

orty-mile-an-hour winds buffeted the truck as we headed west.
Dirt blew, and the truck yawed. I pulled the steering wheel to
the right as I fought to keep the truck on the road. Careful, I
thought, I *must* be careful...carrying such precious cargo.

It was 30 minutes since I'd seen another vehicle on this lonely
highway. Deliberately I unclenched my hands from the steering wheel,
repositioned them carefully, and took a deep breath. My passenger,
Susan Arritt, seemed lost in her own thoughts, so I was forced to
examine my own. What was I doing here anyway with a "payload"
of Mexican wolves, snugly tucked away in the camper shell?

I was being consciously *careful*, that's what...and being grateful
for the privilege of playing a role (albeit a small one) in the reintroduction of the Mexican wolf into the wild.

Just seven hours earlier, Susan and I first observed our wolves,
part of a group of five, at the Living Desert Zoo and Gardens State
Park in Carlsbad. Today, we would transport two of these wolves to
new temporary homes at the Ladder Ranch, where individual third-
to half-acre wolf enclosures awaited them. Just completed in December 1997, the wolf pens are a joint project of the Turner Endangered
Species Fund and the U.S. Fish and Wildlife Service. The pens are
located at the Ladder Ranch, one of Ted Turner's southern New Mexico properties. For an indefinite period of time, the facility will serve
as holding pens for five pairs of Mexican wolves. The U.S. Fish and
Wildlife Service will then evaluate them for their suitability as release
candidates into the Blue Mountains of Arizona.

At Living Desert Zoo and Gardens State Park, park biologist Mark Rosacker gave us the scoop on the lupine cargo we were to carry.

"You'll be transporting wolves 183 and 184," Mark explained. "The number designations represent individual animals, separately listed and held in U.S. and Mexican captive breeding facilities. The animals are part of a cooperative program between the U.S. Fish and Wildlife Service and the American Zoo and Aquarium Association's Mexican Wolf Species Survival Plan. Wolves like these two, which are currently being considered as possible release candidates are animals which may be considered 'genetically redundant.' That means their genetic potential is already well represented within the captive population by animals in other breeding facilities. If 183 and 184 are released into the wild and happen to die before reproducing, their genes will not be lost forever. Wolves 183 and 184 already have what essentially amounts to genetic duplicates in captivity and thus are potentially eligible for release into the wild."

Mark, Susan and I went to look at the wolves through the chain-link fence. The distinctive color marking on their backs put me in mind of blonde ponies fitted with black saddle blankets, topped by silvery-gray English saddles, stirrups and all. Odd markings but definitely handsome.

Mark enlightened us about our wolves. "They're all 3-year-old, full-grown adults who just happen to be brothers—Alpha, Beta, and Gamma."

Enough watching. Time to get on with the business at hand. Mark and a crew of five assistants began herding the wolves into the indoor holding pens so a veterinarian could process them for the trip.

Susan and I joined the team in the wolf service area, along with contract zoo veterinarian Mark Heinrich, the processing crew and wolf 184: Gamma. In the holding pen, Dr. Heinrich gave Gamma a mild tranquilizer injection. "He's still awake and aware but mildly buzzed—like he's had a bit too much to drink. We don't feed them the night before, just in case. Don't want them vomiting from fear and aspirating food particles into their lungs."

Once a Nye tourniquet had been slipped on and tightened about the wolf's muzzle (like a heavy-duty bolo tie), the team lifted wolf 184 onto a sling on an examining table and began working over him.

"Weight 64 pounds...pulse 60...reverse teardrop-shaped scar below his right eye..." (*Such thick fur. Ash-blonde, reverse-frosted with black. I longed to touch it.*) "Respiration 30."

(*Riveting eyes…the color of pale, clear caramel—blinking and glittering at all the commotion…*)

"The less they've been around people, the more submissive they are when we restrain and process them," Mark Rosacker said as he worked, noticing my rapt expression. "They're always that way, even though they may be dominant over other wolves."

Dr. Heinrich drew blood and took a fecal sample from Gamma, while I found myself mesmerized by his huge feet. *Like a puppy's, all outsized in proportion to his body…*

"Temperature 104." Dr. Heinrich vaccinated Gamma against rabies, distemper, hepatitis, leptospirosis, para-influenza, corona virus and parvovirus.

Done. The team carried dead-weight Gamma, nose-tied and lightly sedated, out to his traveling crate, where the wolf was carefully nudged into place, nose-noose removed, door securely fastened, and burlap curtains unfurled over the small barred windows of the crate. Dr. Heinrich seemed satisfied with Gamma's condition. "Giving the wolves the best of care is the *least* we can do for them, I think…when you consider what humans have done to them for so long." I readily assented.

The next wolf was brought in: 185. Beta, second of the three brothers. He didn't know it yet (nor would he until later), but he was to be separated from his siblings and sent to a breeding facility outside of Seattle.

"There's blood on the tip of 185's penis," Dr. Heinrich said. "Could be any number of things—more likely a myoglobinurea from overexertion of the muscles as the wolves ran to avoid capture. It often happens this way. I'll give him a prophylactic antibiotic injection, just in case."

Wolf 185: done. Beta was whisked away in an air kennel, eventually headed for Seattle.

And then came Alpha, wolf 183, bound for the Ladder Ranch—dominant wolf of the three lupine brothers.

"Alpha is the perfect candidate for survival in the wild," Mark Rosacker said with pardonable pride. "Feisty, dominant and strong."

Although he was slightly smaller than Gamma and Beta, Alpha—'Alf'—was more alert than the other wolves, more angry and seemingly affronted. "Weight 62, temperature 105…"

Then Susan asked the veterinarian, "May we touch him?" I was instantly disgusted with myself for not having the courage to ask on my own but silently blessed her for asking.

"Of course," Dr. Heinrich replied. "It would be best on his ruff, though, or on his back—not on his face." Susan and I carefully sank our fingers into the thick, black-tipped fur.

Ahhh. Soft…radiating heat.

Reluctantly, we stepped back from the wolf's warm body. Dr. Heinrich continued his work and assured us that the wolves' initially high temperature readings would soon fall to normal levels, once the mild tranquilizer kicked in.

"This guy could be hypoglycemic from not being fed yesterday, plus all that running around. Again, blood on the tip of the penis. I'm not surprised. He's pretty upset. We'll do an antibiotic, just in case, and put some sugar in his drinking water in the crate. Ask the people at the Ladder Ranch to feed this one immediately."

Then Alpha was done, loaded in his crate. Both wolf crates were stowed in the back of my pickup, out of public view within the camper shell. I opened the windows of the camper shell to make sure the wolves had air. The day was cool, the wind still blowing furiously.

Because of the near gale, we were advised to cut across west Texas to El Paso and avoid the winding mountain roads to the north: a trip of about six hours.

"Check on the wolves every hour or so," Dr. Heinrich urged. "Just peep at them quietly to make sure they're okay. Here's my work and home numbers if you need me." I thought about flat tires, engine trouble, wolf medical crises and other unmentionables and prayed to be equal to the task.

We gave the crated wolves one last peek. Both animals lay on beds of wood shavings, awake and aware but motionless. Coffee cans, wired inside the crates, were filled and ready with water and (in Alpha's case) sugar water.

At least they're not panting or heaving, I thought. Secretly loathe to leave the safety of Living Desert, I could delay the inevitable no longer. *Move it, MacCarter. What are you waiting for?* And off we went.

Here we are now, Susan and I…with Alpha and Gamma, the Mexican wolf brothers…heading across middle-of-nowhere west Texas. As fierce winds buffet the truck, clouds of granular white material drift across the hilly horizon and over the road. I'm guessing it's gypsum, the sacred salt of the Mescalero people, rising from a place still out of our sight.

The time for our first wolf check coincides with a place where the highway bisects a vast dry lake bed—the Mescalero Salt Flats, used since time out of mind for sacred rituals of the Mescalero people. Susan tells me that Mescalero educator and tribal leader Joey Padilla takes the young people of the tribe here each year from Mescalero, where he passes along the ancient rituals, songs and stories.

I stop the vehicle. Taking turns with each wolf. Susan and I lift the edges of the burlap curtains and peer cautiously in at Alpha and Gamma. Gamma is resting quietly, a fringe of wood chips rimming his lower jaw like a reverse mustache. Alpha is lying so still I know a moment's panic. Then he twitches his nose and blinks. *Still alive.*

A short distance from the truck, Susan and I each grasp a small handful of the sacred salt from the dry lake bed. Sprinkling tiny amounts of the material atop each crate, we anoint each wolf with our own personal blessing.

"Go well, be safe, run free!" We whisper baptisms of good wishes for the continuation of this species. Then we drive on, fighting a strong headwind all the way.

After an eternity, we re-enter New Mexico and head north on the interstate. At last, the Hillsboro exit looms out of the darkness *(Almost there)*. West we go in the night with a truckload of Mexican wolves *(Are two considered a truckload?)*. Under a brilliant moon and a billion stars, Susan and I are relieved to finally deliver our precious cargo *(Safe at last!)*.

The lights are on at the Ladder Ranch office where they've been waiting. Ranch manager Steve Dobrott and others stream out to greet us: "The wolves! They're here!" Our precious cargo is inspected. A-OK. The crates are immediately transferred to two ATVs, and Susan and I make sure dry kibbles are placed in Alpha's crate.

Then, *whisk*...wolves, ranch employees, and ATVs melt into the darkness as the animals are delivered to their pens. All night Gamma and Alpha will remain in their crates, burlap curtains still in place, facing the crate of their new mate. (Coming from other wolf-rearing facilities, two female wolves are slated to arrive at the ranch in a couple hours and will be similarly positioned.) Susan and I collapse in our beds in the guest quarters. Big day tomorrow.

Dawn breaks. Pinkish-blue sky. No wind or clouds. *Beautiful!* Susan and I meet with Steve and some 20 other individuals. Most are volunteers who helped build the pens—completely by hand, with almost no disturbance to the land—over the past three-and-a-half months. Today is a celebration for them, too, in appreciation for their extraordinary efforts.

Together we hike into the backcountry and finally arrive at the permanent observation blind from which we can view all five wolf pens spread out before us on the hillside. The 180-degree, up-slanted panorama of the pens puts me in mind of a Greek amphitheater.

As the group watches from the hillside, the wolves' caretaker, Matt Hartsough, and selected volunteers enter Pen 2, where two wolf crates face each other. Here Alpha has spent the night, positioned across from his new mate, Saguaro, who came from the Wild Canid Survival and Research Center in Missouri. Carefully, almost gingerly, Matt opens the door of Alf's crate.

Without hesitation, Alf springs free of the crate, trotting purposefully about the enclosure. Sniffing and pacing, poking and exploring, Alf appears to ignore the humans as he checks out his new home.

Then Matt opens the other crate, and a sprightly specimen of female wolf bounds out and away. Within seconds, the light gray female and Alf are nose to nose, sniffing briefly as tails wag. Alf has never seen nor smelled a female Mexican wolf since his birth. Now he has a new mate. I assume time and instinct will take care of Alf and Saguaro's nuptials.

Whether the strange new female rattles him or pleases him (probably both), Alf decides to urinate, then steps away. Saguaro sniffs his calling-card, then eagerly rolls in the urine puddle. Alf runs back to Saguaro, frisking and begging to play. *Love at first sight, I'd say...*

The gate is locked behind Alf and Saguaro, their new little world now their own. Matt and his crew move on to Pen 3, where Gamma and his new mate wait to be uncrated. Again, as before...Gamma and a large, light-colored female approach one another with cautious optimism...tails wag...they part to sniff and explore their new surroundings...then come together to frisk.

Steve confides to Susan and me, "You know, these wolves are *much* calmer than the first two pairs brought in last week. Those wolves seemed much more nervous—charging into the fence to test its strength, biting at it, running erratically and so forth. These wolves seem so mellow and blasé...as if they've lived here all their lives. I wonder why that is?

I catch Susan's eye. We're thinking the same thing: blessing the wolf crates with sacred Mescalero salt. I just *know* that's what did it.

Suddenly, the crowning glory: We hear the first howl of a wild Mexican wolf in these mountains in more years than almost anyone can remember. It's one of the wolves released the week before.

Howling to greet the four new arrivals, perhaps? Who knows—or cares. We're just thrilled to listen, entranced, as the young male wolf inclines his head and howls...long, and sweet, and slow. Again and again. Hair stands up on the back of my neck. *Perfect. Absolutely perfect.*

CAUGHT TWIXT BEASTS AND BUREAUCRATS: NEW RULES FROM A SOFTER SOCIETY, FAR REMOVED FROM THE LAND

|||||||||||||||||||||||||||||||||||||||||||||||||||||||||||||||||||||||||||||||||||||||||

J. ZANE WALLEY

(1998)

"Behold, I send you forth as sheep in the midst of wolves, be ye therefore wise as serpents, and harmless as doves," Jesus instructed the apostles as he sent them into the world with his word. He knew of the danger wolves presented, and metaphorically used their grim fame to instruct his disciples. American colonists and pioneers experienced the havoc of wolf attacks on humans and livestock and did their best to eliminate the plague.

In recent years, a softer society, far removed from the land, has unwittingly stood idle as nihilist wildlife devotees, championed by politically-correct appointees on federal regulatory boards, have succeeded in reintroducing the wolf scourge.

Wolves running free in America do have a hint of Jack London adventure, a particular seductiveness to the soul, and they are certainly handsome animals. These Disney-like fantasies abruptly evaporate in the physical actuality of a face-to-face attack. Such an attack happened—happened recently—not to woodsmen, or miners, nor cowboys, but to an average urban family on a camping trip. Luckily, they were able campers and defended themselves against the wolf assault. What they were not prepared for was the political aftermath. They found themselves caught between beast lovers and bureaucrats, amidst the wolves of politics.

Over a simple lunch, the Humphrey family falls into easy conversation. The two daughters talk their dad, Richard, into telling stories about his far-flung travels in Micronesia, Southeast Asia and the South Pacific. They love his stories for they are gentle, amusing stories of people he met, befriended, and endeavored to understand.

And Richard doesn't just spin yarns, he shares, and underlying each story is a kindly parable of people getting along with each other. He gently educates as he smiles and talks, and the girls cling to each of his words. They lean their heads against their mother, and Helen unconsciously and fondly strokes their hair, usually not speaking, for she is a lady of few but earnest words.

The Humphrey family and two dogs, Buck and Sam, live in suburban Tucson, Ariz., but it is clear their hearts aren't there. For years, every possible free moment has been spent in the desert and mountains of the West. They hunt, hike and camp often. Camp is like home, a large heavy-framed canvas tent with table, chairs, and a wood stove. It is a cozy, livable shelter that has often been a classroom for the young ladies.

Helen and Richard chose to home-school so even in the wilderness education goes on, with mom and dad as teachers and the wilds as mentor and laboratory.

Richard and his daughters were in the tent studying when the wolf attack began. Helen sweeps silver wings of long hair away from her face as she recounts the harrowing event. Tears flow freely. "Buck saved us and then God saved Buck. If Buck hadn't gotten between my daughters and the wolves, they would have attacked them."

Buck is the venerable family dog. He's a dappled-gray stalwart fellow, the best of breeds, an All-American mutt and treated as a valued member of the family. He sensed danger near the camp, went looking, and discovered two recently released Mexican wolves lurking close to the tent behind a thicket of undergrowth—too close for Buck's protective instincts. He found the wolves exactly where the younger daughter was getting ready to build a playhouse. As Buck confronted the wolves, Helen was several yards away from camp near a stream, reading. "I sensed something wrong, horribly wrong. It was as if a black dread swept over me. I began running toward the tent and screaming, 'Dick, come quick.'"

This camping trip was to be a celebration of Richard's retirement as a U.S. Postal Service letter carrier and the family's newfound freedom. Camp was set up late on a chill April evening, near a well-traveled tourist route, in a spot they had camped for the last 20 years. The following morning Richard was up early, sawing wood for the campfire and tent stove. "I felt something funny, like something was watching me," Richard remembers. "I looked around and saw what I thought at first was a dog. It was close, low to the ground and was stalking me. Then I saw it had a collar and a transmitter box. I assumed it was a hybrid wolf. I noticed a second one in the trees. I thought they had been released in a wilderness area far to the north, near Alpine."

He walked to the tent, woke the family, told them they had wolves in camp, and loaded his wife's rifle. They moved outside the tent and spotted the wolves 30 or 40 yards away. They yelled and made noise, which partially worked. The wolves backed off, but as Richard recalls, "They acted more like dogs than wildlife unaccustomed to humans." Later they heard howling which they assumed was about a half-mile away. "We didn't break camp and leave," Richard explains, "because we thought the wolves were just passing through."

After breakfast, Richard began the girls' lessons and Helen left to read. Almost an hour later, he heard his wife of 23 years screaming. "I stepped out of the tent and she told me to get the rifle." They could hear the sounds of Buck shrieking as he fought for his life with the wolves. Richard began yelling to run them off. One wolf detached from the fray and ran away, but, as Richard chillingly reminisces, "All of a sudden, a wolf came around a tree toward us, and not in a walk but in a run. That's when I shot. I was thinking how fast wolves could run and I couldn't let him get any closer."

Richard's shots stopped the wolf less than 50 feet away from his family. "I didn't have time to get scared. All I could think was, they release five or six at one time and I didn't know how many more were out there. When it was all over...then...I was so, so scared."

Buck staggered out of the undergrowth and came between Richard and Helen on three legs. "He's moving under his own power and not dragging his guts," Richard remembers thinking. Buck was seriously mauled with several deep gashes and a badly shattered front leg. Richard, an experienced hunter, made sure the wolf was dead. The Humphreys bandaged Buck's wounds with towels and rushed to find a veterinarian. They didn't take time to break camp and pack their gear: the family was too concerned about Buck's condition. They stopped at a state highway maintenance yard near their camp and notified a lady of the shooting. "She was shocked," Richard recalls. "She said they had a mule, didn't know that wolves had been released nearby and worried the wolves might attack her mule."

The lady had no telephone. Richard, a by-the-book sort of fellow, knew the mandatory 24-hour reporting period for killing endangered species, so as they drove toward a vet's office in Clifton-Morenci, Ariz., he used a construction worker's mobile phone to notify Arizona Game and Fish of the incident. The doctor was only at his office in Clifton-Morenci two days each week, so they had to drive 100 miles to Safford, Ariz. to get suitable medical attention for Buck. Before leaving Clifton they stopped at a store and borrowed a pencil from a clerk to write down the doctor's telephone number in Safford. They called his office to let him know that they were en route with a dog that had been injured by wolves. "The vet was ready for us," Richard says. "He said it was one of the worse cases he had ever attended."

They left Buck at the animal hospital in Safford and began the long trek back to their campsite. Stopping in Clifton-Morenci to return the borrowed pencil, they met an undercover U.S. Fish and Wildlife (FWS) officer filling a huge cooler with ice, presumably for the wolf cadaver. The investigator was in a rush to get to the scene before dark, so they followed him back to the campsite. When they arrived at camp, their agonizing ordeal began in earnest.

The wolf attack and Buck's brush with death had traumatized the family; even so, the investigator proceeded with his interrogation. "He was undercover so we agreed not to disclose his name," Richard says. "I invited him inside the tent to sit at the table and told my story. An agent from Arizona Fish and Game, John Romero, had arrived and stayed away from the tent as if he didn't want to hear it. I thought he might be on our side a little more than the federal agent so I called him over. He was very hesitant and took no notes."

For six drawn-out weeks the questions and interrogations continued by telephone and in person. The nameless agent and his supervisor even brought the investigation to the Humphrey home. The inquisitors had an unwelcome surprise waiting. Alarmed, Richard had an attorney present and a video camera set up to record the meeting. "I could tell they didn't like that! The supervisor played games with me; he played hard to trip me up," Richard earnestly declares. "They had questions and information from a biologist who obviously knew nothing. They were concerned about the way the bullet went in and weren't even sure if Buck had been attacked. I asked them if they had checked the dead wolf for dog bites. They had not even done that."

Likely the supervisor was making sure he covered his own tracks, for the shooting had developed into a media spectacle, a push and shove soapbox melodrama between environmental activists and the FWS. Richard had accidentally become a political pawn and scapegoat. Facing prison and financial ruin, he was painfully aware of his jeopardous position.

Environmentalist groups were enraged that FWS did not prosecute Humphrey, and they took their views public with the help of willing and often inaccurate media. Richard and his family watched helplessly as a sly leak in FWS released inflammatory, slanted information, and green activists convicted him in a kangaroo court frenzy of newspaper and television interviews. "REAL MEN DON'T KILL WOLVES" charged a bumper sticker printed and supplied to the public by Tucson-based, Wildlife Damage Group. "Federal Wildlife officials are lying and covering up the truth about the killing. The whole so-called official account of this is a lie. I don't believe any of it, not at all," spokesperson Nancy Zierenberg angrily stated to the Tucson Citizen.

"We've got to make an example of this guy," demanded Bobbie Holaday of Preserve Arizona's Wolves. "There is no excuse. It is totally illegal."

Before the facts in the shooting or even Humphrey's name were released, the Southwest Center for Biological Diversity (SWCBD) pressed a demand for indictment. In a series of interviews with the Tucson Citizen, their spokesman, Peter Galvin accused, "This whole thing has turned out to be a travesty. The fact they have failed to prosecute is just another indication that the U.S. government is not making wolf recovery a priority. We are now examining our legal options."

Galvin threatened to charge FWS with "dereliction of duty" because they did not charge the killer. He further indicated they might seek legal action against the shooter. SWCBD used their web site, and perhaps the FWS leak, to further polarize the public by reporting, "The U.S. Fish and Wildlife Service continues to investigate the killing. They apparently do not believe the shooter's story that the wolf attacked his dog. Even if the dog had been attacked, it would not legally or morally justify killing a severely endangered species. It is looking more and more like the killing was malicious, not just ignorant."

During the whole outrage, Humphrey maintained his silence. He sought the advice of confidante, G. J. Sagi, publisher of Outdoor News and an experienced publicist. Sagi had known Humphrey for years. "My mom was homebound and paralyzed because of a stroke," Sagi recalls. "She was in bad shape and dad had to stay with her constantly. They would go for days without seeing anyone except for their postman, Mr. Humphrey. He was concerned and would always drop in with a cheery word and check on them when he delivered the mail. I knew what kind of man I was helping."

Sagi and the Humphreys worked out a plan to counter the negative publicity and inaccurate articles. Humphrey wanted a chance to tell the true story. He and his family are deeply religious and felt a blight on their name would be intolerable. The antagonistic forces Humphrey was between had a lengthy chronicle of clashes. Environmental activists had virtually litigated the U.S. Department of the Interior into the March-April 1998 release, ignoring the objections of those citizens who would be affected. New Mexico Governor Gary E. Johnson vehemently opposed the release, bluntly saying it was based on an "absence of credible information and should not be endorsed by this office." The New Mexico Cattle Growers Association, along with eight other livestock organizations in New Mexico and Arizona, sued in late March 1998 against the release of the wolves. Scant days following the filing of the suit, wolves were covertly released with no public notice.

The vacationing Humphrey family had no hint of the release controversy's magnitude when they inadvertently became the focal point. They did not even know they were in a wolf release area. "It was late afternoon when we arrived and began setting up camp," Richard recounts. "There was nothing posted. I had heard about the release program, but all publicity indicated it was far to the north in a wilderness area."

They had no way of knowing that the release pens, where wolves were being fed road-kill twice per week by FWS, were not more than a mile from their camp. FWS had guaranteed in public meetings that "Notice of general wolf locations will be publicized." If they had followed through with their pledges to the public, the Humphreys' calamitous situation would not have occurred. "Had there been signs identifying the area as a wolf release site," Richard acknowledges, "we would have never camped there!"

After spending years and almost $3 million on the wolf release program, why would FWS release dangerous predators so close to civilization and a major highway without posting warnings? Why would they choose an area traveled by large numbers of tourists where camping was common? One reason is that FWS contends that wolves aren't dangerous. Their official line is, "There are no documented cases of wolves attacking and killing or severely injuring people in North America."

One wonders how much actual research went into that statement. Recently documented attacks by wolves on humans were available in several newspapers and in historical documents at the very time FWS made their doubtful statement. Conceivably, Mr. Humphrey was under criminal investigation for killing an animal technically not a wolf. The science behind the Mexican wolf release program is labeled as tainted by several biologists. They suggest FWS released genetically-flawed animals, which are not really wolves, but rather hybrids. The agency refutes the opposing reports by quoting their own science. If the animals that attacked the Humphrey family were wolf-dog hybrids, attacks on humans were likely and well documented. Even Wolf Park, staunch defender of wolves, circulates wolf-dog warnings. "A person, especially a child who tripped and fell, or who is moaning, crying, or screaming, may be considered wounded prey and attacked. Grave injuries, even death, are all too frequent in such cases."

In a current effort to ban wolf-dogs in Virginia, the Humane Society sent fact-sheets to Virginians urging them to contact their legislature to ban wolf-dogs. The literature portrays wolf-dogs as potential killers and claims attacks are disturbingly common. Six grinding, nervous weeks after the shooting, the nightmare was finally over for the father and husband who simply defended his family. He was informed no charges would be filed.

Richard now resolutely believes the wolf release is dangerous and wrong. He is humble, but serious, when he says, "We didn't have to go public, but wanted to tell people about our experience, and hope and pray it will prevent this from happening to others."

Helen, the lady of few but earnest words, is straightforward in expressing her feelings. "We feel that both the wolf and our family are victims. They put out a potentially dangerous animal—an animal that is not afraid of man, which was fed by man, and put too close to man. There were no warnings that wolves were in the area. The vets say our dog will never fully recover; and I'm just thankful it wasn't my children who were injured. The wolf did go after my husband, daughters, and me. My husband had no choice. He was protecting us. I hope that what happened to us never happens to anyone else."

STRIP MALL LOBOS

||||||||||||||||||||||||||||||||||||||||||||||||||||||||||||||

Alexander Parsons
(1998)

*D*riving through the jagged Organ Mountains and toward Alamogordo, New Mexico, I realize that the most specific picture of a Mexican wolf I can call to mind is the slavering, gray and red mascot of The Lobos, the University of New Mexico's basketball team. The logo, a wolf's profile with canines in sharp relief, bedecks the gleaming boards of the University's basketball court. The expression of the wolf—ferocity in motion—is what you'd expect for an image meant to link the team to an aggressive fierceness. Predatory animals are a favorite mascot for sports teams. We like what they represent and don't seem to feel anything contradictory about idealizing many animals we've historically maltreated. The Mexican wolf is no exception; the wildness and cunning we admire in them didn't prevent us from virtually exterminating the wolves in the American Southwest. This is why the four wolves I will see in Alamogordo are in a zoo, part of a tiny population just back from the edge of extinction.

Until this spring, the entire Mexican wolf population was held captive in zoos or sanctuaries in the U.S. and Mexico. Twenty-one years after it was declared an endangered species, and a decade-and-a-half after the move for reintroduction was instigated, *el lobo* has been released into the wilds. But it is unlikely that the debates, mail campaigns, studies, and lawsuits over the Mexican wolf's reintroduction will be brought to a close with this, although it's convenient to think that the wolf will return quietly to the wilds and we can check one species off the endangered list. More than likely, it will be shot at, harassed, and closely monitored by friend and enemy alike. For the wolf, freedom has conditions, but conditional freedom is better than being caged.

And so the Mexican wolf, both vilified and loved, is beginning to roam a small section of Arizona and New Mexico and the debate over its value and place in our world is raging on. For the debate over the wolf reintroduction has less to do with the wolf than it does with larger issues: what the wolf symbolizes, how we view our relationship to the land, and, most importantly, how we see ourselves.

I crest the Organ Mountains and descend toward the Tularosa Basin, entering the White Sands Missile Range. Replicas of Air Force Nike Hermes missiles jut from either side of Highway 70, marking the border of military territory. Past this, the land levels and soon the gypsum dunes of White Sands pass to my left. White Sands Missile Range is where the atomic age was inaugurated and is one of the largest military testing grounds in the U.S. The highway is often closed to traffic when missile tests are underway.

Alamogordo looks like a run-down Jetsons town, not a sanctuary for the endangered Mexican gray wolf. City streets, lined by one- and two-story, sunbleached buildings, have melted and run a little in the intense desert heat. The place has about it the impermanent air peculiar to western towns situated in physically hostile environments—as if a sudden relocation is still a possibility, perhaps being mulled over by members of the Chamber of Commerce.

In the middle of town, just off the main thoroughfare, I find the Alameda Park Zoo. It is located on a thin strip of land between the raised tracks of the Southern Pacific Railway and the highway. Lola, a Mexican gray wolf, and three of her daughters live here in a chainlink and cinderblock pen. I can imagine that the howls of these wolves echo over the Walgreen's Pharmacy parking lot that abuts the zoo.

The zoo's director, biologist Steve Diehl, lives across the road from the zoo. Steve is well muscled and moves in a restless, springy manner. He confirms that, in fact, the wolves do howl from time to time. Though unsure of the effect it has on shoppers new to town, he says: "When a wolf howls I can feel something in the brainstem, harkening back to when man was not at the top of the food chain. It's like listening to a ghost." By now we stand watching the wolves, having walked the length of the zoo. The wolves perk up at the sound of Steve's voice; he often feeds them. A train rocks past, the noise sudden and deafening, but the wolves and other animals have long since acclimated to this and I am the only one who is startled.

The wolves' pen is near the edge of the zoo, the chainlink section of it offering a tantalizing view of the emus across the walkway. I expected to see something other than the quiet animals before me. Mexican gray wolves average between sixty and ninety pounds; the cinnamon and browns in their fur make them look like very large coyotes or middling dogs, though they do have striking almond eyes that make it impossible to confuse them with dogs. Nonetheless, I'm underwhelmed; it's hard to believe that this animal has generated so much controversy.

It is only when I see one of the wolves rise and circle the enclosure at a slow run that I am struck by the difference between these animals and other canines. The wolf can *move*. It's not that it's fast (coyotes are faster) but that it has a smooth, flawless motion. Oversized paws flip up with each extension of the leg almost as a cyclist's foot does on a pedal, the legs in motion, the body level, the movement so efficient and easy that it looks like the wolf is gliding. A wolf can cover forty miles at a stretch and can range hundreds of miles in a few days. I can imagine what it must be like for such an animal to be confined to an enclosure not more than sixty feet wide. But here I catch myself. Such thinking anthropomorphizes the wolf, and anthropomorphization—seeing the wolf in human terms—has contributed to driving them toward extinction.

⁓

There is not much known about the Mexican gray wolf. While it once ranged through Mexico, Texas, Arizona and New Mexico, it was all but wiped out by ranchers and subsidized wolfers from the U.S. Biological Survey (USBS). Government records show that the last Mexican wolf in Arizona was shot in 1960, the last in New Mexico in 1976 (the same year it was declared an endangered species). The use of a particularly deadly poison in the U.S., Compound 1080, made the border between Mexico and the U.S. far more of a reality for wolves roaming from Mexico than it has ever been for illegal immigrants, and for a time the only population was in the isolated mountains of Durango, Mexico. There has been no documented sighting of a Mexican wolf in the wild since 1980—anywhere.

In the 19th century, buffalo hunters made money on the side by killing the wolves that proliferated in the wake of the slaughter of the herds by seeding buffalo carcasses or pieces of meat with strychnine. Wolf pelts fetched about a dollar. Joseph H. Batty writes in his book *How to Hunt and Trap* (1884), "It takes two bottles of strychnine to a buffalo, costing the hunter a dollar and a half....The hunter is almost sure of a few pelts, and is often richly rewarded. Seventy-eight wolves have been taken in Montana in a single night with one buffalo."

In the wake of the buffalo, wolves became an economic threat to the cattle industry because they hunted livestock. Wolves had learned the hard way not to scavenge meat or return to their own kills as these might be laced with strychnine; instead of feeding on a carcass for a few days, they would eat only meat they had freshly killed themselves, and so they killed more often. To the cattlemen it must have been insult added to injury; bad enough to have their cattle preyed upon, but then for these wolves to kill more than they could eat....Rick MacIntyre, writing of the enraged reaction of ranchers to wolves that "were wasteful of meat," aptly asks, "What right do we have to demand that another species abide by an ethic that we ourselves nearly always fail to achieve?"

Stockmen's associations hired full-time wolfers and out-of-work buffalo hunters and paid them a bounty for each hide; later the federal government contributed to this. That *Canis lupus baileyi*, the Mexican gray wolf, is named after Vernon Bailey, is a savage irony. Bailey is the man who brought the USBS into predator control in the early 20th century and pushed—successfully—for the extermination of Southwestern wolves. Of the five subspecies of the gray wolf that ranged through the Southwest, only *C. l. baileyi* escaped total extinction. Today the Mexican gray wolf is one of the rarest mammals in the world.

~

In the late 1970s, seven wolves from Mexico were captured for breeding in the U.S. (including a pregnant female) in response to the Endangered Species Act. Now, roughly 180 Mexican gray wolves are held in 31 zoos and refuges in the U.S. Eleven wolves—three breeding pairs, two of them with pups—have been moved from refuges to the Apache National Forest since January, 1998. All are considered "genetically surplus," meaning that other wolves with the same genetic makeup are held in captivity in case these die. This designation also gives the U.S. Fish and Wildlife Service (USFWS) greater flexibility in managing the animals. As "genetically surplus," they can be relocated or even shot for attacking cattle.

Unlike the arctic wolf or the timber wolf, the Mexican gray wolf is an entirely captive population. Some debate the ability of a wolf reared in captivity to adapt to the wild, but captive red wolves released in 1987 in North Carolina have done well. In fact, the Mexican wolf reintroduction is partly modeled on the release of the red wolf; it will likely also benefit from the knowledge gained from the timberwolf reintroduction program in Yellowstone.

The Mexican wolves in the release site are referred to only by number—never by name—in an attempt to distance them from people. Their interaction with humans is kept at an absolute minimum with the hope that this "defamiliarization" with people will work to their advantage in the wild. And, indeed, it will be useful if the wolves do keep clear of humans, for their range falls squarely in an area where ranching and hunting are the major industries, and where the local populace has been outspoken in its opposition to the wolf reintroduction.

Through the year 2000 the USFWS plans to release ten Mexican wolves each year into the Blue Mountain Wolf Recovery Zone, an area of 6,854 square miles that straddles the Arizona–New Mexico border and is comprised of the Apache and Gila National Forests. Of these released wolves, three animals in each set are expected to quickly die, disappear or disperse, and not contribute to population growth. By 2001 the USFWS estimates there will be twenty wolves breeding in the wild; the goal is to have a population of 100 wolves— roughly what the wolf population in the area was estimated to be at the turn of the century.

Each day the wolves in the release site pens are fed roadkill (to accustom them to game meat) brought in by workers and volunteers. The release of each breeding pair/family is staggered; the first at the release site, relocated there on January 26, are now hunting for themselves. The collared wolves are kept in pens for four to six weeks, then allowed to wander and acclimate themselves to their new surroundings, and provided with fresh meat until they are able to fend for themselves.

The high cottonwoods shading the zoo cast long shadows in the late afternoon light. Steve turns to head to his office and I take another look at Lola and her daughters, hoping for something that's hard to put a finger on. I realize that what's been so underwhelming, so at odds with the impassioned literature I've read both for and against wolves, is their demeanor. A caged tiger or lion has a menacing energy—it makes you glad for the separation of a cage; but these wolves look, at most, mildly curious, perhaps wistful now that Steve's departing and he's left no food in his wake. Reluctant. That's exactly it. As if there is something embarrassing about being seen by the likes of me, much less being seen in such reduced circumstances. I follow Steve and make a mental shrug; you can't help but anthropomorphize a little.

Wolves, like American Indians, were considered threats to civilization at one time, emissaries of a wild in need of conquest, and were attacked accordingly. Barry Lopez, in his excellent book *Of Wolves and Men*, describes our antagonistic relationship to the wolf:

> In the Bible, wilderness is defined as the place without God—a sere and barren desert. This twined sense of wilderness as a place innately dangerous and godless was something that attached itself, inevitably, to the wolf—the most feared denizen of gloomy wilderness. As civilized man matured and came to measure his own progress by his subjugation of the wilderness—both clearing trees for farms and clearing pagan minds for Christian ideas—the act of killing wolves became a symbolic act, a way to lash out at that enormous, inchoate obstacle: wilderness. Man demonstrated his own prodigious strength as well his allegiance to God by killing wolves.

Why wolf reintroduction has been so fiercely contested, and why wolves were driven to near extinction, has largely to do with our perception of them. Wolves are intelligent predators, and very social, and in these similarities to humans there is the temptation to ascribe human emotion or rationale to their behavior. It's something we've long done, much to the wolves' detriment. Indeed, it's seemed impossible for humans to look at these creatures dispassionately. Teddy Roosevelt, model American, outdoorsman and cattleman, wrote a book in which he called them "the arch type of ravin, the beast of waste and desolation." He, like others, hunted them on the Great Plains with packs of greyhounds. And the tenor of his description holds for many ranchers today just as it did for ranchers a century ago. As Phil Harvey, a New Mexico rancher and a former Head of the Board of Directors of the American Hereford Association—a well-spoken and intelligent man—says: "It just makes you sick when you see it—ripped up udders and teats. And a coyote is mild compared to a wolf. Coyotes don't have the bravado of wolves. They're not ruthless and voracious like the wolf."

But to see the wolf in such terms, to call it ruthless, raises certain questions. One question that might have been asked in Roosevelt's time, that should be asked now, is: If a wolf is seen in human terms, if we ascribe it the same moral sense we attribute to ourselves, can we justify its continued persecution?

Back in Steve's small office, which is disconcertingly festooned with a variety of animal skulls, I ask him about his opinion of the wolves under his care. "When I came here I had a lot of preconceived ideas. I had to go in to feed them raw meat I'd prepared, and I smelled like it, and I thought, 'My life is going to be very short.' The wolves were curious, but shy and reclusive at the same time. They want to stay away. And this is true of the vast majority of wolves I've worked with. They have an instinctive fear or respect of man." He smiles and shifts in his chair and I'm struck by how his manner resembles that of the wolves: a lot of energy and not enough room. He continues, "I thought of Jane Goodall and Diane Fossey, and how they must have felt at certain times. And I said, 'I'm going to champion this animal. I like this animal.' The way it looks at you, the way it moves—it's human-like in terms of its social behavior."

The question often raised by opponents of wolf reintroduction is why such animals can't be preserved in captivity, where the curious can go see them if so inclined. While ranchers worry about predation, many hunters maintain that the wolf will diminish deer and elk harvests. The implicit argument here is that humankind has altered the wilds in such a way that there is no longer a place for the wolf, and more, that such an arrangement is worth sustaining. Protected herds of cattle and sheep have displaced buffalo and other herbivores to feed on prime southwestern grasslands, and hunters control the populations of deer and elk. But such a model is biologically flawed and reductive.

Mexican wolves occupy a high montane zone between 4500 and 6000 ft., where grazing is good for the ungulates (hooved animals) on which they prey. In areas where there are wolf packs, mountain lions are confined to the higher elevations, while coyotes keep to the flats. When the wolf, which is the controlling predator, is removed, it creates a vacuum. In Yellowstone, for example, coyotes flourished in the wolves' absence. With their return, half the coyote population has been killed and this has led to a surge of rodent life (coyotes eat more rodents than wolves do). Such a shift has benefited foxes, hawks, owls, eagles, badgers and pine martens. As a result species diversity has improved—animals with small populations are growing in number, and those with large populations are shrinking, creating a stronger balance between them. Longstanding, carefully balanced trophic relationships are recovering.

Hunters argue that they, as the controlling predators in the wake of the wolf, can maintain the populations of deer and elk at healthy levels. But they have proved to be incomplete predators at best. They don't effectively limit the ranges of mountain lions or coyotes, and they pursue a very limited range of animals. Thus, imbalances from the absence of the wolf, in combination with the presence of large numbers of cattle—overgrazing has long been an issue in the West—leaves us with an ecosystem that is stressed and damaged to varying degrees.

Studies at Yellowstone demonstrate, fairly conclusively, that wolves are good for the environment. But the question of whether restoration of our wilderness areas is biologically desirable or realistic is not the issue. As Steve Diehl succinctly states, "What is biologically sound is of secondary importance in the political arena. It comes down to land use. Who's going to control the land. The wolf becomes an insignificant pawn." Al Schneberger, of the New Mexico Cattle Growers' Association, while against wolf reintroduction, agrees with this point: "It's land control. The wolves are really almost a side issue. It's control by the government."

~~◦~~

In part, the debate over wolf reintroduction has to do with preserving the status quo. There are both economic and cultural reasons for this, and these combine with the volatile issue of the role of the government in private life to make a strong case for leaving things alone, or at least for eliciting strong resistance.

Steve pulls at the brim of his cap, looking from the wolves to me and back again. He's spent years arguing on his own for the Mexican wolf reintroduction at meetings throughout New Mexico, often to hostile crowds. "Mining, logging, and hunting have sided with the ranching and livestock industry. They see wolf reintroduction as a way that the government can control large areas where these animals will live, thus curtailing the use or exploitation of these areas. Do we want to use the land for wolf reintroduction or endangered species reintroduction, or do we want to use it for economic and more recreational kinds of situations?" He shrugs unhappily.

On an economic level, public lands provide resources for the mining, logging, hunting, and ranching industries. Land in this country has long been viewed as an economic resource—aesthetics and preservation fit the picture, if at all, in a minimal way. When Congress created the National Park Service in 1916, it was with the intent of using the public lands' resources while conserving them for later generations. The reintroduction of timber wolves in Yellowstone was aided by the fact that Yellowstone is a national park, and therefore closed to industry. Conflict with land use was not an issue. However, in national forests, like the ones in which the Mexican wolves will find themselves, such use is a concern, and so this reintroduction effort has had to contend more directly with commercial interests.

The industries that benefit from these public lands' resources fear that restoring these lands will prevent them from enjoying the revenue they currently receive. Issues like wolf reintroduction are viewed as the thin edge of a wedge that could open up debate over land use, which would threaten the existing arrangement. This may well be true. While the Mexican wolf reintroduction doesn't directly affect these industries (in fact, ironically, it may lead to increased logging and clearing to provide more "early successional" vegetation—shrubs and the like—that deer consume), the move toward restored wilderness seems to logically imply an end to much of the logging, cattle, mining, and hunting on these lands. It's not that this will necessarily happen, but it does become more plausible as incremental steps toward restoration are taken. One Catron County man—the county is part of the Mexican wolf release site—warns, "They want things to go back to the nature like it was before the white man got here, and if they're going to release that wolf, they ought to release some Indians down here and some buffalo and put these *gringos* across that ocean back where they belong. That's where it's coming from."

Reserve, a small New Mexican town in the heart of the Gila National Forest, lost much of its employment base when the Stone Container Corporation sawmill shut down in 1992; much of the money in town now comes from visiting hunters. Surrounding Catron County relies primarily on ranching as a means of support. The wolf is perceived as a threat to these industries and can expect a chilly reception. The final environmental impact statement on the reintroduction of the Mexican wolf by the USFWS states that the decline in legal kills of deer will be 5–13%, and for elk 4–9%, which is not inconsiderable. Combine this with a drop in hunting expenditures and it translates into a loss of between one and two million dollars annually. This may, of course, be offset by increased tourism by those eager to glimpse a wolf in the wild—howling tours are already popular in areas where there are wolves. There also is the fact that much of the money spent comes from local hunters and is likely to find its way back into the economy via another route. Cattlemen seem to have less room for complaint: they could suffer an annual loss of .001–.04% of their herds—17.5 per year out of a population of 82,620 cows—due to wolf predation—verified losses will be covered by the Defenders of Wildlife Depredation Compensation Fund. The organization has created the fund to reimburse ranchers for cattle lost to wolf predation throughout the nation, as well as an incentive program to reward landowners when wolf pups are born on their property.

Phil Harvey points out that this fund, while useful, won't necessarily work as intended. "Wolves would rather kill cattle than anything else. When you come up on a carcass, eaten by wolves, then coyotes, then buzzards, how do you prove wolf sign?" Cattle in this mountainous area wander into inaccessible areas and it can be days or even weeks before a dead cow is found, by which time wolf depredation is hard to prove. Harvey, who has raised registered Herefords most of his life, also maintains that the fund pays only the going commercial rate for depredated cattle. For someone raising registered cattle, where individual bulls can be worth as much as $20,000 and calves can represent an initial $300–500 in artificial insemination costs alone (and with bloodlines that place their value at $5000–7000) such compensation is cold comfort. Of course, the vast majority of cattle are not, in fact, of such distinguished lineage.

The cattlemen likely to suffer most from the reintroduction are those of the San Carlos and White Mountain Apache tribes. Both groups have opposed the reintroduction. The San Carlos reservation is extremely poor and it is difficult for ranchers to keep close tabs on their cattle there, which will leave their animals more vulnerable to predation. The White Mountain Apache have the same problems but also rely on money from licenses sold to hunters for trophy elk, an arrangement that the wolves could harm.

In the face of all this, pro-environment groups are attempting to reclaim the debate through economics. For example, in addition to paying for verified cattle predation by wolves, Defenders of Wildlife wants to help cattlemen market their beef as "wolf country" certified beef in return for wolf-friendly ranching practices. Pro-wolf literature discusses how wolves increase tourism and provide an opportunity for new research, which will bring in money. Yellowstone National Park is held up as a shining example. In 1995, the year the timber wolves were released in the park, annual visitations were up by 36,000, and the sale of, and market for, wolf memorabilia had also grown substantially. Thus, while wolf reintroduction will adversely affect some industries, it's not a foregone conclusion that the venture is bad news economically.

Cowboys embody the frontier spirit that has so defined our culture, fusing rugged independence with entrepreneurial spirit. During the conquest of the West, government aid to cattlemen in the form of soldiers to deal with hostile Indians, cheap (or free) grazing rights, and predator control allowed the U.S. to establish ownership of the area. That time and need has passed, but the mystique and image of these frontier men is deeply ingrained in our culture, dictating how many Americans see themselves. To pursue something that threatens this way of life is to attack a cultural icon and attempt cultural redefinition. That the agent of change is the federal government becomes even more problematic; even though the cowboy way of life came about with government underwriting, it defines itself as being independent of and even opposed to the interests of the very same government.

Much of the news of the '90s has involved people in conflict with the government. Waco, the Freemen, Ruby Ridge, all of these have highlighted a deep ambivalence among Americans over the role of the federal government in private life. Republican—and now Democratic—rhetoric has as a touchstone the idea of a new federalism, a smaller national government that won't interfere with the rights of the state or of the individual.

So perhaps it is not surprising that an undertaking that is perceived to be bad economics, anti-cowboy, and pro-government has come under attack, or that the scientific justification for reintroduction has been relegated to the periphery of the debate.

Adam Shriver, a resident of Reserve, states, "Reserve, like any other small town, has its radicals. Some feel so strongly about wolf reintroduction that they might go out and hunt wolves. I could really see that happening. Poaching is a big deal in Reserve. You can get fined or imprisoned. The Forest Service sets up fake elk, and they catch a lot of people. But it still happens. It's not going to be different for the wolves."

The Mexican wolves will end up roaming an area that, while sparsely populated, has one of the most active anti-wolf constituencies in the country. It seems that anti-wolf sentiment is strongly wedded to a feeling that outsiders—city dwellers and the federal government—have no place regulating programs that will affect their way of life. As Phil Harvey said to me: "People in the East view this part of the country as empty public lands and think it should stay that way. They don't have a clue what it's like. All this is done on a whim.

Why should ranchers be prepared to take losses just so some New York City guy can sleep well knowing there's wolves in the wild?"

Seen in this light, the desire among those working to defamiliarize the wolves with people makes more and more sense. Commenting on the wolves' reintroduction into the Blue Range Wolf Recovery Zone, where they will learn to fend for themselves, Steve Diehl says, "Wolves are going to have problems in terms of predation from humans and other predators. The wolf will have to displace mountain lions and coyotes—you're going to have some unhappy animals. And coyotes get big. They have actually started to pack up more. Hunters shoot each other, they shoot cows—you can bet there will be some wolves in there, too." He grins bleakly.

Shriver states that he'd obey the law against killing these endangered animals, but he says, "I wouldn't like it if I saw one. It's lessening the population that we enjoy hunting and that helps support us."

The federal penalty for killing a wolf carries a fine of up to $50,000 and a year in prison. Enforcement, however, is another issue, and some wolves will inevitably be lost to poachers. Part of the reason that the wolves being released are genetically surplus is so that if they die or are killed, the loss will not be irreplaceable. The USFWS study stoically notes, "However, although the wolves will be more protected legally, enforcement difficulties and local sentiment against the wolves may result in a high rate of killings that could impede wolf recovery."

Phil Harvey sums up rancher sentiment thus: "There are quite a few ranchers fed up with the government telling them what to do, fed up with endangered species. Frankly, it all amounts to the government taking private property. You'll see some file lawsuits over the wolf reintroduction; you'll see some start to shoot."

One rancher I spoke with prior to visiting the zoo joked, "Shoot the wolf you see hanging around your cattle and then tie the damn transmitter to a truck. Let them [USFWS agents] track it to Canada."

⤳

The most powerful aid to reintroduction has not been science, but popular opinion. The majority of Americans live in urban settings, and for them the reintroduction is a compelling idea. One has only to view the vast traffic jam that is Yellowstone in the summer months to know that recreational use of public lands is booming, and people like the idea of escaping from crowded cities to untrammeled wilder-

ness. In this there is a tendency to idealize the wilds as a place syn-
onymous with vacation, a place where one can relax and is never at
risk. It will be interesting to see how people revise this notion as wild
animal populations grow and the land surrounding these enclaves
becomes more densely populated.

In California, where the mountain lion population is increasing,
there have been a number of documented mountain lion attacks, and
the victims are not always housepets. While the number of attacks is
small and human fatalities are rare, it affects our perception of wild
animals—will we become more ambivalent or hostile toward them?
Coyotes attack and eat housepets, bears rummage through garbage.
Rebounding populations of seals and sea lions have caused some fish
stocks—already reduced by humans—to decline. By some estimates
there are more white-tailed deer in America now than when the settlers arrived, many of which can't be hunted in densely populated,
suburban areas. As sparsely populated, privately-owned buffer lands
disappear and developed land abuts public lands, predator and prey
alike may become a common sight; managing them may require more
effort than we realize.

Wolves, well, wolves make many people nervous even though
there's never been a documented account of a healthy wolf seriously
injuring a human in North America. As with other animals, we can't
expect them to recognize park boundaries or recovery zones. In the
case of the Mexican wolf, can we really keep them all collared, especially when they begin reproducing in the wild? Will we always be
able to track them when they venture from protected areas? James
Bednarze, a biologist at the University of New Mexico who has studied *C. l. baileyi*, says of them, "Data dealing with the behavior, ecology, and other aspects of the biology of the Mexican wolf essentially
do not exist." Given this, can we truly expect to control these animals, or is there a certain arrogance to this assumption?

What seems clear is that reintroducing the wolf into its native
habitat will continue. There is enough land to support viable populations. The main question is not over making room for the wolf, but
over shifting away from the age-old prejudice we hold for this creature to allow it a better place in the wilds and in our psyche.

But even if the old prejudices do fade, there remains the pressing issue of land use and where we, as Americans, stand. How will
we come to define a "wilderness"? Will the desire or compulsion to
preserve the wilds and the animals in them remain strong during
times of economic hardship, or in the face of increased population

pressure? Will these developing situations with wild animals come to be viewed as nuisances, as something beneficial, or as something threatening?

I thank Steve for his time and walk one last time to the wolf pen. I get a disinterested once-over from one of Lola's daughters before she resumes her nap; the others are out of sight. As I unlock my car, I pause, clinging to the hope that a wolf howl will waver over the sound of evening traffic; none does. But I have the memory of the wolves in motion, that beautiful glide, and I watch this again and again as I drive west toward the Organ Mountains

The wolf-wildlands debate will continue on the pages of newspapers and the screens of TVs this year and next, and as it does the wolves will establish themselves in the forests of the Apache and Gila National Forests. They will howl just as their captive cousins do near the Albertson's parking lot of Alamogordo. In both cases the why behind the howl will remain unclear. We know surprisingly little about these animals, having viewed them as vermin and having exterminated them; not much time was spent observing them. Howling may be to assemble the pack, to express alarm, loneliness, anxiety, camaraderie, celebration, or mood synchronization. Maybe it's a way of calling long distance—a loud chat. We don't know. But we can learn—as long as they're left in the wild to be studied, to be glimpsed, to be listened to. And in this, perhaps, we will learn something of ourselves.

THE WASTING OF CATRON COUNTY: BLUEPRINT FOR THE DESTRUCTION OF RURAL AMERICA?

|||||||||||||||||||||||||||||||||||||||||||||||||||||||||||||||||||||

J. Zane Walley

(2000)

Catron County Commissioner Auggie Shellhorn is a big man, rugged, callused, and tough from years of ranching high country and fighting forest fires with "Hot Shot" teams. He faces a task equal to his size and spunk in rescuing his economically ravaged New Mexico county.

Auggie stops his aging pickup truck on a slight rise overlooking a large abandoned and rusting sawmill, the ruins of the industry that was the very lifeblood of his community. He sighs heavily. "When the mill was running, everyone who wanted to work had a job. People could afford to raise their families here and our county could afford to provide a decent education for the children. But that is all gone—gone thanks to the spotted owl and the Endangered Species Act." Shellhorn is silent for a few moments then perks up. "Someday, and we pray it is soon, America is going to need our timber again, and so the county bought the mill. It's our investment in the future. We gotta believe in it."

From the old mill we drive into the county seat at Reserve, New Mexico, and enter Uncle Bill's, a local saloon that proudly displays its motto. "Kids that hunt, fish, and trap don't mug little old ladies!"

Auggie introduced me as a writer for *Range* magazine and Paragon Foundation, which eased the tense looks I was getting from the grizzly clientele. The heated and controversial U.S. Fish and Wildlife Service (FWS) wolf reintroduction hearings were scheduled to be held in Reserve, so big city journalists had beleaguered the tiny population. It seemed that everyone in the bar had a 60 Minutes II, Discovery, or other network camera stuck in their face over the past week. "We sure are glad we finally got some press in town that'll tell our side of the story," smiled a tiny lady tipping her beer mug to me. "We just 'bout had enough of them wolfers."

Catron County indeed has had enough of the media and the "wolfers." The citizens have been assailed without mercy and without pity, from environmentalists, the federal government, and biased media for over a decade.

The economy is wholly devastated, the school system de-funded and, most sadly, Catron has lost its greatest treasure, the children. As communities declined, families left, and with the families go the children. Shellhorn relates, "The spotted owl didn't just affect the sawmill workers. Truckers, fallers, planters, thinners, and construction workers lost their jobs. We lost so many children because of families moving away that we shrunk from a 12- to a 6-man football team. In 1998 only eight boys and one girl graduated from Reserve High School. Before the spotted owl, our graduating class was 20 to 25. We have such limited funds for education that we had to shorten the school week to four days."

The county seems to have been singled out as a testing ground for every new land-taking concept based on the Endangered Species Act. Perhaps it is even more than a random singling out. Conceivably, it is as rancher Hugh McKeen believes, "a federal test-bed for like-actions in other rural communities."

The actions by the U.S. Forest Service, FWS, and federal courts have been so continuous, so uncompromising, that they could be interpreted as a deliberate retaliation for the Herculean independence displayed by Catron citizens. These good people have resisted, and still defy, the heavy hand of the federal government on their personal lives and lands.

Catron County caught the nation's attention with its effort to return to a regulation-free life. It birthed the county independence movement. It was the first to pass statutes resisting federal reign over national land within its boundaries. The message has been plain: "Get the federal government out of our people's lives."

Jim Catron, the county attorney, is a fourth-generation New Mexican and a distant relative of Thomas Benton Catron, for whom Catron County is named. "There is a culture in the American West," he says. "It lives and it breathes and it is under assault in the name of environmental protection. Under the guise of environmental conservation, we're attempting to destroy the last vestige of people who resist central government in the world. If those one-worlders and those federal imperialists really believe they've got us whipped, that the final resistance to centralized government is over, they're wrong. We don't use bullets and swords; now we use lawsuits and injunctions. When these people see government getting strong enough to push them off their lands, destroy their culture and their livelihoods, when these people see the federal government protecting owls and fish instead of humans, they tend to fight back."

Reserve, with its empty streets and boarded up windows, seems an unlikely place to ferment a rebellion and the citizens certainly don't see themselves as revolutionaries. They are common working folks who were pushed against the wall, put out of work, and watched their lives being destroyed by over-zealous regulatory agencies and environmentalist lawsuits. Their county leaders merely passed ordinances they believed would defend the citizens' livelihoods. It hasn't worked. Instead federal agencies continue tightening the noose to the point of perceptible discrimination.

Back in Uncle Bill's bar, Gary Harris, owner of the last tiny, one-man sawmill in Catron County explains how absurd the Forest Service regulations have become. "We had a fire in the Gilas a couple years back. Sixteen thousand acres of prime large trees burned. Out of that the Forest Service only allowed five acres of Douglas fir to be salvaged. We only cut for two weeks. As we were salvaging, the enviros got a court order to quit cutting and quit skidding the burned timber. So the rest, and it was choice wood, simply rotted. Outside of that, the Forest Service has only had one timber sale in 10 years. It is ridiculous. We have 60 percent more acreage in tree cover today than in 1935. We are surrounded by timber, but people are building houses with lumber trucked in from Canada."

Gary stares into his beer for a long moment, shakes his head, turns to me with a somber face, and says, "Look, here is how it is. There is no timber for sale, after the wolf reintroduction ranching will dry up, the wolves have limited game to eat so after the deer and elk are gone we'll lose our hunter income. It boils down to the fact that ways to make a living are vanishing. People are suffering. These are proud folks who won't ride welfare and they have nothing left. We have suffered a lot of casualties. Some turned to the bottle, some blew their brains out, and many gave up and went away. I guess it has got me too. I'm out of logs to cut so I'm closing my mill."

The wolf reintroduction into the Gila Wilderness is viewed by most Catron citizens as the final kiss of death to the county's economy. Con Allred, old-time rancher and former New Mexico State Representative, sits by the window at the Golden Girls Café in Glenwood, a small village down the road from Reserve, drinking coffee and talking politics. He sums up the dilemma posed by the wolves.

"We have almost no deer left and the elk population is so small the wolves will wipe them out fast. We'll lose our hunters and the damn wolves will continue killing our cattle."

Con's son, Darrell, a rancher and realtor specializing in ranches, forcefully adds to his dad's observations. "Nobody wants to purchase a working ranch where wolves are a threat to livestock. The effect is that ranching properties are seriously devalued. Those folks who need to sell are going to be forced to subdivide. This pristine land will be turned into a sprawl of summer home subdivisions. We don't want that; we'd like to see the old ranches kept intact. By reintroducing the wolf, the environmentalists and federal agencies are instrumental in increasing the population pressure on our resources. It's back to the question, 'Whadda you want, condos or cows?'"

Catron County resisted the Mexican gray wolf reintroduction plan to the bitter end. In March, they hosted a rally in Glenwood to provide alternative information on the reintroduction program. A thousand peaceful folks from all walks of life showed up for the meeting to protest the wolf reintroduction. The major media swarmed the assembly, obviously hoping to further reinforce the "violent redneck" image of the Catron folks that has been carefully choreographed by federal agencies, and environmentalist-driven media over the last decade. They seemed disappointed that nothing bad happened. An Albuquerque newspaper reported the rally as "remarkably sedate." A television station in Albuquerque showed five seconds of the Glenwood rally, then allowed an environmentalist considerable air time on how ranchers destroy the land. Skewed sound bites and a prejudiced notion of what was going to be reported was painfully obvious. The only media that gave accurate accountings of the events were small and independent.

The final inputs into the Wolf Reintroduction Environmental Impact Statement (EIS) were conducted in Reserve and Silver City, New Mexico, by the U.S. Fish and Wildlife Service shortly after the Glenwood Rally. They were extraordinarily tense meetings because shortly before the hearings official reports indicated that FWS baiting with elk and deer cadavers had lured a pack of reintroduced wolves across the Arizona border. Once in New Mexico, the pack promptly started killing livestock.

Bud Collins and his partner Judy Cummings of the Cross Y ranch near Glenwood were hit first. Collins said a fetus calf was taken from the cow by the pack of seven wolves, possibly before she was dead. "She ran about two miles from the pasture to the line camp," he said.

"They were chewing on her all the way, and she died close to the cabin. She was looking for protection. It was pretty grisly."

Judy's take on the slaying of the Cross Y livestock was one of shock and betrayal. She was new to ranching and had invested a lifetime of savings from her former position as a vice president of The Bank of America in California. Ms. Cummings was a life member of Defenders of Wildlife, The Nature Conservancy, and the Environmental Defense Fund. "Suddenly, reality hit me," she said. "All the green groups I had been contributing to were working with the government to put me and every rancher like me out of business!"

A few days later, the pack downed a 1,400-pound bull on Smoothing Iron Mesa. The wolf pack seemed unafraid of the two hunters who happened upon the scene of its kill. "They were calm and reluctant to leave," according to a sheriff's report.

Bud Collins said, "The wolves don't appear to be afraid of humans and seem to prefer hanging around the ranch line camp. It's very disconcerting. It's hard to get the horses to come up here anymore."

The wolves killed the bull about two miles from the Glenwood Elementary School. Then a solitary male was spied several times wandering through the tiny village of Alma eating pet cats and hanging around the school bus stop. The alarmed communities were suddenly held hostage by the rogue wolf and fear that the pack might attack a child. The threat was so real that they kept their children inside until the FWS trapped the pack and sited the lone wolf well away from the locale.

It was under these incensed conditions that the final hearing on the EIS was held. The Wolf Reintroduction Team, after presenting formal statements, turned the meeting over to a stern professional facilitator and sat stone-faced and mute in their chairs, refusing to answer or in any way acknowledge questions from the hundreds of angry people in the audience. Dozens of representatives from New Mexico agencies, county commissions, city officials, hunters, ranchers, mothers, and children stood and voiced to the emotionless panel of FWS employees that they did not want the wolves reintroduced into their backyards.

None of this outpouring by citizens against the wolf reintroduction was heeded. Shortly after the hearings, the wolves were unleashed.

Is Catron County a blueprint for the destruction of rural America? Certainly the havoc wreaked there can be effectively applied anywhere. It would be simple, because the fiats to effectively accomplish such a plan are in place. Use the Endangered Species Act to shut down major industries and destroy the tax base.

When the tax base is destroyed, funding for schools and public services are diminished. Working people are forced to leave for lack of employment. Private lands found to be habitat for endangered species would be so devalued that owners would be forced to sell them to governmental agencies or nonprofit groups like The Nature Conservancy, further reducing the tax base. Private citizens cannot afford to defend themselves against the power, might, and the unlimited monetary resources of the federal government and a judicial system that seems to have predetermined the course of environmental-takings lawsuits.

The Catron County blueprint is spreading to rural communities across our country. It's not confined just to the West. The U.S. Fish and Wildlife Service is forcing hundreds of farmers in Ohio off their private land. West Virginia recently watched helplessly as the EPA decimated the coal mining industry. As West Virginia Senator Rockefeller recently said, "It sure looks like the War on the West is moving East."

LIVING WITH WOLVES

||||||||||||||||||||||||||||||||||||||||||||||||||||||||||||||||||||||||||||

Johnny D. Boggs
(1999)

*B*ergin Riddle doesn't want Mexican gray wolves anywhere near his home, and can't fathom why the U.S. Fish and Wildlife Service has been so determined to rebuild the population in the Gila and Apache national forests of southern New Mexico and southeastern Arizona—Riddle's backyard. "We've got the bubonic plague here, too," Riddle says at the 3 Trees store in Reserve, owned by friend Jess Carey, "and you don't see them reintroducing that."

Across the street sits the Black and Gold convenience store, owned by Elena Gellert of Luna. She's much in favor of the wolf recovery program. "I think people have been taught fear about wolves, and they've been gone for so long that people just don't realize how 'in place' they really are here," she says.

The wolves are here now. Wildlife officials began releasing Mexican gray wolves near the New Mexico–Arizona state line last year. The controversy found the national spotlight when five of those animals were shot to death, but the recovery program continues. And despite strong differences of opinion, the people of Reserve are getting along peacefully. They seem to know that pro-wolf or anti-wolf, they must learn to live with wolves.

Reserve sits off state Highway 12 in the rugged, mountainous terrain of southwestern New Mexico. Nearby Starkweather Canyon is well-named. This is tough, wild country. With a population of only 319, Reserve nonetheless serves as the county seat of Catron County (population 2,657). A quiet town founded in 1874, Reserve has seen its economy pounded by sawmill closings to protect the Mexican Spotted Owl. The fragile economy is one reason some residents oppose the wolf recovery program.

"If you don't have that economic base coming in, then that means every business in this town is gonna die; we cannot pay our mortgages on our homes or our businesses, and the bottom line is we're gonna be displaced by an animal," Carey says.

This is hunting country. Many residents depend on wild game not only for business, but for food in the winter. Ranchers fear for their livestock.

Gellert understands.

"But I feel like there has been enough effort from the environmental community nationwide to cover those kind of depredation costs," she says.

Both sides agree on one thing, however: The victim in this debate is the wolf.

Of the five shootings last year, only the first has been solved. Camper Richard Humphrey of Tucson, Arizona, reported shooting an adult male wolf on April 28, saying the wolf was coming at his family. He was not prosecuted.

Killing a Mexican gray wolf, except in defense of a human life, is a violation of the Endangered Species Act and punishable by a fine of up to $100,000 and up to a year in jail. Rewards totaling $50,000 have been offered for information about the killings.

Few people believe the residents of Reserve are responsible for the shootings.

"We've got more decent, law-abiding citizens here than anyplace else," Carey says. "We have different values. Everybody sends their kids to school to get an education. They know where their kids are at; they ain't joining gangs, they ain't on the streets drive-by shooting, all of that. The people here have pride in what they do."

Many believe the wolves were mistaken for coyotes, and killing coyotes is common in this part of the country. Others say ranchers, many of them strong opponents to the program, are responsible for the deaths. After all, ranchers were primarily responsible for driving the species to near-extinction in the late 1800s and well into this century.

In December four wolves, wearing splotches of bright paint and fluorescent radio collars for easier identification, were released in Arizona. More releases have taken place this year.

Two questions remain: Do the wolves belong? And why are people afraid of the animals when there has never been a documented case of a wild wolf attacking a human?

Kieran Suckling, director of the Southwest Center for Biological Diversity in Tucson, Arizona, spent a lot of time around Reserve and Luna as an owl and goshawk surveyor for the U.S. Forest Service.

"I spent many cold, rainy nights tromping around those mountains, so I have a real soft spot in my heart for the area."

These days, he has been one of the most vocal supporters of the wolf recovery program.

"We have a moral responsibility and a desire to live in balance with other species, to give other species a chance to simply live their lives," he says, "and to do that we've got to reintroduce the wolf because otherwise we're sentencing it to die in a zoo."

An answer to the second question can be found at the Alameda Park Zoo in Alamogordo.

"I was brought up on the myths and legends, Little Red Riding Hood, the same as everyone else," Director Steve Diehl says. "I think once people learn a little more about these animals, some of their concerns will be addressed."

Wolves aren't the menace we're taught to fear as children, Diehl says.

"They're very shy," he explains. "They learn quickly to stay away from people. They're very alert, very acute to their surroundings, with a complex social schedule in their group. They're compassionate to each other and with their young. And in 13 years, I've never even had one snap at me."

Alameda Park Zoo is one of more than 30 zoos in the United States and Mexico in the Mexican gray wolf captive management program. Biologists and wildlife officials make sure the wolves are as genetically diverse as possible, with the hope that some day the animals will be reintroduced to the wild.

"No matter what happens with the wolf recovery program, we will make sure this species does not become extinct," Diehl says.

That has been an uphill battle. The Mexican gray wolf once roamed from central Mexico to southern New Mexico, southeastern Arizona, and southwestern Texas before being place on the endangered list in 1976.

"It's the most endangered species on the planet," Diehl says. Only 177 are known to exist in captivity.

The wolves have human contact only for medical, dental, or transportation purposes. "We have a hands-off policy with this species," Diehl says. Once the wolves are almost ready for release, they are held in "acclimation pens" before being turned loose. "So they learn quickly to stay away from people," Diehl says.

But human nature being what it is, doubts remain about releasing the animals.

Riddle points out that the mountains around Reserve have bobcats, mountain lions, bears, and the omnipresent coyotes. "Why introduce another predator?" he asks.

Ironically, however, wildlife officials claim that wolves have proved to be one of the best ways of controlling the coyote population.

Carey says he would feel more comfortable if Interior Secretary Bruce Babbitt would take personal responsibility if someone's child is killed by a wolf.

Suckling shakes his head. "Humans have lived with wolves in North America for hundreds and hundreds of years," he says. "If wolves were a huge threat to the human populace, I think we'd know it by now."

But wolves are wild animals. Environmentalists, hunters, and ranchers alike say living with the animals requires common sense.

Riddle and Carey remain opposed to the program, but they're learning to accept it.

"To me," Gellert says, "the greatest gift of this area is that it's truly wild. I guess that's why I'd like to see the wolf here, because I'd like this country to be as wild as it can."

Diehl agrees.

"I'll be sitting outside in my house nearby and I'll hear a wolf howl," he says. "It's sort of a ghostly moan that sends a tingle to the base of the spine. I think it's a carry over from when man wasn't at the top of the food chain.

"I'm looking forward to the day when I'm out camping with my son and I hear a wolf howl in the distance."

SIGNS OF THE WILD

||||||||||||||||||||||||||||||||||||||||||||||||||||||||||||||||||||||||||||

DASHKA SLATER
(1999)

ountain lion pee, said Andy Holdsworth, smells like cat pee but on a grander scale. At his insistence, I pressed my face into the duff and gave a good sniff, but all I could smell was the fragrant, summer-camp scent of pine needles. Still, right next to my cheek was a dry, segmented turd—incontrovertible evidence that a mountain lion had been using this very section of eastern Arizona ridgeline as a litter box.

"It's an old one," Andy explained as I gave a last snort and stood up. "You can tell by the pine needles on top. But it's definitely a mountain lion scrape. The clue is the pile." Here he pointed with a twig at the line of bare ground the cougar had cleared as it kicked the duff into a heap with its back paw.

Andy, a program coordinator with Tucson-based Sky Island Alliance, was teaching me and 13 other Sierra Club members the rudiments of animal tracking in preparation for a week of data collection in the Blue Range Primitive Area of Apache-Sitgreaves National Forest. The alliance planned to use the information we gathered to make a case for giving the area permanent protection under the federal Wilderness Act, which would restrict roads, logging, and motorized vehicles in the mountain lion's habitat.

A five-hour drive from the nearest major city, the Blue Range has been too unknown to have many partisans besides ranchers, loggers, and miners. But events in 1998 changed all that. In March, the U.S. Fish and Wildlife Service released 11 Mexican gray wolves into Apache-Sitgreaves National Forest as part of a plan to bring the wild wolf back to the Southwest, where it had been extinct for more than 50 years. By the time our Sierra Club group set out at the end of September, only 6 of those original 11 remained in these woods.

The agency chose the Blue Range for the wolves' release because of its diversity of prey—a well-stocked larder of 16,000 elk and 57,000 deer, as well as innumerable rabbits, hares, and javelina. It is part of one of North America's most diverse ecosystems, the Sky Islands, an archipelago of mountain forests that rise above the desert. Extending from the Sonoran and Chihuahuan deserts in the west to the Rocky Mountains in the east, the islands form a kind of ecological melting pot, where grizzlies once cavorted with jaguars and goshawks mingled with thick-billed parrots. The grizzlies are gone now, but a few jaguars remain, along with cougars, bobcats, black bears, ring-tailed cats, coatimundis, and some 85 other mammal species. While the chances of us encountering wolves were slim, the knowledge that they were somewhere nearby convinced us to bury our noses in the duff of this little known corner of Arizona.

As I walked along the trail with Andy and the rest of the group on that first day, it was hard to imagine that this forest of pine, oak, and aspen was teeming with wildlife. Descriptions of the forest's diversity made it sound almost as if the animals would be peering out from behind the trees and batting their eyes at us, Disney-style.

But it turned out that if we wanted to know they were there, we would have to learn to read their tags, the mammalian versions of "Kilroy was here." Animals, we were told, left signposts for each other in the same kind of obvious places we would choose: the meeting of two streams, the junction of two trails, a saddle between a pair of mountains, a large tree like the Douglas fir that had fallen across the trail ahead of us.

⚬

"If you come down a trail and you see a big tree like this, something unusual, take a few minutes and really look at it," Andy suggested. We all surrounded the tree, studying its surface until someone noticed the four claw marks etched into the bark.

With the help of our Sky Island Alliance guides, the landscape began to reveal itself to us. A bear had taken the time to chew an eight-inch chunk out of a fence post at a trail junction nearby and then rubbed against the gnawed wood, leaving a tuft of kinky brown fur tangled in the barbed wire. A triangle of bark neatly lifted from a dead log might mean that a bear had foraged here for grubs, although the absence of claw marks made it hard to say for certain. Pocket gophers were responsible for the mounds of dirt at the base of a spruce, while an elk had used the tines of his antlers to chafe a row of dark abrasions in the bark of a young aspen. Bull elk, Andy explained, have a handy trick: they urinate on their manes and then scour the scent into the raw bark. When we looked closely, we saw that the scrape was matted with long coarse hairs.

It was late afternoon when we began walking back to camp, and the woods seemed dappled with things we hadn't noticed on our way in. Lying in the middle of the trail, for instance, were the furry bottom quarters of a vole. "Neat," Andy said, probing it with a twig. The vole's brown belly and pink feet had yet to stiffen in rigor mortis. Whatever creature had been lunching on vole tartare may have been startled by our footsteps. Maybe it was the coyote that had left a twisted turd nearby, shaggy with undigested fur. I picked up a stick and poked at the abbreviated vole, wondering if its killer would come back to get it after we left. Perhaps it was watching us from the shadows behind the trees, or around that rock. I hoped so.

That night as I lay in my tent, I listened for the howl of wolves, the "deep, chesty bawl" that ecologist Aldo Leopold described as "an outburst of wild, defiant sorrow, and of contempt for all the adversities of the world." In the months since their release, the wolves had been seen not far from Hannigan Meadow, where we were camped, and a sign at the campground reminded campers and hunters that it was not permissible to kill a wolf, not even if you mistook it for a coyote, not even if it was fighting with your pet.

In 1909, when Leopold was a young forester mapping timber tracts in the Blue Range, no right-thinking out-doorsman would let a wolf cross his path without reaching for his rifle. Leopold himself once believed that wolves and other predators should be exterminated from the wilderness, because they, unlike human hunters, could not be persuaded to respect the posted seasons for hunting deer. "It is going to take patience and money to catch the last wolf or lion in New Mexico," he told delegates to the National Game Conference in 1920. "But the last one must be caught before the job can be called fully successful." There were then about 30 wolves left in New Mexico. In the previous five years, bounty hunters in New Mexico and Arizona had killed 900 of them.

New Mexico's last wild wolf was killed in 1942, but by then Leopold had begun to see the folly of a wilderness without them. In 1944, he wrote the famous essay "Thinking Like a Mountain," in which he recalled a female wolf that he had shot in the Apache Forest while she frolicked on a riverbank with a half-dozen grown pups. "We reached the old wolf in time to watch a fierce green fire dying in her eyes," he wrote. "I realized then, and have known ever since, that there was something new to me in those eyes—something known only to her and to the mountain. I was young then, and full of trigger-itch; I thought that because fewer wolves meant more deer, that no wolves would mean a hunters' paradise. But after seeing the green fire die, I sensed that neither the wolf nor the mountain agreed with such a view."

By 1944, the southwestern forests that Leopold loved were overrun with deer, deer that had forgotten how to flee and knew only how to feed. "I have watched the face of many a newly wolfless mountain, and seen the south-facing slopes wrinkle with a maze of new deer trails," he wrote. "I have seen every edible bush and seedling browsed, first to anaemic desuetude, and then to death. I have seen every edible tree defoliated to the height of a saddle horn. Such a mountain looks as if someone had given God a new pruning shears, and forbidden Him all other exercise."

When the Fish and Wildlife Service returned wolves to these remote Arizona mountains, it hoped that there would eventually be a hundred of them, moving stealthily, steadily, as wolves do, from the Apache Forest into the Gila Forest in New Mexico, teaching the deer and the elk about fear and flight over a range of almost 7,000 square miles. In theory, the wolfless years of 1942 to 1998 would be just a hiccup in the mountain memory of the Southwest. After all, the wolves had been here since the Pleistocene, adapting to this dry, tough country by growing smaller and scrappier than their northern relatives, 60 to 80 pounds at full weight, and about five feet long (including their tails).

Wherever wolves have returned, they have begun to correct ecological imbalances, not only by culling deer and elk, but also by making room for other species. Two years after returning to Yellowstone, wolves had killed half of the park's coyotes, allowing foxes, hawks, owls, eagles, badgers, and pine martens to thrive on the small rodents that the coyotes used to consume. Grizzlies have prospered as well, feeding with their cubs off the remains of wolf kills, then leaving the carcasses for eagles and ravens. There are more birds and trees in the canyons because the elk are vigilant now—they no longer linger on low ground and overbrowse saplings. "Too much safety leads to danger," Leopold concluded in his essay. "Perhaps this is behind Thoreau's dictum: In wildness is the preservation of the world."

We set out for the mountain the next day, traveling from a moist, stream-cut canyon lush with meadow grasses and wildflowers, up through ponderosa forests thinned by a recent fire that left grove after grove of trees contorted and hollowed like melted snowmen. As I walked, I imagined the wolves moving through this terrain, scenting for deer and elk, nervous, alert, the instinct to roam and hunt battling the familiarity offered by human settlements.

The wolves released in the Blue Range were captive-born, and while they had been chosen for their fierceness, independence, and fear of humans, they were still learning to be wild wolves. Regular updates released by the Fish and Wildlife Service described their painstaking education as they traveled from their release pens into the wilderness in three separate packs: Hawk's Nest, Campbell Blue, and Turkey Creek. Living at first on roadkill left by FWS personnel, they gradually learned to chase and then to kill elk. Although, like all wolves, they chased more than they killed. They still had much to learn, particularly, to learn to fear humans. In April, the wolves in the Turkey Creek pack spent the night near a retired postal worker and his family, who had camped near the town of Clifton. In the morning, the male wolf got into a scrap with one of the family's dogs, and the man shot it through both back legs. The dog survived but the wolf died. The wolf's mate, which was two days away from delivering a litter of pups, had to be recaptured and returned to the refuge where she was born because she and her pups couldn't survive on their own.

From spring into summer the wolves continued learning the ways of the wilderness, the younger ones discovering independence by leaving their natal packs for days and sometimes weeks. In May, two young females were caught and returned to the refuge after they wandered too far from the pack and began lingering near the towns, killing some chickens and injuring a miniature horse. (Defenders of Wildlife is compensating livestock owners for losses.) A pup was seen with the Campbell Blue pack in July, the first Mexican wolf born in the wild in the United States for more than 50 years, but a few days later the pack's alpha female was dead, killed while fighting a mountain lion over the carcass of an elk calf. Her mate was seen with the pup for several weeks, but then the pup disappeared and is presumed dead.

As I walked, I thought about how much the wolves had progressed in less than six months. They were figuring out where the game was, how far its range extended, and how to raise pups. They had learned that it was good to chase rabbits and squirrels but not all the way into a hollow log (the Hawk's Nest alpha female had gotten stuck one day and had to be dug out by the rest of the pack), that it wasn't necessarily a good idea to steal dinner from a mountain lion, that it might be better to stay away from campers and their guns. In their bulletins, wildlife officials warned the wolves' supporters not to be discouraged by the setbacks; the animals were still doing better than expected. They would get the knack of it, soon enough.

We camped that night by Franz Spring and set out the next morning in groups of four to scout. Each group had two or three destinations arranged in regular intervals; at each stop we were to take careful notes about the topography, tree mix, and the presence of food plants, and then fan out looking for animal sign.

I knew how to hike and how to take notes, but as we began looking for animal indicators I discovered that my eyes would not pay attention to the right things. I knew I should be looking for scat and tracks, for clawed and rubbed trees, and for piles of duff where a mountain lion might have made a pit stop. Instead I noticed a blond and orange bumblebee humped over the pincushion center of a purple daisy, butterflies with red and black wings like Spanish fans, the pale green of the downy meadow grass, the ridged, jigsaw-puzzle bark of an alligator juniper.

It was only when the others began showing off their finds—a marshy puddle rimmed by the print of a big cat; dark, pebbly clumps of elk droppings; teardrop-shaped deer prints; a clump of coyote scat—that I remembered the goal of this scavenger hunt. I decided that the trick must be to think like an animal: What would I eat? Where would I go? I was certain that any creature in its right mind would avoid the thorny thicket of New Mexican locust and stay in the open meadow, and by following that logic I soon stumbled onto the largest pile of crap I had ever seen. "Is it bear scat?" I asked Matt, worried that the grassy turds would turn out to be run-of-the-mill horse pucky.

"Let's see," he said. Using twigs, he dissected the excrement, revealing the undigested ant exoskeletons buried inside. "Now, do horses eat ants?"

Buoyed by my find, I grew more diligent at the succeeding observation sites, locating a coyote print, some browsed leaves, and an upended boulder that might have been moved aside by a foraging bear. I was starting to tire of keeping my eyes on the ground when I noticed something moving. A dozen deer were bounding across the meadow, leaping up out of the tall grass with their necks arched and legs tucked high under their bellies. When they were gone, I walked through the tangled grass where they'd been and scanned for droppings and hoofprints. I found nothing. Had I come through two minutes later, I would never have known that they'd been there.

I spent the next afternoon scouting the saddle of WS Mountain with Andy and another trip participant named Tim. The ridge had been heavily burned in recent years and was now filling in with thorny locusts that embroidered our shins with scratches as we walked. There were few food plants and even fewer signs of animals, just a squat horned lizard that Andy said can shoot blood through its eyes to scare off coyotes.

After about an hour of walking, we came to a ring of four Gambel oaks with a litter of branches in the center. Andy stopped and grinned. "Hoo boy, this looks like some activity," he said as he lifted one of the fallen branches so that we could see the green acorn caps that had been meticulously denuded of their acorns. The branches lay in a splintery heap, like linens and dishes piled up after a banquet. Nearby was a pile of acorn-studded scat, so fresh Andy put his hand over it to check for warmth, and then looked around as if expecting to find its author squatting behind a tree, waiting for someone to pass the toilet paper.

"You can see how they climbed all the way up here," Andy said, scrambling into the tree to get a better look at the claw marks the bears had left in the bark. "They went all the way onto these little branches. Crazy old creatures," he said wistfully, like someone who has just learned about a party to which he hadn't been invited.

We spent our last two days camped by Hinkle Springs, in an open meadow ringed by ponderosa pines that had recently been the bedding ground for a herd of elk. The ground was divoted by their heavy hooves, and they had dug themselves a shallow bed not far from where I pitched my tent. One afternoon as I walked across the meadow, it occurred to me that I had begun to read the ground's inscriptions in the unconscious way we read street signs and billboards. I knew it had rained recently by the way the grasses had been swept into clumps by roils of water. And the bloom of locust and daisy told me a fire had come through, taking out some of the trees and most of the understory. A sandy wash was marked by a clumsy filigree of elk prints, and I found myself bending closer to see if anything had followed them as they made their way across the meadow.

It was like living in a foreign country and suddenly discovering that you understand the language. I knew now what Leopold meant when he wrote about the "hundred small events" that indicated a wild presence on the mountain: "the midnight whinny of a pack horse, the rattle of rocks, the bound of a fleeing deer, the way shadows lie under the spruces." I had seen where bears had foraged for honey, ants, and acorns, the print a bobcat leaves after drinking at a lake, the scrape a mountain lion makes in the duff. I had seen the deep troughs elk had dug in the ground as they rubbed their antlers against a tree and noticed where a pack of coyotes fed on rodents and when they had tasted berries. My vocabulary was as limited as any foreigner's, but for the first time in my life, I was able to eavesdrop on the conversation the wilderness has with itself. I shouldn't have been surprised to discover that the discussion revolved around the usual subjects—food, sex, and the weather.

On our last day, a few of us rose before dawn and tiptoed into the woods. "I'm sure you're all getting tired of bear scat," Andy had said the night before. "But very few animals are out when we're out—it's too hot for them. The best times are dawn and dusk." Now we were out at the animal hour, the slate-gray sky still flecked with stars. We walked single file, keeping the beams of our flashlights low to the ground and listening for something thrashing into the underbrush or heaving itself into a tree. But all I could hear was the racket our boots made as we skirted the underbrush, and the sound of our tempered, cautious breathing.

After a time the sky lightened to a pale blue, and we each went off to find a quiet place to sit and watch. I picked a rock near the edge of a ridge and willed myself to sit quietly. The greens and browns of the tall pines were just beginning to emerge as the trees brightened out of silhouette, and I imagined that if I were patient the wolves would come trotting through the clearing, ears up, noses down, scenting for elk. Flies buzzed me, investigating the accumulated odors of campfire, sunscreen, and sweat, and a white moth circled the limb of a Douglas fir. After nearly an hour, a solitary jackrabbit capered into the clearing. When I stood up to get a better look, it veered back into the brush, hind quarters kicking furiously.

It occurred to me that in a wilderness this remote, the animals had no reason to be seen, and plenty of reasons to stay hidden. The mark of a wilderness is its elusiveness, its secrecy, and those of us who believe that wild creatures are what gives a wilderness its mystery can only be thankful when the animals elude us. We have to be content to glimpse them on their own terms, by reading the calligraphy they leave on the terrain.

CAUGHT BETWEEN THE PACK
AND THE HARD CASE

LAURA SCHNEBERGER
(2002)

rizona ranchers Gary and Darcy Ely have had a tough six months. It shows in their faces. Gary spends most of his time in the saddle, and Darcy spends most of hers coordinating meetings, kids, and trying to keep the normally calm Gary from losing his cool.

The Elys were fully aware they lived in close proximity to the Mexican wolf Francisco pack; even dealing with wolf depredations on their livestock. Over the course of the past summer, something happened to the Francisco pack that has the Elys scrambling for help. The wolves had a successful litter of pups, and things drastically changed for the worse in the Elys' pastures.

In July, Gary Ely put 165 heavy and mother cows with 70 branded calves into their summer pasture on the 4-Drag ranch in eastern Arizona. In November, after gathering for over a month, his found tally is so low that he is not optimistic about remaining in business. Found so far are 158 cows and 31 calves, 6 of those were born in the pasture.

Last week, after finding a partially consumed calf, one of the few that could be found, the U.S. Fish and Wildlife Service (USFWS) informed Gary that he was really dealing with the combined forces of two packs of wolves. Nine of the wolves have collars and are definitely part of the Mexican Wolf Recovery Program; at least 5 are possible pups, 3 have been trapped and have temporary collars, and 2 of them are unknowns. Of these unknowns, one is so big that it has earned the name Bigfoot. To date, no one has been able to trap Bigfoot to determine whether he is actually a Mexican wolf born to the packs in the last year or two, or if he is a feral hybrid released to supplement the gene pool. If the wolf turns out to be a hybrid, the question will be: how did it get there, and has it mated with any of the other wolves?

Across the fence from the Elys, on the San Carlos Reservation, just 5 miles from the Elys' livestock allotment, the livestock that provides the San Carlos Apache tribe with income and a food supply for ceremonies has all but disappeared. Tribal leaders want to know why the U.S. Fish and Wildlife Service has ignored their plea to remove the marauding wolves. So far, answers have not been forthcoming.

GOBBLED UP

According to the final rule of the Mexican Wolf Recovery Program, the expected livestock depredation numbers were supposed to remain at 30 head a year, once 100 Mexican wolves were recovered into the Blue Range wolf recovery area. On the 4-Drag, 16 wolves have likely slaughtered nearly 50 calves and several cows since late spring, many of them since July. This count gives the pack the benefit of the doubt by not including the unknown depredation numbers from reservation losses. This count also ignores the Elys' missing adult cows and the calves that were due to be born in the pasture, yet didn't show up. The count is far over the expected depredations, from less than a quarter of the wolves.

Using those conservative numbers, the super pack has eaten 3 to 4 calves each, in 120 days. If this is any indication of the need for prey, 100 wolves in cattle country, with a free buffet of livestock, will eat at least 1600 calves per year, and likely many more. These numbers are closer to historic data on Mexican Wolf depredations, but much higher than the current environmentally-correct school of thought expressed in the wolf recovery plan.

The USFWS would like to blame the damage on other predators. Lion kills have historically been a problem on the 4-Drag, but the Elys say their depredations have increased from a bad-year high of 25 percent depredation attributed to lion, coyote, and bear, to an overwhelming 70 percent, in just two years.

Back in the good old days of 25 percent, the newcomer wolf packs were not as successful at providing for themselves and less capable of bringing down livestock. Instead, they preferred to live off hunter leavings and lion kills, many times driving the lions to kill more livestock and wildlife, and driving hunters off their game.

While gathering cattle, rancher Doug Stacy in Arizona watched a different pack of five wolves chase six elk not more than 75 yards from his truck and trailer while gathering cattle, proving that it isn't just ranchers with something to lose.

"All the sportsmen need to get on the bandwagon before they don't have any game to hunt. Just think about the future picture as these damn things multiply," said Stacy.

Animal Damage Control (ADC), the agency responsible for capturing problem wolves and other livestock killers, has its own wolf troubles. In late October, three members of the super pack ambushed employee J. R. Murdoch while he watched from horseback. They appeared out of nowhere, and badly mauled one of his female lion hounds before he could intervene.

EXPERIMENTING WITH SOMEONE ELSE'S LIVELIHOOD

The advent of an unknown number of pups in 2002 has lent a successful air to the project; three collared pups live in the super pack. However, with mouths to feed, the wolves have hit their predatory stride. The Elys and the San Carlos Reservation Apaches are paying the bill, given that the super pack territory has expanded deeply into the reservation in the last two years.

Both wolf packs involved in the massive depredations are confirmed livestock killers. Experimental 10-J status allows the USFWS to remove them, but nothing substantial has been done to limit the nightmare to a manageable scope. Arizona Wildlife Services feels it is becoming impossible to trap them, leaving helicopter removal as the only option.

USFWS has considered bringing in contract trappers, but this idea seems to create an agency scuffle that no one wants to broach as of yet. The past year alone, ADC trappers spent hundreds of fruitless hours babysitting wolves and trying to find what little evidence was left of ranchers' high calf losses in wolf recovery areas.

Acting on orders from the Mexican wolf recovery leader, who has faced two years of demands that he remove the wolves from the San Carlos Reservation, Animal Damage Control, a division of Wildlife Services, was ordered to play musical wolves, trapping wolves from the reservation, only to release them back into the forest, where they could roam right back to the reservation or deeper into the 4-Drag. Wildlife Services believes that the constant manipulation and shuffling of wolves has trained them to avoid traps, and has intensified the problem.

The education of Mexican wolves is not news to ranchers who, before the project was begun, warned that history showed us that too much trapping would habituate the wolves to traps.

BUREAUCRATIC TUG OF WAR

With the sudden increase in wolf numbers, lethal control is an option; however, USFWS refuses to give the state agencies the authority to make normal management decisions, much less a lethal take decision. Ranchers offered lethal take permits often refuse, because of threats to their operations and livestock by wolf activists and environmental extremists, who see wolf reintroduction as a political and biological weapon against land use in the west. The Elys want nothing to do with what they feel is USFWS responsibility.

⌒

There is no doubt the recovery program is in the midst of a major power struggle. Both the Arizona and New Mexico Fish and Game commissions have been unhappy with the project and are determined to have more of a say in how it is managed.

Arizona game commissioner, Joe Carter, says the program is clearly in disarray. "Over the past two years, the program has continued to disintegrate in fulfilling the obligations of the U.S. Fish and Wildlife Service. The Arizona Commission, myself included, have discussed this with H. Dale Hall and we would like to see him turn this around and make full partners of the state agencies so we all know who is responsible for what."

Mr. Carter calls the wolf reintroduction the only real problem project they have conducted with the USFWS; other projects have worked well in the past. This lends credence to rancher claims that the original wolf recovery plan was unrealistic and compiled with faulty data. As Mr. Carter points out, "When a grazing permittee is losing 70 percent of his calf crop, and we can tie the cause to wildlife, the state game agencies bear a responsibility for dealing with that problem. With things going the way they are, if we cannot control and manage the 10 or 25 or 40 wolves that are out there, how are we going to manage 100 animals?"

Arizona and New Mexico state agencies are insisting on a set protocol for dealing with problem animals, including identifying who has the authority to deal with depredation problems, removal and lethal control issues, and dangerous situations. As things stand, no decision to remove an offending wolf can happen at the state level. All management decisions are being made at the top of the USFWS food chain. USFWS is reluctant to relinquish control of this authority.

While major project renovations languish in bureaucratic splendor, the wolves in Arizona have taken this season to establish themselves as record-breaking livestock killers, living off the labors of the few remaining ranchers in Arizona and the helpless people on the Apache reservation.

Gary Ely says Fish and Wildlife Mexican Wolf Recovery Coordinator Brian Kelly told him that the Arizona game department does not want to help deal with the Elys' problem, and that Gary needed to talk to them and find out why. This information was a big surprise to Commissioner Carter. His impression was that a plan to begin dealing with the super pack should be in place within days, though USFWS only provides for the removal of three uncollared wolves.

Whether that gives the Elys enough relief to stay in business remains to be seen. It is entirely possible that if they stay the Elys will have to feed wolves for free, into perpetuity, and they aren't inclined to furnish the chuck that long. Defenders of Wildlife, who reimburses ranchers for lost livestock, has bowed out of the process, since even they cannot continue to write the checks the wolves are cashing at the Ely chuckwagon. So far, the Elys say they have gotten one check amounting to $1,000 dollars, in 2001, for heifers they lost. This year there have been many promises, but nothing else, for one badly-bitten ranch horse and two baby calves. Of course, the missing cows and calves are considered to be a donation by the Elys.

The Mexican Wolf Recovery Program is proving, once again, that those who do not learn from history are destined to repeat it. Doing the same thing over and over again and expecting different results is indeed the definition of insanity. Ultimately, rural Arizona and two separate cultures are being destroyed. The bill falls squarely on those who had no choice in the matter.

WELCOMING HOME
AN OLD FRIEND

||||||||||||||||||||||||||||||||||||||||||||||||||||||

Peter Friederici
(2002)

*W*ading through tawny, knee-high grasses, Apache tribal biologist Krista Beazley raises a radio telemetry receiver overhead. Wind sighs through the boughs of the pines that cloak the surrounding ridges, which run through the Apache-Sitgreaves National Forest and toward the White Mountain Apache Reservation. Radio-collared Mexican wolves were here recently, and Beazley hopes to hear the electronic signal that would indicate they are still around. Elk pellets litter the ground. A raven calls, but the equipment makes no sound.

In March 27 a remarkable ceremony took place in the Hon-dah casino and conference center on the White Mountain Apache Reservation in east-central Arizona. Representatives of the tribal government signed an agreement with the U.S. Fish and Wildlife Service (FWS) to make their reservation part of the official recovery area for the endangered Mexican gray wolf.

Relations between the tribe and FWS have not always been good. As recently as the 1990s, the tribe threatened to stop cooperating with FWS officials because of disputes over the agency's mandate to protect threatened and endangered species on tribal land. But the political and cultural work that lay behind the scratching of pens to paper in March just may herald a new era of cooperation in eastern Arizona—both among people and between people and wildlife. Today Beazley works in the field with biologists from FWS and other agencies, and the tribe and the agency regularly share information about wolf locations and activities.

Mexican wolves, which were extirpated from the Southwest in the last century, have been the subject of an ambitious reintroduction program. FWS biologists captured the five remaining animals in Mexico in the 1970s and bred them in captivity, beginning reintroductions in the Apache National Forest in Arizona in 1998. The agency designated a 7,000-square-mile recovery area encompassing wilderness areas in the Apache Forest and the adjacent Gila National Forest in New Mexico. The wolves are deemed a "nonessential, experimental" population under the Endangered Species Act, which offers FWS biologists more flexibility in dealing with their management; for example, they can remove wolves that prey on livestock.

Though the wolves have been successful in hunting wild prey and in rearing young, many have been shot or hit by cars. Although Defenders of Wildlife has pledged to reimburse landowners for any livestock killed by wolves, a strong anti-wolf sentiment remains among some locals, and biologists agree that the wolves will benefit from access to more remote wild land.

In fact, to wolf advocates, the White Mountain reservation land is integral to recovery efforts. According to tribal chairman Dallas Massey, it's "a beautiful reservation, and there's a lot of wild country left. Wolves can survive out there."

The reservation, located along the western boundary of FWS's original recovery area, contains more than 1.6 million acres of forest, woodland, grassland and riparian areas that comprise ideal wolf habitat. Unlike national forest land, access to reservation land is strictly controlled, reducing the likelihood of encounters between wolves and people.

"The reservation provides a much-needed sanctuary for wolves that are having a difficult time surviving," says Craig Miller, Defenders' Southwest representative. "The reservation has far fewer humans and fewer chances for conflicts."

Wolves have strayed onto reservation land almost since the beginning of the recovery program. Working with Defenders and with state and federal agencies, the tribe has allowed those wolves to remain. One naturally bonded pair has spent most of its time on the reservation for the last year. The new agreement commits the tribe to allowing up to six family groups of wolves on its land.

The reservation also supports ample prey for wolves in the form of deer, elk and other wildlife species. This abundance was a hurdle for wolf advocates, since revenue from hunting is an economic mainstay for the tribe. Some hunters pay tens of thousands of dollars for the opportunity to hunt trophy elk, and tribal wildlife management officials worried that the wolves would disrupt that lucrative business by preying on the elk.

The decision to support wolf recovery, says Massey, "was not something simple. We had a lot of concerns, especially with cattle.

Would they hurt our cattle? Our elk? But the more we talked the better it sounded. Wolves were here before; they were always here. At the end we finally decided we want to live with them."

The decision was hammered out over several years, during which a tribal task force studied the contentious issue and eventually made recommendations to the tribal council. A thorough assessment of likely wolf impacts on elk, cattle and other species yielded no definite answers. In the end, the decision was made partly because officials recognized that wolves were in the area to stay, and wanted some say in how they were managed.

Mary Jo Stegman, a FWS biologist who consults with the tribe on endangered species issues, hopes the decision will be noted by others who live within the Mexican wolf's range. "If this wolf program is successful," she says, "maybe it'll help with some of the private landowners as well."

Some tribal officials also saw the possibility for new enterprises that would take advantage of wolf populations. Defenders is exploring the possibility of eventually including the tribe in its "Wolf Country Beef" program, which rewards ranchers who agree to allow wolves on their land with higher prices from conservation-minded consumers. And the tribe is already working on creating a dude ranch at which vacationers will be able to ride horses, herd cattle and enjoy luxurious camping. The potential of also being able to hear wolves howl in the distance may make the reservation even more enticing for those who want to experience the wild Southwest.

Defenders has already supported the tribe's wolf program by helping to provide field training and housing—in Alpine, a small town in the heart of wolf country—to Beazley and other biologists. The group is also working to help set up a wolf exhibit at the tribe's casino.

Acceptance of the wolf's presence may also be related to something of cultural revival. At the March 27 ceremony, Beazley's father, Joyner George, sang a traditional Apache wolf song—with lyrics "Let me be powerful like the wolf"—that warriors once sang for strength and inspiration. The song had been forgotten by all but a few tribal members until a medicine man taught it to George. Ramon Riley, the tribe's cultural resources official, notes that some still remember songs about bison even though bison haven't shared the same living space as Apaches for generations.

Riley and other tribal members hope that wolves will again become part of tribal culture. "For the elders, the traditional people, their opinions have always been the same. Traditionally predators weren't viewed as bad," says Doreen Gatewood, a tribal member and activist who has long supported wolf recovery. "That view is now getting a voice."

"Some days you get lucky, some you don't," says Krista Beazley after yet another attempt to get a signal on her radio tracking equipment. On her first day working in this area, a pair of wolves ran right in front of her truck. This afternoon we're not so fortunate. The wolves have roamed elsewhere. But in a couple of places, on the old two-track road that runs up the valley, we spot scat filled with elk fur.

The late afternoon grows cold. We head back to the car.

My mind is filled not with the sound of wolves howling, nor with a glimpse of a sleek gray shape darting between pines, but with the image of the wild country the wolves traverse here—and with the feeling that it may be the wolves, for a change, that are getting lucky.

MEXICAN WOLF FATE TEETERS
BETWEEN SCIENCE AND POLITICS

||||||||||||||||||||||||||||||||||||||||||||||||||||||||||||||||||||||||||||||||||||||||||||||||||||

MICHAEL J. ROBINSON
(2001)

*T*he saga of the troubled Mexican gray wolf recovery program can be traced through the life of M166, a seven-year-old male lobo who at birth in the Wild Canid Survival and Research Center in Eureka, Missouri, was given the more romantic and even hopeful name, Rio, "river" in Spanish.

Until recently, every known Mexican wolf was born in captivity, the progeny of the last five wild wolves trapped in Mexico between 1977 and 1980, interbred with two lineages already held in captivity in the U.S. An emergency captive breeding program raised the world's Mexican wolf population to around 200 animals, but until reintroduction began in March, 1998, there were no wolves known in the wild in either Mexico or the southwestern United States.

Rio was one of the first eleven animals released that historic spring. The recovery area for the Mexican wolf comprises 4.4 million acres, split between the Apache National Forest in Arizona and the Gila National Forest in New Mexico. Unlike Yellowstone National Park and central Idaho, more than two-thirds of the Mexican wolf recovery area is grazed by cattle; the Gila contains the largest chunk of ungrazed terrain and three-quarters of the recovery area.

However, to meet the opposition of the livestock industry-dominated New Mexico Game Commission, wolves from the captive population would only be released in the Arizona portion of the recovery area, with allowance for translocating animals into New Mexico following their recapture from the wild.

A second equally-unprecedented management provision, also demanded by ranchers, called for removal of any wolves that establish territories outside of the recovery area—even on other public lands and even if the wolves are not killing livestock.

Finally, in contrast to the Northern Rocky Mountain Wolf Recovery Plan, there are no provisions requiring livestock operators to assume any responsibility for cleaning up the carcasses of cattle that die from other causes before wolves scavenge on them and become habituated to stock. In the Southwest, where many allotments are grazed year-round, it is not uncommon to stumble upon dozens of dead cattle that succumbed to starvation, disease and other factors.

Shortly after the first eleven pioneering Mexican wolves were released in the Apache National Forest, they started getting shot. Rio's mate was one of five wolves killed within half a year. A sixth wolf disappeared and is presumed dead, and Rio's pup, thought to be the first Mexican wolf born in the wild in the U.S. in over 70 years, disappeared and is also presumed dead after its mother was shot. (There has been one conviction from these [first] five shootings—that of James Rogers, a member of a local ranching family, who served four months in prison.)

Over the next two years, Rio was successively provided four new mates, the first of which was killed by a mountain lion and the next two recaptured after showing insufficient fear of humans. But the last mate displayed suitable wild behavior: The pair avoided people and domestic animals. Then they crossed out of the recovery area.

As a result, Rio and this last mate found themselves back in captivity. After four months, they were re-released in the Gila National Forest in December, 2000. But the once-established pair split up shortly after their release.

Rio's experience wasn't unusual. Three other packs were released in Arizona but recaptured and held in captivity for several months, and two of those have been re-released. Each split apart after re-release, with most of those animals subsequently recaptured, killed in vehicular hit-and-run incidents, or dying or disappearing suspiciously.

During Rio and his mate's peregrinations alone in the first half of 2001, each separately scavenged on livestock carcasses. A rancher refused to allow Fish and Wildlife Service biologists to remove a bull Rio had been feeding on, even though the bull (when alive) was not supposed to have been in that part of the national forest. He was one of a number of trespass cattle in the area; a necropsy revealed he had died from a fall, not from wolf predation.

This also is not atypical. The first three wolf packs to be recaptured had each scavenged on cattle. One pack's scavenging had taken place in a region closed to grazing by the Forest Service but with cattle still present in defiance of that order. Two of those packs went on to kill cattle. The third pack was recaptured to prevent possible future depredations, resulting in an injury that required the amputation of the alpha female's leg (perhaps a factor in that pack's dissolution upon re-release and her eventual disappearance and presumed demise.)

Then, in May of this year, Rio and his mate re-united and began killing cattle, leading to their recapture in June. They have been separated in captivity, and Rio has been assigned a new mate—his sixth—in preparation for another release.

The Mexican wolf recovery area spread across parts of two states aptly illustrates the difference a state line can make. In Arizona, where wolves have been released directly from the captive population, five packs with around 25 wolves are now established, and several litters of pups have been born this year. But in New Mexico only one pair survives.

In June, 2001, four biologists led by Dr. Paul Paquet, released an 86-page study of the first three years of the reintroduction. The scientists concluded that "survival and recruitment rates...are far too low to ensure population growth or persistence. Without dramatic improvement in these vital rates, the wolf population will fall short of predictions for upcoming years."

They recommend eliminating artificial management boundaries. "By far the most important and simplest change the Service can make," they write, is "obtaining the authority to conduct initial releases in the...Gila National Forest." They also recommend allowing wolves that are not "management problems" to roam freely outside the recovery area, noting that "in sharp contrast with the Service's approach elsewhere, the Mexican wolf project developed a rule that requires wolves to be removed from public and private land outside the...recovery area, even in the absence of a problem."

Another recommendation is to "Require livestock operators on public land to take some responsibility for carcass management/disposal to reduce the likelihood that wolves become habituated to feeding on livestock." They note that "At least 3 packs were removed from the wild because they scavenged on dead livestock left on national forest lands. Such scavenging may predispose wolves to eventually prey on livestock."

Unfortunately, Mexican wolves have seldom benefited from scientific-based decision-making. The first Fish and Wildlife Service Mexican wolf recovery coordinator lost his job in 1999 when he proposed allowing wolves from captivity to be released in the Gila. After Clinton Administration officials finally agreed to this change, the agency failed to follow through with the requisite amendment to the management rule, and still has not initiated the legal process to do so. Now, rancher-congressman Joe Skeen (R-NM), infuriated by the scientists' recommendations, is pushing legislation to conduct a new study of the recovery program to be conducted by non-biologists.

Whether sonorous howls will continue to echo along southwestern canyon walls will depend on whether politics continues to hold sway or whether we finally heed the scientists' warnings. For North America's most imperiled mammal, the stakes couldn't be higher.

THE MEXICAN WOLF

||||||||||||||||||||||||||||||||||||||||||||||||||||||||||||||||||||||||||||

Tom Dollar

(2002)

A hundred years ago on the Arizona frontier, just about everyone—prospectors, stockmen, hunters, trappers, and foresters alike—agreed that the only good wolf was a dead one.
Even Aldo Leopold, the putative godfather of conservation biology,
killed wolves. He wrote about it in "Thinking Like a Mountain," an
essay in his seminal book, *A Sand County Almanac.*

As a rookie forester with self-described "trigger itch," Leopold
thought that killing wolves saved game for hunters, so he "pumped
lead" into a pack of cavorting wolves, fatally wounding the alpha
female and crippling a yearling pup. Thirty years later, he wrote mov-
ingly of the "fierce green fire" dying in the eyes of the she wolf.
Over the years, Leopold said, he had seen state after state, with
the acquiescence of foresters like himself, eradicate wolves. And in
wiping out key predators such as wolves and grizzlies, humans had
"toppled the spire off an edifice a-building since the morning stars
sang together."

As early as 1893, Arizona offered a bounty for wolf kills, but
eradication didn't begin in earnest until 1914 when Congress created
Predatory Animal and Rodent Control (PARC). Extermination was
quick. By the 1930s breeding populations of the Mexican gray wolf,
El Lobo, were eliminated in the Southwest, and lone wolves wandering up from Mexico's Sierra Madre were hunted down remorselessly.
Though sightings of wolves were reported in Arizona and New Mexico into the 1970s, the last documented wolf kill in the Southwestern
United States was near Alpine, Texas, in 1970.

It's midsummer in Arizona, a time when "cabin fever" afflicts
residents of valley cities who drearily check off the days as the temperature rips past 100° F. by noon and keeps climbing. But it feels
like spring here in the White Mountains along the state's eastern
edge, where yesterday's summer thunderstorm hit hard with light-
ning, slashing rain, hail, and a few vagrant snowflakes.

Now, in the early morning as I drive north on the Coronado
Trail, U.S. 191, a serpentine route ascending the Mogollon Rim

toward the village of Alpine, gray mist wreathes steepled conifers and patchy ground fog lies in roadside swales. Just ahead, a cow elk sprints across the blacktop, a calf at her heels. I brake and steer onto the narrow shoulder. A small creek threads through a large meadow where several elk cows, a few calves, and a single antlered bull graze on dew-spangled grasses. They raise their heads and stare, flight ready. Steamy vapors rise from their nostrils.

Seeing these elk, the main ungulate prey of gray wolves, I recall a sign posted at a trailhead announcing WOLF COUNTRY in bold letters. Beneath it is a list of wolf info: Wolves live in family groups of two to eight, are curious by nature, and may come calling. They're rarely aggressive toward humans but will attack other canids, especially when rearing pups. Drive slowly, the sign advises, and lists hotline numbers to call if you see a wolf. I don't expect to be so lucky.

I drive on slowly through strands of broken fog. Suddenly, in the right-hand ditch, I catch a glimpse of something crouched in the brush, a bushy ruff round its neck. A wolf! I whip my truck into a U-turn and idle past the spot, scanning the brush. Nothing. Probably just someone's ranch dog, I think, as I swing round, heading north again. But just at that instant, a small wolf wearing a bright orange radio collar, darts across the road, clears the ditch, and disappears into the thicket. The collar is a giveaway; it's a wolf. Though smaller than I'd pictured, it's probably the alpha female of the Lupine Pack, released only days ago in the nearby Bear Wallow Wilderness.

I stop where I saw her enter the underbrush, and there she is!— perhaps six feet beyond the ditch, standing broadside, head turned, yellow eyes unblinking. She seems curious, not fearful, but when I switch off the ignition, she trots into the steamy woods, pausing briefly to glance over her shoulder.

After an absence of nearly half a century, the endangered Mexican gray wolf, *Canis lupus baileyi*, has been reintroduced here in the Blue Range Primitive Area of the Apache National Forest. I have seen the living proof with my own eyes. On March 28, 1998, more than 20 years after the Mexican gray wolf was listed as endangered under the Endangered Species Act, 11 wolves were released from their holding pens into the Blue, as the region is known hereabouts.

Now, midway through the third year of the recovery program, approximately 35 Mexican wolves, including wild-born pups, inhabit the Blue. The goal of the interagency recovery team, headed by U.S. Fish and Wildlife Service (FWS), is a sustainable population of approximately 100 wolves by the year 2005. The team also includes USDA-Wildlife Services (formerly Animal Damage Control), the

Turner Endangered Species Fund, the U.S. Forest Service, the Arizona Game and Fish Department, and the New Mexico Department of Game and Fish.

The shooting started again as soon as the first wolves hit the ground. During the recovery program's first year alone, five of the original eleven wolves were shot and killed. The first killed was an alpha male. The wolf had attacked his dog, the shooter said. But upon learning that it was a crime to shoot an endangered wolf for attacking a pet, he insisted that the wolf had actually threatened his wife. A necropsy refuted the gunner's claim, showing clearly that the wolf was motionless, standing broadside to the shooter.

Wolf advocates were outraged when FWS declined to prosecute. Bobbie Holaday, founder of the grass-roots, all-volunteer PAWS (Preserve Arizona's Wolves), who worked tirelessly for wolf restoration, said of the shootings, "It's terrorism. Somebody's trying to sabotage the program and terrify the U.S. Fish and Wildlife Service...into abandoning wolf recovery."

Others saw it as one more example of the agency's feckless performance on behalf of the wolf, pointing out that only after citizens' groups sued did the service draft the required Final Environmental Impact Statement on wolf recovery.

Though investigations are still pending, only one wolf assassin has been brought to trial. A man near rural Nutrioso, Arizona, was sentenced to four months in prison, six months of house arrest, and community service after he admitted shooting a wolf and dumping its body in New Mexico to conceal the crime.

Depending on which side you take on conservation issues, Catron County, New Mexico, is either notorious for know-nothing opposition to the Mexican wolf or famous for brave resistance to "federal bureaucracies in Washington." In the 1990s Catron County attracted national headlines by attempting to pass a law annulling the authority of the federal government to manage the county's public lands and another that would have required every homeowner to bear arms.

Curious about the depth of hostility that would spur someone to shoot a wolf, I attended a FWS-sponsored open house on wolf recovery in Reserve, the county seat. When I arrived at the meeting hall I parked behind a battered pickup plastered with bumper stickers: "I love spotted owls. They taste like chicken." And "To protect and care for his creations, God made ranchers. No wolves!" I'd come to the right place.

The explosive atmosphere that once encouraged outsiders to swarm to Catron County to volunteer as militiamen has simmered down some. Whereas this kind of meeting would have been standing-room-only a few years ago, tonight fewer than 50 ranchers, hunting guides, and townsfolk were gathered.

Fear of the wolf—depicted in folklore as a snarling canine, red in tooth and claw—is deeply etched in the human psyche, and one ranch woman who had seen wolves on her property asked, "How do I know one of these wolves won't run up on my porch and snatch my three year old?"

While it is true that captive-reared wolves are more habituated to humans than their wild kin and a few Mexican wolves have approached people, there has never been a documented wolf attack on a human in the lower 48 states. "Lions or feral dogs may do that," said former Arizona Game and Fish commissioner Beth Woodin, "but not wolves."

I expected to hear a lot of anti-wolf and anti-government venom at the Reserve meeting. And there was some. One rancher heatedly accused the recovery team of fudging data, concealing its activities, and outright lying. But the economic impact of wolf depredations on livestock economy seemed to be the biggest fear. Ranchers might be put out of business, some said, and government agents didn't care.

There was only a little grandstanding, and most of the questions were thoughtful and measured. A recurrent subtext of many comments, even from those who favored wolf recovery, was that no one tells them anything or listens when they speak. And people who feel disenfranchised, especially if they perceive their grievances as foisted upon them by outsiders, namely city folk and representatives of remote government bureaucracies, are uncooperative

Afterwards, driving away from Reserve, I wondered if there were wolf killers among the people with whom I'd sat elbow-to-elbow. A couple of days later I posed the question to Don Hoffman, a Forest Service wilderness specialist who has lived and worked in the Blue for 25 years. "I don't think there are guys driving around in pickups, rifles bristling out the windows, looking to blast a wolf," Don said. "More likely it's just hunters who see something that looks like a coyote and start banging away." Trigger itch again.

Despite determined opposition to wolf recovery by the Arizona and New Mexico Cattle Growers Associations, a few ranchers welcomed the Mexican wolf back on the land. Will and Jan Holder run the Anchor Ranch, a two-and-a-half-hour drive from the closest settlement, and so remote it's off the power grid. A cell phone, which captures a signal sporadically, is their only contact with the outside.

Though Will and Jan are latecomers to ranching after careers in advertising, the Anchor has been in Will's family for four generations. His mother was born here, and Ervin's Natural Beef, the organic, predator-friendly brand they produce, is named for Will's maternal grandfather, Ervin Hicks.

From the start they consulted rangeland experts, wolf biologists, even environmentalists, which other ranchers saw as a defection to "tree huggers." The Holders, some accused, would ruin ranching for "real" ranchers. But Will says, "We've been trying to eliminate predators for years; maybe it's time to try something different."

The first step was to practice sound animal husbandry. "It's not brain surgery," Jan says, "but it takes work to make it harder for wolves to kill a cow than an elk." When they discovered wolves on their land, they bunched up their cattle and stayed with them. A tight herd is more formidable to predators than isolated cows, and human presence in itself is a deterrent.

They kept the wolves off balance by moving their cattle around. After a few weeks, the wolves lost interest and moved on. "If you just let cows sit out there, in a few days the wolves pick a favorite," Will says. "By herding and moving them, we simply emulate how ungulate prey—buffalo, caribou, elk—naturally behave when predators appear."

As an example of bad husbandry, the Holders mention negligent disposal of animal carcasses, and they tell about wolves scavenging the carcass of a horse that died on a neighbor's grazing allotment. Soon, a rumor started that wolves had actually killed the horse. "If you don't remove carcasses, wolves will scavenge them," Jan says. "Next they'll attack a weak animal on its way out. Why not? It's easy." According to many wolf supporters I talked to, a major flaw in Mexican wolf recovery management is the absence of a provision requiring the timely disposal of dead livestock.

Wolves have killed cows, but Defenders of Wildlife, which compensates ranchers for losses, says that wolf depredations are a minuscule fraction of all livestock in the recovery area. The Holders are skeptical of the compensation program. "The idea of compensation is good," Will says, "but what's not good is that the wolf has to be either shot or removed. We're trying to get along with wolves, to come to sustainable terms with them, to coexist. Ranchers who have trouble with wolves are often those whose animal husbandry is poor."

During the first three and a half years of the recovery program 69 wolves were released into the Blue. Of those, six were shot, three run down and killed on roadways, and another slain by a mountain lion.

Two were recaptured and translocated into the Gila National Forest in New Mexico. Several others, including an undetermined number of wild-born pups, simply vanished and are presumed dead. Coursing after and trying to bring down a 400-pound bull elk is a tough way to make a living, even for seasoned predators, and some of the captive-bred wolves weren't up to it.

At one point during the program's first year, there were no wolves in the Blue; all 11 of the initial release had either been killed or returned to captivity for harassing livestock. The latter practice especially incensed environmentalists. As former Arizona Game and Fish commissioner Beth Woodin puts it, "This business of catching and removing every wolf that looks cross-eyed at a cow turns the program into a zoo without bars."

All in all, these fourth- and fifth-generation captive-bred wolves have adapted amazingly to life in the wild—forming pair bonds, organizing into packs, and killing ungulate prey. "It is apparent that these wolves are capable, which we questioned at first because they're all captive reared," says Dave Parsons, who was coordinator of the recovery program for nine years before retiring. "There's ample proof that the wolves still have what it takes physically and instinctively," he continues. "Within three weeks of their release we documented their killing elk. They've successfully reproduced in the wild and done all the other things that wild wolves do, such as establishing and defending territories. There've been very few problems with livestock depredation; in fact, wolves are out there whacking elk left and right and walking right past cows to do it."

But unless flaws in wolf management policy are soon corrected, El Lobo may be fated to live in what Beth Woodin described as a "zoo without bars." As mandated by the Federal rule governing Mexican wolf recovery, FWS commissioned a three-year independent scientific review of the program by the Conservation Breeding Specialist Group, led by acclaimed wolf biologist, Paul Paquet. The CBSG assessment was unequivocal in urging two immediate rule changes. The first would enlarge the primary wolf recovery zone; the second would allow for wolf dispersal outside the Blue Range Recovery Area.

While recommending that wolf releases continue for at least two years to ensure a sustainable population, the science review notes that because wolves have already settled much of the area, few suitable release sites remain in the primary wolf recovery zone. Currently, only problem wolves, those that commit such sins as loitering in the vicinity of human habitation or harassing livestock, can be translocated into the so-called secondary recovery zone, New Mexico's vast Gila National Forest. The Gila comprises about 75 percent of the 4.3-million-acre Blue Range Recovery Area and contains 700,000 roadless acres, free of livestock.

Early critics of the recovery plan argued that restricting the primary release zone to the relatively small Apache National Forest portion of the Blue would needlessly handicap wolf recovery. And one year into reintroduction, a panel of experts commissioned by FWS recommended enlarging the primary recovery zone to include the Gila. The service endorsed but did not implement that finding. The CBSG three-year review asserts that immediately changing the final rule to allow wolf releases directly into the Gila is "by far the most important and simplest change the Service can make."

What is often omitted from commentaries on Mexican wolf recovery is that wolves wander; it's how they form new pair bonds, create packs, and extend territories. The dispersers are usually young wolves, yearlings or two year olds, that travel amazing distances seeking mates. In the summer of 2001, for example, a radio-collared female wolf may have roamed up to Durango, Colorado, some 500 road miles from her Arizona release site. Unlike wolf recovery programs elsewhere, the Mexican wolf program recaptures wolves that disperse outside the Blue Range, a practice that the scientific review saw as detrimental to the recovery of *Canis lupus baileyi*. Urging FWS to modify the rule to permit wolves to wander and even to establish territories on private lands, the CBSG review refers to "extensive tracts of land" contiguous with the Blue Range that are excellent wolf habitat. Species recovery, the report states, preempts private property rights.

But will the service actively pursue a Federal rule change? When I asked current wolf recovery coordinator, Brian Kelly, he said, yes, definitely, the rule would be changed. But when I pressed for a timetable, he spoke of "adaptive management" and of input from all the "stakeholders"—ranchers, hunting guides, environmentalists, county officials, and others—as being just as important as "ivory-tower" science.

But others are pessimistic. Following a four-day, facilitated stakeholders' workshop on the three-year science review, several participants dissented from the FWS draft report, arguing that science should lead the way, that more public forums are redundant, and that wolves are being held hostage to bureaucratic stalling.

Michael Robinson of the Center for Biological Diversity set the tone: "Many hours were spent bemoaning constitutional issues, the plight of rural people in general, and other irrelevancies to the legal obligation to fashion an effective recovery program," he said. "One result of this...is the mind-numbing array of new studies, information gathering tasks and reviews...recommended within the various work groups. This workshop was part of an ongoing pattern...to delay and ultimately thwart...[recovery] of Mexican gray wolves.

And in the opinion of Terry Johnson, Chief of the Endangered Wildlife Program for the Arizona Game and Fish Department, "The majority of participants came to the Workshop armed only with personal opinions and little to no factual information on which to base their positions and comments....The resultant Draft Report thus represents a compilation of raw data...mixed with 'noise.'"

Finally, former wolf recovery coordinator, Dave Parsons, wrote, "The Endangered Species Act emphasizes the importance of scientific data...in the listing and recovery of endangered species....I am concerned that the scientific review conducted by independent scientists will not receive...appropriate...consideration."

Mexican gray wolves were eradicated from the Southwest before we had a chance to study them, to know their historic range, their natural history. "The recovery program was developed on hypotheses about wolf behavior," says Craig Miller, Southwest Director, Defenders of Wildlife. "If it's going to work, FWS has to stop heavy-handed management against dispersal and allow the wolves a...role as guides in developing a plan that does not ignore wolf habitat preferences."

Listen to the wolves? Perhaps. And one lone wolf may be trying to put an exclamation mark on Craig's point. He's wolf #m578. When I was up on the Blue, he was last heard from only a few miles from the Mexican border, heading south. When I learned about m578, I dropped in at the Alpine field office where I met Dan Groebner, an Arizona Game and Fish biologist who formerly worked with wolves in the Great Lakes region. "If that wolf was headed to Mexico, where presumably there are no longer any wolves," I said, "he's got to be going the wrong way, right?"

Dan arched his brow, smiled, and said, "I don't know. These wolves know how to find each other."

A government trapper was sent down to catch m578, but he eluded capture and turned back north. He's still out there, on the move, looking for something.

MEXICAN WOLF GUARDIAN REPORTS, 2002

|||||||||||||||

Jon Trapp

JANUARY 7–20, 2002

On January 7, I began my position as the new Mexican Wolf Guardian. I am an Arizona native and after spending six years overseas in the Air Force it is good to be home. In addition to working on this very worthwhile project, I am pursuing a master's degree in conservation biology–environmental education through Prescott College.

The last few weeks have been spent learning the ropes—telemetry, GPS, ATV, snowmobile, documentation, and office procedures. The staff and volunteers here are a great bunch of people who truly care about the success of these wolves. I am definitely learning the social, political, and economic complexities involved in a reintroduction program like this one.

The first week I was here, Melissa Peer (volunteer) and I posted area closure signs around a pen where we were holding a yearling male that was recaptured in New Mexico (m632). He was originally a member of the Lupine Pack. Since I taught survival and land navigation in the Air Force, I was the de facto navigator. The terrain was rugged and full of many parallel drainages. During our excursion, we happened upon a black bear cub that was searching under rocks for food.

I spent much of the second week with Rich Bard (volunteer) monitoring m632. The highlight was going into the pen to refill the water and check the fence line. It is one thing knowing that there are wolves somewhere out there in the forest, but it is quite another thing to be inside an enclosure with a wild wolf. Just about every evening the Saddle pack (M574, F510, and f646) came to the enclosure to visit m632. There was some concern that there may be violent interactions through the fence so Rich and I stayed close when the pack came near the enclosure. During the visits, we observed that f646 seemed to spend the most time visiting m632. Since breeding season is soon approaching, we decided to release m632.

While snow-shoeing into KP Cienega Campground on January 20, my wife Barbara and I found evidence of a recent elk kill as well as wolf tracks, scat, and blood splotches from a menstruating female. After we left there, we headed toward Blue Vista Lookout to see if we could pick up any wolves with the telemetry equipment. As we drove there, we noticed a very strong signal from the Saddle pack. As we rounded a corner, I saw them standing in a clearing. Three wolves with bright orange radio collars looked at us with curiosity as we stared back. Within moments they headed off into the woods. After they were gone, we studied their tracks for several hours. What a treat!

As a side note, m632 was nowhere near.

JANUARY 20–FEBRUARY 8, 2002

This period has been extremely busy, starting with a trip to Albuquerque to meet Brian Kelly, the Mexican Wolf Recovery Coordinator for the USFWS. Brad Bartet, a volunteer; Dan Stark, acting field coordinator; and I made the trip. It was very interesting to meet Brian and see where he works. I have a much greater appreciation for the work he does on the political side of the project. Endangered species recovery is always surrounded with political controversy, especially when a large carnivore is involved. It is good to have someone like Brian dealing with those issues.

While out in the field in New Mexico, we utilized a Radio Activated Guard (RAG) box in a calving pasture. The RAG box is an aversive training device that is activated by the radio collars on the wolves. When the wolves get within a certain radius of the RAG box, a flashing strobe activates and loud, obnoxious sounds are emitted from two speakers. The RAG box appeared to be successful; however, it was very difficult to place the device exactly where the wolves would be entering the 650-acre pasture. In that situation we would have needed about five more RAG boxes to effectively cover the area. The RAG box is best suited for smaller pastures or along known travel corridors of the wolves.

The next day we went to the Sevilleta National Wildlife Refuge where the pre-release wolf facility is located. The facility holds the wolves that have been selected for release from the captive breeding population. After this phase, the wolves are moved to pens in the area where they will be released. The purpose of this visit was to "process" eight wolves for their annual checkups. Processing involves capturing, sedating, drawing blood, giving vaccinations, taking measurements, and then returning the wolves back to the pen. It involved close contact with wolves, and I learned a great deal. Some of these wolves may be released within the next several months.

We were welcomed back to Alpine with a fresh road-killed elk. The Mexican gray project utilizes road-kill to feed wolves that are in holding pens and supplementally feed newly released wolves until we are sure they are hunting on their own. This helps the wolves in their transition to the wild. When we are notified of a road-kill, several of us will go to the kill, gut it and remove the limbs. Everything, except the gut pile, is then moved to a storage freezer for later use.

A few days later Paul Overy, Arizona Game and Fish wolf technician; Melissa Peer, volunteer; and I went to a remote area to look for wolf sign and study the vicinity where the Francisco pack denned last year. We spent several days there and learned the area pretty well, but due to heavy snow we did not find much wolf sign. We will probably be returning to this area depending upon the wolves.

The last major event involved a trip to the Slash Ranch in New Mexico. This ranch is in a highly remote area involving an 80 mile drive on a dirt road. The Slash Ranch currently has about 200 calving cows. Fresh calves and the associated afterbirth can be a strong enticement to wolves. Wildlife Services wolf management specialist, Alan Armistead and I were called in to discourage the Pipestem pack (M190 and F628) from preying on the fresh-born calves. This process uses aversive techniques such as pyrotechnics, sirens, vehicles, and firing weapons in the air. Several times the wolves entered the pasture. Alan and I did our best to scare the scat out of them. I've never seen a wolf run so fast. It is important to stop these wolves from preying on calves before they start, especially since the ranch is slated to have 1,800 more pregnant cows in the next few months. Volunteers Rich Bard and Brandon Barr replaced us.

In wolf recovery programs the stereotype "ranchers versus environmentalists" is often thrown around. I think it is important to understand that these stereotypes many times do not apply. The cowboys I met at the Slash Ranch were not opposed to wolves; they were just opposed to their cows being killed. I have a strong respect for the ranchers I met. They were good people who want to do the right thing.

FEBRUARY 10–MARCH 3, 2002

A majority of this reporting period has been spent at the Slash Ranch in New Mexico. Before I continue, it is important that I put this situation into context. Currently, there are only five wolves in New Mexico: M632 (Lupine), F621 (Cienega), M578 (Wildcat), and the Pipestem pack (M190 and F628). The Pipestem pack appears to be the only wolves who have established a territory. The other wolves travel between New Mexico and Arizona. Also, since all the other wolves are singletons, Pipestem is the only breeding pair in New Mexico. That is why the project has been focusing so much energy on this pair. Our efforts have largely been a success, since we have not documented any depredations on calves or cows. Soon it will be time for the female to choose a den site. We are hoping that she will choose a site somewhere in the Gila Wilderness area.

We have a good working relationship with the cowboys at the Slash Ranch. In fact, we often help around the ranch when the wolves are out of the area. Unfortunately, there are some ranchers in the area who are not supportive of the wolf project. Sometimes this can make for fairly tense situations. Some of the ranchers see the wolf as one more obstacle to a successful ranching operation. Some even see it as a larger conspiracy to drive them off their land. I understand that it is becoming harder and harder for them to make a living on the land, and I can empathize with them. However, I know that healthy ecosystems are more important for the global community as a whole. I do not want to see ranchers put out of business. I hope that the decision-makers can find a way to support ranches and healthy ecosystems.

We did have a scare one day when we found a dead calf that had its stomach eaten out. Alan Armistead, Wildlife Services; Brad Bartet, volunteer; and I performed a necropsy to determine the cause of death. By completely skinning the calf we could determine that coyotes had been the culprits. Canids bite their prey in two fundamentally different ways: 1) to bring the prey down (usually deep, high-pressure bites); and 2) to feed on the prey. When canids begin to feed they must tear through the hide. Often they do this by raking their canine teeth across the hide until it tears. In doing this, they leave very distinctive rake marks on the hide. By skinning the animal, we can clearly see these marks and measure the distance between the two canine teeth. In this case the rake marks were definitely coyote size. Additionally, we were able to tell that the calf was dead before the coyotes began feeding on it. This was determined by the absence of hemorrhaging near the bite marks. Basically, if the calf's heart had been beating at the time, there would have been hemorrhaging.

Things to look forward to in the next several months include two releases in New Mexico, pen sitting, den monitoring, trapping, and gathering telemetry data.

MARCH 4–APRIL 21

The first two weeks were fairly slow, but then picked up considerably. The first week I spent monitoring wolf packs that are near Alpine, Arizona. When I say near, I mean that I can return to my home each night. Most of the wolves have been exhibiting "good" behavior, with several exceptions. M632 (the wolf that had been at Engineer Springs Pen) had localized just east of Springerville. Unfortunately, he was hanging around cattle and feeding on cow carcasses on private land. At the request of the landowner, we decided to recapture him. After we attempted to trap him for about a week, he moved east where he began the same unproductive behavior on another ranch. It was then decided that we would use a helicopter and a net-gun to capture him. Alan Armistead was chosen to fire the net-gun from the helicopter. After he fired one net and missed, M632 ran into an abandoned chicken coop. The ground crew quickly surrounded the coop and captured him. M632 is now at Ladder Ranch.

M190 and F628 (Pipestem) have been causing some problems as well by killing cow calves. During this period, we have confirmed that these wolves have killed two calves. Once again, the landowner requested that we remove the wolves. Alan and I attempted to trap these wolves, but they were very wary of the trap sets. A large fire in the Gila National Forest caused us to pull our traps and return home for a short while. We will continue to attempt to trap these wolves.

During this period, I also attended an animal handling and chemical immobilization course at Sevilleta National Wildlife Refuge. This course was taught by Mark Johnson who was the wildlife veterinarian for Yellowstone National Park during its wolf reintroductions. His level of knowledge and commitment was very impressive. His number one goal was to prevent any handling of the animals. Handling and drugging of animals, however, is often necessary. His second goal was to minimize the stress and potential physical harm to the animals. His empathy toward the animals was very refreshing and empowering. It is wonderful to meet a wildlife professional who looks beyond the pure science of data collection.

The project released two mated pairs into the Gila Wilderness, New Mexico. The wolves were carried into the wilderness on mules and placed into soft pens. There were separate release sites for each pack. The two new packs are named Luna (M583, F562) and Gapiwi (M584, F624). Both packs are currently free of the soft pens. We will supplementally feed the wolves until we are sure that they are making their own kills.

This is an exciting time for the project since there is the potential for eight wild-born litters. We will be watching this situation closely.

MARCH 18–MAY 19

A majority of this period was focused on the Pipestem pack (M190, F628) in New Mexico. As mentioned in an earlier report, it had been decided that Pipestem needed to be removed from the wild due to the fact that they had killed calves and were on private property outside of the recovery area. It was decided to allow F628 to den to help facilitate the safe removal of the adults and the pups. Alan and I spent many hours using telemetry to try and pinpoint the den site. The den site was located in a big boulder pile. We set many traps near the den and a helicopter was available as a back up. We did end up utilizing the helicopter to dart gun the adults. I assisted in the processing of the wolves. The mission was a success, and the pups and the adults were all safely reunited at Sevilleta National Wildlife Refuge by the end of the week.

During this period we had an ecology class from Prescott College visit the wolf project. We spent several days tracking the Hawks Nest pack (F486, M619) using telemetry equipment. The class was very eager to help us to get more position data on the pack. I enjoyed instructing the students on how to use the telemetry equipment in conjunction with maps, compass, and GPS.

I also attended the Southwest Carnivore Committee at the Grand Canyon. At this conference I learned the status of other carnivores in this region, including foxes, coyotes, bobcats, jaguars, lynx, ocelots, mountain lions, and others. Other topics covered included habitat fragmentation, bilateral agreements with other countries, carnivore diseases, and habitat modeling.

For the next week, I will be focusing on the Hawks Nest pack.

MAY 20–JUNE 23, 2002

This reporting period primarily involved intensive monitoring of two wolf packs: Hawks Nest and Bluestem. The first two weeks were spent with the Hawks Nest Pack (M619, F486). We had not noticed this pack localizing in any particular area and wondered if they had produced any pups this year. During the first week I followed Hawks Nest from about 4:30 a.m. to 10:30 a.m. I obtained good telemetry data and identified some possible travel corridors. I found an interesting location in a narrow portion of a drainage called Coyote Creek. From an observation point near the wolves location, I noticed four elk carcasses of various ages. One of the carcasses still had some meat on it. I sat at this observation point for many hours hoping to get a view of F486 with the binoculars. If there were a clear view of her, I might be able to see if she had swollen nipples. I never did get to see the wolves from that location, but I did see some beautiful sunrises.

This first week also included a day spent constructing the soft pen for the soon-to-be released Bluestem pack. The enclosure was about a half an acre and made of plastic fencing. Electric wires were woven through the fencing to slow the impending exit of the wolves. This sort of enclosure is a compromise between a hard release (simply opening the kennel door) and a soft release (an eight-foot high chain-link fence). After a full day of work on the pen, Brian Kelly (USFWS Recovery Coordinator), Dan Stark (acting USFWS Field Coordinator), and I tracked Hawks Nest. We just happened to be at the right place at the right time when we noticed the wolves running through a meadow. M619 was carrying an elk leg in his mouth. It was quite impressive.

The second week Hawks Nest monitoring was conducted from approximately 5:00 p.m. to 11:30 p.m. At this point the wolves had moved approximately five miles to a new location. They were feeding on an elk carcass that was adjacent to a large meadow. Several nights I moved to the edge of this pasture before the wolves started moving. From this vantage point I was able to view the wolves for a couple of nights. The wolves did not notice my presence as they moved through this meadow. I was able to see them sleeping, grooming, and sniffing through the tall grass. Unfortunately, due to the tall grass, I was unable to get a good view of F486's underside. We are still unsure if F486 produced any pups this year, but we will continue to monitor the pack to be sure.

The last two weeks were spent supporting the release of the new pack named Bluestem. This pack consists of an alpha male and female (M507, F521), two sub adults (m639, f637), and five pups. These wolves spent only one hour in the enclosure before breaking through the plastic fencing. Due to the extreme fire conditions throughout the southwest, the fence was not electrified. Once the wolves were free of the pen, I monitored them with telemetry equipment to determine if they would leave the area. We provided elk carcasses and water to aid them in their transition to the wild. I also spoke with forest visitors to inform them of the closure area around the release site.

One evening while monitoring Bluestem, I picked up telemetry signals on Saddle Pack (M574, F510, f646). The release area for Bluestem was actually on the edge of three other wolf-pack territories (Saddle, Bonito Creek, and Francisco). It was possible that the Saddle pack had sensed these new wolves, and were coming in to investigate. No altercations were noted. Within a few days, the other pack left the area. The Bluestem pack is still near the release site.

Currently there is a complete forest closure order in effect due to the extreme fire danger. At this time we may only access the forest to bring in meat for Bluestem once a week. Until the forest closure is lifted, I will be working around the office.

Coda

WILL THE WOLF SURVIVE?

DAVID HIDALGO AND LOUIE PÉREZ (LOS LOBOS)

Through the chill of winter
Running across the frozen lake
Hunters are out on his trail
All odds are against him
With a family to provide for
The one thing he must keep alive
Will the wolf survive?

Drifting by the roadside
Climbs a strong and aging face
Wants to make some honest pay
Losing to the range war
He's got two strong legs to guide him
Two strong arms keep him alive
Will the wolf survive?

Standing in the pouring rain
All alone in a world that's changed
Running scared now forced to hide
In a land where he once stood with pride
But he'll find his way by the morning light
Sounds across the nation
Coming from your hearts and minds
Battered drums and old guitars
Singing songs of passion
It's the truth that they all look for
Something they must keep alive
Will the wolf survive?
Will the wolf survive?

ACKNOWLEDGMENTS

I'd like to thank the many writers who are included here for allowing their works to be reprinted in this collection with little or no remuneration to themselves. Without such generosity this project would not have been possible. And I'd like to extend a special thanks to those writers who oppose the reintroduction of the Mexican gray wolf. Their essays make this a stronger, more interesting, and more honest collection. They did not have to allow their work to appear in an anthology whose overall tilt conflicts with their own views, and I am especially grateful for their willingness to participate in this dialogue.

Thanks, too, to Dylan for a several-days excursion to the Blue Range of Arizona. We didn't see any wolves, but we had fun looking. And to Margaret, Cody, and Riley, who have had to put up with my obsession with this project, my love and gratitude.

RICK BASS, "The Feds," from *The New Wolves*. Copyright © 1998 by Rick Bass. Reprinted by permission of the author and Lyons Press.

JOHNNY D. BOGGS, "Living with Wolves." Copyright © 1999 by Johnny D. Boggs. Originally published in *Southern New Mexico Magazine* 4, no. 3 (Fall 1999). Reprinted by permission of the author.

DAVID E. BROWN, "The Long and Dismal Howl," excerpt from *The Wolf in the Southwest: The Making of an Endangered Species*. Originally published 1983 by the University of Arizona Press. Copyright © 2002 by High Lonesome Books. Reprinted by permission of the author and High Lonesome Books, Silver City, NM.

DAVID E. BROWN, "A Tale of Two Wolves," from *Out among the Wolves: Contemporary Writings on the Wolf*, edited by John Murray. Originally published 1992 in *Game Journal* (January/February). Copyright © 1993 by David E. Brown and Graphic Arts Center Publishing Company. Reprinted by permission of Graphic Arts Center Publishing Company.

JAMES C. BURBANK, "Great Beast God of the East," from *Vanishing Lobo: The Mexican Wolf in the Southwest*. Copyright © 1990 by James C. Burbank. Reprinted by permission of the author and Johnson Books.

TOM DOLLAR, "The Mexican Wolf." Copyright © 2002 by Tom Dollar. Reprinted by permission of the author. Originally published in *Wildlife Conservation* (September/October 2002). Reprinted from *Wildlife Conservation*®, published by the Wildlife Conservation Society.

AMADEO M. REA, *"shee'e, [pl.] sheshe'e,"* excerpt from *Folk Mammalogy of the Northern Pimans.* Copyright © 1998 by the University of Arizona Press. Reprinted by permission of the University of Arizona Press.

MICHAEL J. ROBINSON, "Mexican Wolf Fate Teeters between Science and Politics." Copyright © 2001 by Michael J. Robinson. Originally published in *International Wolf* 11, no. 4 (2001). Reprinted with permission of the author.

SHARMAN APT RUSSELL, "The Physics of Beauty," excerpt from *Kill the Cowboy.* Copyright © 1993, 2001 by Sharman Apt Russell. Reprinted by permission of Perseus Books Publishers, a member of Perseus Books, LLC.

LAURA SCHNEBERGER, "Caught between the Pack and the Hard Case." Copyright © 2002 by Laura Schneberger. Reprinted by permission of the author.

DASHKA SLATER, "Signs of the Wild." Copyright © 1999 by Dashka Slater. Originally published in *Sierra* 84, no. 5 (September/October 1999). Reprinted by permission of the author.

BEN TINKER, "Timber Wolf (*Canis lupus*)," from chapter 7 "Life Sketches of Major Predatory Animals," from *Mexican Wilderness and Wildlife.* Copyright © 1978. By permission of the University of Texas Press.

ESTELA PORTILLO TRAMBLEY, "Wolf Boy" excerpt from *Trini.* Copyright © 1986 by Bilingual Press/Editorial Bilingüe. Reprinted with permission of Bilingual Press/Editorial Bilingüe, Arizona State University, Tempe, AZ.

JON TRAPP, "Mexican Wolf Guardian Reports, 2002." Copyright © 2002 by Jon Trapp. Reprinted by permission of the author.

J. ZANE WALLEY, "Caught Twixt Beasts and Bureaucrats." Copyright © 1998 by J. Zane Walley. Originally published in *Range* (Fall 1998). Reprinted with permission of the author.

J. ZANE WALLEY, "The Wasting of Catron County: Blueprint for the Destruction of Rural America?" Copyright © 2000 by J. Zane Walley. Originally published in *Range* (September 2000). Reprinted with permission of the author.

CONTRIBUTORS

|||||||||||||||||||||||||||||||||||||||||||||||||||||||||

NORMA AMES worked for the New Mexico Game and Fish Department. In 1971 she acquired several Mexican gray wolves from the "Ghost Ranch" lineage, which she raised in captivity. Because of her professional position and personal experience with wolves, she was hired by the U.S. Fish and Wildlife Service in 1979 to form a team to write a plan for the restoration of the Mexican gray wolf to portions of its former territory. This plan, the basis for the current restoration program, was published in 1982 as the *Mexican Wolf Recovery Plan.*

RICK BASS is the author of eighteen books of fiction and nonfiction, including the nonfiction works *The New Wolves* and *The Ninemile Wolves,* and a fiction collection, *The Hermit's Story.* He lives in northwest Montana's Yaak Valley where, despite it being one of the most biologically diverse valleys in the Lower Forty-Eight, there is still not a single acre of designated wilderness.

JOHNNY D. BOGGS is a Spur Award-winning writer who specializes in topics—from historical and travel to personalities and environmental—about the American West. He has written more than twenty novels and books, and has been published in more than fifty newspapers and magazines. His novels include *Arm of the Bandit, Lonely Trumpet,* and *Ten and Me.* He lives in Santa Fe, New Mexico, with his wife and son.

DAVID E. BROWN is an adjunct professor of zoology at Arizona State University and a former biologist for the Arizona Game and Fish Department. He is the author of many books on southwestern wildlife, including *The Wolf in the Southwest: The Making of an Endangered Species* and coauthor of *Borderland Jaguars/Tigres de la Frontera.*

JAMES C. BURBANK holds a lectureship in the English department at the University of New Mexico. He is also the Executive Director of American Land Publishing Project Inc. (ALLP), a publisher of large-format books dealing with land conservation and policy issues. He has published over 200 articles in major magazines and newpapers, as well as books on national energy policy and conservation and the environment, including *Vanishing Lobo: The Mexican Wolf in the Southwest.* His book *Retirement New Mexico* is the leading seller for New Mexico Magazine Press.

TOM DOLLAR, who specializes in adventure travel and natural history, has written hundreds of feature articles for both national and international publications. His most recent book, *Guide to Arizona's Wilderness Areas,* is a bestseller among backcountry guide books. An earlier travel book, *Tucson to Tombstone: A Guide to Southeastern Arizona,* won the Publishers Marketing Association 1996 Best Travel Book of the Year Award. He lives in Tucson, Arizona.

G. W. "DUB" EVANS moved to the Gila country of New Mexico in 1919. He owned the Slash Ranch, later also known as the Beaverhead. In addition to being a rancher, he was a noted houndsman, hunter, and guide. He published his memoirs, *Slash Ranch Hounds,* in 1951.

PETER FRIEDERICI is a writer and editor who lives in Flagstaff, Arizona. He is the author of an essay collection, *The Suburban Wild* (University of Georgia Press, 1999) and a coauthor of *The National Audubon Society Field Guide to the Southwestern States* (Knopf, 1999). He recently edited *Ecological Restoration of Southwestern Ponderosa Pine Forests* (Island Press, 2003). His articles and essays have also appeared in such periodicals as *Audubon, Wildlife Conservation, Mountain Gazette,* and *High Country News.*

DALE D. GOBLE is the Margaret Wilson Schimke Distinguished Professor of Law at the University of Idaho. His teaching and research focus on the intersection of natural resource law and policy, constitutional law, and history. He has written more than fifty articles, chapters, reports, and reviews; edited a collection of essays on the environmental history of the Pacific Northwest, *Northwest Lands, Northwest Peoples: Readings in Environmental History* (University of Washington Press, 1999); and coauthored the casebook *Wildlife Law: Cases and Materials* (Foundation Press, 2002). Before arriving at the University of Idaho, he worked in the Solicitor's Office in the Department of Interior in Washington, D.C.

GRENVILLE GOODWIN (1907–1940) was a well-known and respected ethnographer of the Apaches. He was the author of *The Social Organization of the Western Apache, Myths and Tales of the White Mountain Apache,* and *Western Apache Raiding and Warfare.*

DAVID HIDALGO and LOUIE PÉREZ are founding members of the Chicano rock band Los Lobos, one of America's great eclectic musical groups. David and Louie write most of the band's songs.

ALDO LEOPOLD (1887–1948) is one of the most important figures in the history of American conservation. His book *A Sand County Almanac* has influenced several generations of environmentalists and laid the groundwork for environmental philosophy and ethics. He worked for the U.S. Forest Service in New Mexico and Arizona from 1909 to 1924 and was responsible for the establishment of the world's first protected wilderness area, the Gila Wilderness, in 1924.

A. STARKER LEOPOLD (1913–1983), son of Aldo Leopold, was professor of Zoology and Forestry at the University of California, Berkeley. By the time of his death in 1983, he had become a leading figure in the study of the land and wildlife, receiving honors for his contributions to biological science, conservation, and education.

JANE SUSAN MACCARTER is the Share with Wildlife coordinator for the New Mexico Department of Game and Fish.

ROY MCBRIDE is a wildlife biologist who is involved internationally in endangered species research and recovery. He holds three U.S. and three international patents on capture and control tools that focus on humaneness and selectivity, and his company manufactures a padded trap that is used by wolf researchers worldwide. He captured the Mexican wolves used as founders for the captive breeding program. Roy is currently under contract with the Florida Fish and Wildlife Conservation Commission to capture the endangered Florida panther.

JOAN MOODY has worked in the conservation field for more than thirty years as a writer, editor, and public affairs specialist in the public and private sectors. Wolves hold a special place in her heart.

ALEXANDER PARSONS was raised in Santa Fe, New Mexico. He is currently an assistant professor of English at the University of New Hampshire. His first novel, *Leaving Disneyland*, won the 2001 A.W.P. Award for the Novel, the Texas Writers' League Award for Best Novel, and was a finalist for the PEN West Fiction Award. He recently completed his second novel, *El Malpaís (The Badlands)*.

STEVE PAVLIK teaches American Indian studies and environmental education at Vision Charter High School in Tucson, Arizona. He is the editor of *A Good Cherokee, A Good Anthropologist: Papers in Honor of Robert K. Thomas*, published in 1998 by the UCLA American Indian Studies Center.

AMADEO M. REA is a taxonomic ornithologist and ethnobiologist whose work is focused on the Greater Southwest. He worked as Curator of Birds and Mammals for thirteen years at the San Diego Natural History Museum. His papers deal with the taxonomy and distribution of birds, avian paleontology, and zooarchaeology and he is the author of *Once a River: Bird Life and Habitat Changes on the Middle Gila*. His work in ethnobiology includes two published volumes on the O'odham, a Southwest Uto-Aztecan group: *At the Desert's Green Edge: An Ethnobotany of the Gila River Pima* (1997) and *Folk Mammalogy of the Northern Pimans* (1998), all published by the University of Arizona Press. *Wings in the Desert: A Folk Ornithology of Northern Pimans* is forthcoming. He is past president of the Society of Ethnobiology.

MICHAEL J. ROBINSON represents the Center for Biological Diversity and lives in Pinos Altos, New Mexico, on the edge of the Gila National Forest. He is completing a book tracing the political and cultural history of the federal wolf extermination campaign.

SHARMAN APT RUSSELL is the author of numerous books, including *An Obsession with Butterflies: Our Long Love Affair with a Singular Insect* (2003); *Anatomy of a Rose: Exploring the Secret Life of Flowers* (2001); *The Last Matriarch* (2000); *When the Land Was Young: Reflections on American Archaeology* (1996); *Kill the Cowboy: A Battle of Mythology in the New West* (1993); and *Songs of the Fluteplayer: Seasons of Life in the Southwest* (1991), which won the Mountain and Plains Booksellers Award. She teaches writing at Western New Mexico University in Silver City, at the edge of the Mexican wolf recovery zone, and at Antioch University in Los Angeles, California.

LAURA SCHNEBERGER is the owner of a ranch in the Gila National Forest near Winston, New Mexico, and a fifth-generation rancher. She is president of the Gila Permittees Association, which represents ranchers operating on Forest Service land.

DASHKA SLATER is the author of a novel, *The Wishing Box*, as well as numerous articles and essays. She lives in Oakland, California.

BEN TINKER was an American rancher who lived in the upper Yaqui basin of Sonora, Mexico. Because of his knowledge of and concern for the wildlife of Sonora, he was appointed by Mexican President Obregón in 1923 to be the Game Guardian of Sonora. In an early example of international cooperation in the conservation of wildlife, his salary was furnished by the Permanent Wildlife Protection fund of New York. In 1978 he published his recollections in *Mexican Wilderness and Wildlife*.

ESTELA PORTILLO TRAMBLEY (1936–1999), a pioneer in the development of Chicana literature, was born in El Paso, Texas, in 1936. Her books include the novel *Trini*, a collection of short stories titled *Rain of Scorpions*, and a compilation of plays titled *Sor Juana and Other Plays*.

JON TRAPP is a graduate student studying conservation biology at Prescott College. His graduate research focuses on den-site selection of wolves in the Northern Rockies. He has an undergraduate degree in political science and spent seven years in the Air Force as an intelligence officer. His wife, Barbara, is also a biologist concerned with the preservation of wild places and carnivores. In 2002, he spent nine months (January–September) working on the Mexican wolf project as a U.S. Fish and Wildlife Service volunteer and as a Defenders of Wildlife wolf guardian.

J. ZANE WALLEY travels internationally writing investigative articles, which have appeared nationally in such diverse publications as *World Net Daily*, *News Max*, *Range Magazine*, *Agri-News*, *The McAlvany Intelligence Advisor*, *The Christian Science Monitor*, and others. Among his proudest accomplishments was his aid to the Amish when, in December 2000, he was invited by the Amish Community in Lancaster County, Pennsylvania, to expose the destruction of their culture and farms by restrictive zoning. He is the executive director of the Environmental Conservation Organization, Inc., a rural rights advocacy group. He serves on the advisory boards of Take Back America, The Everglades Institute, and other grassroots associations. A former U.S. Marine Sergeant and litigation investigator, he and his wife Sara live in Lincoln, New Mexico.

ABOUT THE EDITOR

TOM LYNCH is an assistant professor in the English department at the University of Nebraska, Lincoln, where he teaches environmental and Western American literature. His primary scholarly interests lie in examining the relationship between literature and ecology, and he has published numerous scholarly articles on the role of the environment in the literature of the American Southwest. He has also published a variety of creative nonfiction essays recounting his explorations of the landscape and ecology of the region.